The Political Economy of Universal Healthcare in Africa

The global rise in pandemics, most recently COVID-19, and other health challenges, some of which are due to climate change, have imposed significant challenges on the healthcare systems in economies around the world. Thus, this book deals with an issue that is very timely and relevant, not just in Africa but globally. It critically assesses healthcare reforms in Ghana under the Fourth Republic, since 1993. Although it focuses on Ghana's National Health Insurance Scheme of 2003, the book instructively goes beyond this program.

The book argues that, although Ghana is a bellwether of healthcare reforms in Africa, its healthcare initiatives are still far from the service haven of healthcare as a human right. Themes that animate the book's argument include the need to translate human rights law, such as the right to health, into practical policies that work for ordinary citizens. Key highlights of the book include an increased accent on health as a human right, emphasis on comparative analysis in healthcare studies, and the formulation of a four-hallmark framework, embedded in economics, law, politics, and human rights, to act as a guide for assessment of healthcare reforms in Africa in particular, and Ghana more specifically.

Using Ghana as a case study and analytical window into the world, the book offers a valuable and timely resource for academics, students, and policymakers across the disciplines of development and healthcare economics, law, public policy, political science, sociology, and African and Caribbean studies, as well as in various fields in health science.

Philip C. Aka is former Professor and Dean of the Faculty of Law, International University of Sarajevo, Bosnia and Herzegovina.

Hassan Wahab is Senior Lecturer of Political Science at the University of Ghana, Legon, Accra, Ghana.

Yvette M. Alex-Assensoh is Vice President for Equity and Inclusion and Professor of Political Science at the University of Oregon, Eugene, Oregon, USA.

Routledge Studies in Development Economics

162 Fiscal and Monetary Policies in Developing Countries
State, Citizenship and Transformation
Rashed Al Mahmud Titumir

163 Law and Development
Theory and Practice (Second Edition)
Yong-Shik Lee

164 The Economic Consequences of Globalization on Thailand
Juthathip Jongwanich

165 Cities and Economic Inequality in Latin America
Intra-Urban Inequality in Argentina
Lena Simet

166 Neoliberalism and Unequal Development
Alternatives and Transitions in Europe, Latin America and Sub-Saharan Africa
Edited by Fernando López Castellano, Carmen Lizárraga and Roser Manzanera Ruiz

167 Industrialization and Economic Diversification
Post-Crisis Development Agenda in Asia and Africa
Banji Oyelaran-Oyeyinka and Kaushalesh Lal

168 Digitalization and Economic Development
Edited by Mohamed Sami Ben Ali

169 The Political Economy of Universal Healthcare in Africa
Evidence from Ghana
Philip C. Aka, Hassan Wahab, and Yvette M. Alex-Assensoh

For more information about this series, please visit: www.routledge.com/series/SE0266

The Political Economy of Universal Healthcare in Africa

Evidence from Ghana

Philip C. Aka, Hassan Wahab and Yvette M. Alex-Assensoh

LONDON AND NEW YORK

First published 2022
by Routledge
4 Park Square, Milton Park, Abingdon, Oxon OX14 4RN

and by Routledge
605 Third Avenue, New York, NY 10158

Routledge is an imprint of the Taylor & Francis Group, an informa business

© 2022 Philip C. Aka, Hassan Wahab, and Yvette M. Alex-Assensoh

The right of Philip C. Aka, Hassan Wahab, and Yvette M. Alex-Assensoh to be identified as authors of this work has been asserted in accordance with sections 77 and 78 of the Copyright, Designs and Patents Act 1988.

All rights reserved. No part of this book may be reprinted or reproduced or utilised in any form or by any electronic, mechanical, or other means, now known or hereafter invented, including photocopying and recording, or in any information storage or retrieval system, without permission in writing from the publishers.

Trademark notice: Product or corporate names may be trademarks or registered trademarks, and are used only for identification and explanation without intent to infringe.

British Library Cataloguing-in-Publication Data
A catalogue record for this book is available from the British Library

Library of Congress Cataloging-in-Publication Data
Names: Aka, Philip Chukwuma, author. | Wahab, Hassan, 1965- author. | Alex-Assensoh, Yvette M., author.
Title: The political economy of universal healthcare in Africa : evidence from Ghana / Philip C. Aka, Hassan Wahab, and Yvette M. Alex-Assensoh.
Other titles: Routledge studies in development economics.
Description: Abingdon, Oxon ; New York, NY : Routledge, 2022. | Series: Routledge studies in development economics | Includes bibliographical references and index. | Contents: Introduction – Analytical Framework – Ghana's National Health Insurance Scheme (NHIS) – The Politics of Healthcare in Ghana – The Economics of Healthcare in Ghana – Healthcare as Human Rights in Ghana – Conclusion and Prospects for the Future.
Identifiers: LCCN 2021055240 (print) | LCCN 2021055241 (ebook) | ISBN 9781032205502 (hardback) | ISBN 9781032205519 (paperback) | ISBN 9781003264125 (ebook)
Subjects: LCSH: Health services accessibility--Ghana. | National health insurance--Ghana. | Medical policy--Ghana. | Medical economics--Ghana.
Classification: LCC RA395.G4 A38 2022 (print) |
LCC RA395.G4 (ebook) | DDC 362.109667--dc23/eng/20211115
LC record available at https://lccn.loc.gov/2021055240
LC ebook record available at https://lccn.loc.gov/2021055241

ISBN: 978-1-032-20550-2 (hbk)
ISBN: 978-1-032-20551-9 (pbk)
ISBN: 978-1-003-26412-5 (ebk)

DOI: 10.4324/9781003264125

Typeset in Bembo
by Taylor & Francis Books

For our families all across the United States, Ghana, and Nigeria.

Contents

List of tables viii
Abbreviations ix
Table of Ghanaian National and International Laws xi
Preface xii

1 Introduction 1
2 Analytical Framework 15
3 Ghana's National Health Insurance Scheme (NHIS) 36
4 The Politics of Healthcare in Ghana 58
5 The Economics of Healthcare in Ghana 68
6 Health as Human Right in Ghana 77
7 Conclusion and Prospects for the Future 104

References 109
Index 127

Tables

1.1	Regions and regional capitals of Ghana	3
2.1	Health system statuses and performances of WHO members in 2000 (estimates for 1997): Juxtaposition of Ghana with 13 neighboring and non-neighboring countries	25
2.2	Recap of Ghana's performance on the four hallmarks	26
3.1	Leaders of Ghana's Fourth Republic since 1993	41
6.1	Ghana under the NHIS: Recap of health as human right	84

Abbreviations

ACA	US Affordable Care Act (2010)
ACHPR	African Charter on Human and Peoples' Rights
ACRWC	African Charter on the Rights and Welfare of the Child
AU	African Union, successor of the OAU (see below)
CHI	Community Health Insurance
COVID-19	The novel coronavirus, a respiratory disease that can result in serious illness or death. The disease is caused by a new strain of coronavirus not previously identified in humans and easily spread from person to person. The World Health Organization declared it as a pandemic.
DALE	Disability-adjusted life expectancy
DMI	District Mutual Insurance
DRG	Diagnosis-related grouping
ECA	UN Economic Commission for Africa
FFS	Fee-for-Service
GHS	Ghana Health Service
GIIF	Ghana Investment Infrastructure Fund
GRA	Ghana Revenue Authority
ICESCR	International Covenant on Economic, Social, and Cultural Rights
ICT	Information and Communication Technology
IMF	International Monetary Fund
MDGs	UN Millennium Development Goals. Replaced after 2015 by Sustainable Development Goals (SDGs)
MDSD	Most-different-systems design
MHO	Mutual Health Organization
MRI	Magnetic Resonance Imaging
MSSD	Most-similar-systems design
NDC	National Democratic Congress
NGOs	Non-Governmental Organizations
NHIA	National Health Insurance Act
NHIF	National Health Insurance Fund
NHIS	National Health Insurance Scheme

NPP	New Patriotic Party
OAU	Organization of African Unity
ODA	Official/Overseas Development Assistance
OECD	Organization for Economic Cooperation and Development
PCHI	Private Commercial Health Insurance
PIAC	Public Interest and Accountability Committee
PMI	Private Mutual Insurance
PRMA	Petroleum Revenue Management Act (PRMA), Act 815
SAP	Structural Adjustment Program
SDGs	UN Sustainable Development Goals
SHI	Social health insurance
SSNIT	Social Security and National Insurance Trust
UDHR	Universal Declaration of Human Rights.
UHC	Universal Health Coverage
UK	[The] United Kingdom [of Great Britain and Northern Ireland]
UNO (UN)	United Nations Organization
US	The United States of America
VAT	Value-added tax
WCC	Within-case comparison
WHO	World Health Organization

Table of Ghanaian National and International Laws

African Charter on Human and Peoples' Rights (Banjul Charter). OAU Doc. CAB/LEG/67/3 rev. 5, 21 I.L.M. 58 (1982). Adopted June 27, 1981. Entered into force October 21, 1986.

African Charter on the Rights and Welfare of the Child. 1990. OAU Doc. CAB/LEG/24.9/49 (1990). Entered into force November 29, 1999.

Constitution of the Republic of Ghana 1992. *Reprinted* in Constitute Project, Ghana's Constitution of 1992 with Amendments through 1996. August 26, 2021.

GAOR, Supp. No. 16, U.N. Doc/6316, 999 U.N.T.S. 171, 6 I.L.M. 368 (1967).

Ghana Independence Act 1957. 1957 CH. 6. February 7, 1957.

International Covenant on Civil and Political Rights. 1966. G.A. Res. 2200A (XXI), U.N.

International Covenant on Economic, Social, and Cultural Rights. U.N. General Assembly Resolution No. 2200A (XXI) (December 19, 1966), 993 U.N.T.S. 3 (1976).

Mental Health Act, Act 846, 2012.

National Health Insurance Act, Act 650, August 2003.

Universal Declaration of Human Rights. G.A. Res. 217A. December 10, 1948.

Preface

Health is wealth and expanded healthcare is a known tool of choice for poverty alleviation in progressive countries around the world. Taking this proposition as a starting point, this book critically explores the political economy of universal healthcare in Africa, a region of high disease burden matched against a relatively modest provision for healthcare, using Ghana as case in point and analytical window into the world. The book's argument is that under Ghana's latest instalment of democratic rule since 1993, known as the Fourth Republic, Stage 3 of its healthcare reform initiative—after out-of-pocket expenses, colloquially known as "Cash and Carry," and the National Health Insurance Scheme (NHIS)—should squarely be the pursuit of health as human right. The book is filled with insights on means that Ghana could use to work toward that goal, even if, for some reason, it did not reach that final destination. Key highlights of the book include articulations of the right to healthcare as a tool of social struggle, and the negative impacts of rapid population growth on the provision of healthcare and other social services in Ghana. Our option for human right is in due cognizance of the transformational advantage that, as a reform tool, this model has over the traditional economic approach of venture capitalism embedded in supply and demand.

The book develops its argument in six chapters, plus an introduction. Chapter 2 defines the key terms of the study, provides a statement on the comparative method that informs the work, and lays down four hallmarks that we propose as a heuristic guide for assessment of healthcare reforms in Ghana. Chapter 3 is a discussion on the NHIS, the current face of healthcare reforms in Ghana with a narrative that begins with the period before the program. A highlight of the discussion is an advocacy for Ghana to transition to a single-payer, tax-funded healthcare system. Chapters 4 to 6 provide the justification for our rating of the healthcare program in Ghana, incarnated in the NHIS, as suboptimal: Chapter 4 on the politics of the program, Chapter 5 on its economics, and Chapter 6 on health as human right.

Key features, which set this book apart from similar or comparable works, include an increased accent on health as human right, emphasis on comparative analysis in healthcare studies, and the formulation of a four-hallmark framework embedded in law, politics, economics, and human right as a guide for assessment of healthcare reforms in Ghana. From the standpoint of comparative analysis, this study anchored on Ghana has teachable lessons, positive as well as negative, that other African countries can tap. The positive is how to build a shared vision and consensus on healthcare reforms among stakeholders in a given polity. The negative revolves around the need for more balance between expansion in health and other social programs on the one hand and population control on the other.

This growth work has been in the making for more than a decade. Ideas beget action. The insights which laid the seeds for its birth date back to mid-2011, soon after the signature of the Affordable Health Care into law by then US President Barack Obama on March 23, 2010. The bill was passed into law by the US House of Representatives on December 24, 2009, and by the Senate on March 21, 2010. On June 28, 2012, the US Supreme Court upheld the law as constitutional.

Every book is a work of collaboration and tribute to the solidarity of numerous parties whose antecedent energies made the work possible. This book is no different. Among the parties who deserve acknowledgment in this preface are the authors of the numerous sources in the references, whose ideas we drew upon to support our argument. We thank each and every one of these individuals and groups. We are also indebted to the team of anonymous reviewers whose perceptive evaluations of our proposal immensely improved the overall book. We hope that they like this final product from our collective sweats. Others that we would like to acknowledge are Thomas Parker Afferi, Hassan Wahab's Research Assistant, for his help during the period of Wahab's eye treatment in the US; and Aliya Amatul-Latif Wahab, for her understanding and continued support for Wahab.

We equally appreciate Alison Kirk, who we started this book with before she changed employment, for the opportunity to publish with Routledge; and Kristina Abbotts, Senior Editor for Economics, Finance, and Accounting, who replaced Alison, for her deep interest in this project as well as for her unmatched conviviality. Kristina, you are a pro and a joy to work with! We also thank Christiana Mandizha, Editorial Assistant for Economic titles, with whom we worked directly in preparing this book, for her conscientiousness. Last but not least, we express our deep gratitude to Brother A.B. Assensoh for his numerous gestures of encouragement in our academic lives that go back a long time. Consistent with the canons of academic practice, no one but ourselves take the blame for any errors of analysis and interpretation in this work. We gratefully acknowledge the permission of the Department of Geography and Resource Development at the University of Ghana to reproduce the map of Ghana on page xiv.

Park Forest, Illinois; Legon-Accra, Ghana; and Eugene, Oregon
October 2021

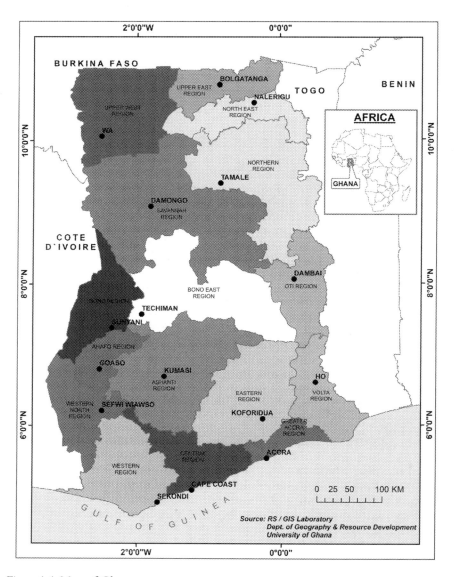

Figure 1.1 Map of Ghana
Source: This map is reproduced with grateful permission from the Department of Geography and Resource Development at the University of Ghana.

1 Introduction

Consistent with the customary tenets of any introductory material, this chapter comprises four key items: primer on Ghana, argument of the book and animating theme, recent developments within the context of the healthcare debate in Africa that inspired and lent impetus to the research, and the organization of the book. Collectively, these issues squarely revolve around the political economy of healthcare in Ghana,[1] reflected in the proposition of how, in the healthcare sector, "government institutions, an economic system, and a political environment affect and influence each other."[2] The missing element this book integrates, as we explain shortly below, is health as human right.

Primer on Ghana

Ghana is a West African country located in the Gulf of Guinea to the south of the Atlantic Ocean.[3] With a landmass of 239,540 square kilometers, Ghana is comparable in size to the UK in Europe, or to the State of Oregon in the US.[4] Ghana is bordered by Togo to the east, Côte d'Ivoire to the west, Burkina Faso to the north, and the Atlantic Ocean to the south.[5] Ghana has a population of 31.8 million people as of July 2021.[6] Like many African countries, Ghana has a population of mostly young people. In 2020, about 57 percent of the country comprised persons under 25 years of age, with little over 10 percent of the population 55 years and above.[7]

Modern-day Ghana is a merger of two territories, old Ashanti (later the Gold Coast), and German Togo (the Volta Region),[8] that, at independence, took on the name *Ghana*.[9] The name derived from an ancient empire, located 500 miles northwest of the contemporary state, which reigned until the thirteenth century.[10] Residents of modern-day Ghana believe themselves to be descendants of the inhabitants of the old Ghana Empire.[11] After World War I (1914–18), following the defeat of Germany, the victorious Allies, under the auspices of the League of Nations (1920–46), divided Germany's colonies in Africa among themselves.[12] The victorious powers instructed that these former German colonies be held and prepared for independence as "mandates" under the League of Nations.[13] Togoland was split longitudinally, and farmed out to the UK and France, while the UK received the Trans-Volta Togoland territory, which it administered, along with the

DOI: 10.4324/9781003264125-1

Gold Coast, until May 9, 1956.[14] That was the date when, in a plebiscite supervised by the United Nations Organization (UNO or UN), successor of the League of Nations, a majority of 58 percent of residents from the area voted to integrate with the Gold Coast.[15] Based on the plebiscite, in December 1956, the UN General Assembly approved the union of British Togoland with the Gold Coast to be consummated upon the latter's independence in 1957.[16] For its part, French Togo became Togo, in which form it received independence from France on April 27, 1960.[17]

Ghana gained independence from the UK on March 6, 1957,[18] after nearly 60 years of British colonial rule.[19] This is counting from 1900 when the British government proclaimed the colony of the Gold Coast.[20] It became a republic on July 1, 1960, little over three years later, in a move designed to eliminate remnants of British control and consolidate its newly-won "political kingdom,"[21] to use the famed expression of Kwame Nkrumah, Ghana's first indigenous leader.[22] Under its current Fourth Republic or phase of civilian rule, free of military intervention, since April 1993, Ghana operates a presidential system of government modelled after the US.[23] However, unlike the US, Ghana is a unitary state. The context dates back to 1955 when, in response to demands for a federal government in the country, British colonial authorities set up a commission of inquiry, headed by Sir Frederick Bourne, to look into the matter. The commission recommended, and the colonial government accepted, that federalism was an inappropriate constitutional arrangement for a small country like the Gold Coast.[24] Specifically, "[t]he Bourne Report recommended a compromise formula of a unitary system with devolutionary powers to regional assemblies, which formed the basis of the 1957 Constitution."[25]

Administratively, Ghana is a country of 16 regions, subdivided into 216 local districts. Table 1.1 is a list of the 16 regions, in alphabetical order, with their capitals. From just five at independence, the regions grew to ten in 1987, and to sixteen in December 2018.[26] Ghana's population is spread unevenly within its area, with almost 80 percent of the population residing in the south or in the far northeast and northwest.[27]

Accounting for about 55 percent of formal employment and contributing to more than one-third of GDP, agriculture still forms the mainstay of Ghana's economy,[28] as it did at independence. Products that Ghana exports to the world economy include cocoa, coffee, gold, diamonds, manganese, bauxite, timber, coconuts, palm products, shea nuts, and, most recently, oil.[29] Gold gave Ghana its name before independence and, in 2019, the country ranked with South Africa among the five top gold-producing countries in Africa.[30] Next to cocoa, Ghana is the second-largest cocoa-producing country in the world after Cote d'Ivoire.[31] Cocoa production accounts for 30 percent of the country's exports and Ghana is home to a chocolate industry worth $US 103 billion.[32] Oil was discovered in commercial quantity off the Western coast of the country in 2007,[33] making it the seventh-largest oil-producing state in Africa—after Nigeria, Libya, Angola, Algeria, Egypt, and

Table 1.1 Regions and regional capitals of Ghana

Item No.	Name of Region	Regional capital
1.	Ahafo	Goaso
2.	Ashanti	Kumasi
3.	Bono	Techiman
4.	Brong East	Sunyani
5.	Central	Cape Coast
6.	Eastern	Koforidua
7.	Greater Accra	Accra
8.	Northern	Tamale
9.	North East	Nalerigu
10.	Oti	Dambai
11.	Savannah	Damongo
12.	Upper East	Bolgatanga
13.	Upper West	Wa
14.	Volta	Ho
15.	Western	Sekondi Takoradi
16.	Western North	Sefwi Wiawso

Source: "Map and Regions of Ghana," The Permanent Mission of Ghana to the United Nations, www.ghanamissionun.org/map-regions-in-ghana/.

the Republic of the Congo (Congo Brazzaville).[34] We will return to this discovery of oil and its ramification for healthcare funding in Chapter 5 on the economics of healthcare reforms in Ghana.

Three previous republics preceded the Fourth Republic, each like it, marked by the adoption of a new constitution: the First Republic from 1960 to 1966; the Second Republic from 1969 to 1972; and the Third Republic from 1979 to 1981.[35] These previous republics involved a combination of parliamentary and presidential rules.[36] Ghana is a state and society which, until recently, was rife with military rule, some of it bloody and repressive.[37] There were three such periods totaling 22 years: 1966–69, 1972–79, and 1981–93.[38]

A figure in Ghanaian politics, whose mercurial personality bestrode both military and civilian dispensations, was Flight Lieutenant Jerry J. Rawlings (1947–2021).[39] Rawlings ruled Ghana for 20 long years: from 1981 to 1993 as military dictator, and 1993 to 2001 as a civilian.[40] He founded the National Democratic Congress (NDC),[41] one of Ghana's two largest political parties under the Fourth Republic, the other being the New Patriotic Party (NPP). The NDC is a left-of-center social democratic party, while the NPP is center-right and liberal-conservative.[42] Both political parties were formed in 1992 on the eve of the Fourth Republic.[43] Given his longevity in office spanning military and civilian eras, it is instructive that the National Health Insurance Scheme (NHIS) was adopted only *after* Rawlings' departure from office.

Argument and Animating Theme

Argument

This book explores healthcare reforms in Ghana under the country's Fourth Republic since 1993. In a seminal 2011 study of healthcare reform, referred to repeatedly in this book, Oxfam International quipped: "[i]f the introduction of 'Cash and Carry' health care was stage one, and the NHIS stage two, it is now time for stage three[.]"[44] That third stage is health as human right. We may not know precisely when Ghana, under the NHIS, reaches that destination or whether it will get there,[45] but to realistically approach that destination, Ghana's leaders must get the politics and economics of healthcare reforms in the country right. Herein lies the argument—and significance—of this book. Our option for human right is in due cognizance of the transformational advantage that, as a reform tool, this model has over the traditional economic approach of venture capitalism embedded in supply and demand.[46]

The NHIS is the face of health reform in Ghana. The program is an anti-poverty initiative designed to minimize the barriers that impede access to healthcare for poor people in the land, and, under the Fourth Republic, is the vehicle of choice that Ghanaian leaders have used to promote expanded healthcare delivery. There is consensus among political parties on social service programs that include healthcare. And contrasted with many of its neighbors in West Africa, of which Nigeria, because of its vast material and human resources comes to mind,[47] healthcare features repeatedly in the platforms of political parties in the land. Most issues in political economy are relative and Ghana has made reckonable progress in healthcare where many African countries are lagging. Despite these impressive achievements, Ghana still has a long way to go to reach the service haven of healthcare as human right. After nearly two decades of experimentation with the NHIS, the politics and economics of healthcare in Ghana remain direly suboptimal. These difficult problems make any talk about health as human right in the country premature.

Since its passage in 2003, many published studies have analyzed the NHIS.[48] This book joins and updates these studies. However, although anchored on this most obvious of Ghana's healthcare reform initiatives since independence, at the same time, this work goes beyond the scheme. For one thing, it puts more accent on the human rights ramifications of the program. This is an aspect of the literature that, for Ghana and other African countries which strive for universal healthcare coverage, "remains significantly unexplored."[49]

Animating Theme

This book is driven by the notion of realizing human rights, tied more or less by the possibilities of expanded access to healthcare. We begin with realizing human rights. Oxfam International comes in here. It is an international confederation of 18 affiliate organizations from across the world, working together with partners and local communities in more than 90 countries.[50] Incidentally, none of these affiliate organizations is from Africa, although the group plans to move its headquarters from Oxford to Nairobi in Kenya.[51] The conglomerate works to combat poverty in the world by various means, including "mobilizing the power of people against poverty," and "end[ing] the injustices that cause poverty."[52] Oxfam was formed in 1995 by a group of non-governmental organizations (NGOs) with the aim of working together for greater global impact to reduce poverty and injustice.[53] Its roots go much further back in time. The name Oxfam comes from the Oxford Committee for Famine Relief founded in Britain in 1942.[54] During World War II, the Committee campaigned for food supplies to be sent through an allied naval blockade to starving women and children in enemy-occupied Greece.[55] Given its belief that "respect for human rights will help lift people out of poverty and injustice, [while] allow[ing] them to assert their dignity and guarantee sustainable development," Oxfam International's approach to combating poverty is human rights–oriented.[56]

Samantha Power and her colleagues come in next with their appeals for scholars and policymakers to move from inspiration to impact in the attempt to realize human rights in a world where human rights atrocities remain pervasive, despite a flurry of domestic and international activities aimed at protecting and promoting these values.[57] As they indicated perceptively,

> if a key challenge of the second half of the twentieth century was gaining universal acceptance of the idea that human rights existed or mattered, *the* key challenge for the decades ahead is to identify the policies and actions that most effectively realize human rights.[58]

Most recently is Paul Hunt, UN Special Rapporteur on the Right to Health from 2002–2008, with his comment on the key challenge facing the health and human right movement. The context was a foreword in a comparative volume on the right to healthcare. That challenge, he said, is an operationalization one, namely, how to translate numerous national and international human rights laws into operational policies that work for citizens—within the context of finite national allocations and budgets for healthcare.[59] Hunt praised the volume he wrote a foreword on for "break[ing] new ground while emphasizing the need for deeper analysis and more studies."[60] This book, focused on healthcare reforms in Ghana since 1993, emblematized by the NHIS since 2003, hopefully answers some of the calls for more extensive analysis.

Amplifying and crystallizing these strands of thought is the notion the economics scholar and Nobel laureate Amartya K. Sen expressed many years ago regarding the possibility of expanded access to healthcare.[61] Sen noted that, if unregulated or laxly regulated, private insurance companies "have a strong financial interest in excluding patients" determined to be "high-risk."[62] Given this reality, he said, access to affordable healthcare is possible in any society, if the leaders, including public intellectuals, "can get [their] act[s] together."[63] This is true regardless of the mode for producing goods and services in a country—whether capitalist or socialistic or a combination of these two conventional systems.

Acknowledging the contributions of the NHIS to healthcare reforms in Ghana, yet transcending it, is a wisdom that drives this book. With healthcare now part of the policy agenda, the next challenge is to maintain and improve it until it becomes a human right. The lethargic responses of many governments to COVID-19 speak to the necessity of a human-rights–oriented healthcare system and the critical role of good laws, funding (economics), and politics, in the sense we use them in this book, in maintaining a vibrant healthcare system.

Recent Developments Which Inspired and Lent Impetus to This Research

One recent development which inspired this research and lent impetus to its message of healthcare as human right anchored instructively on a critical examination of the NHIS is the COVID-19 pandemic.[64] The first confirmed case of the pandemic in Africa, involving Egypt, was reported on February 14, 2020.[65] By May 13, 2020, all 54 countries in the region reported confirmed cases of the virus, the last being Lesotho.[66] As of July 6, 2021, Ghana Health Service (GHS) reported that Ghana recorded over 97,000 infections, with 799 deaths and over 94,000 recoveries.[67]

While, thus far, compared to other regions of the world, the pandemic has affected Ghana, along with other African countries, mildly in terms of the rates of infection and deaths,[68] nevertheless, its mayhem portends new challenges on various fronts—socioeconomic consequences, food insecurity, and maintaining peace and security—that African leaders must respond to through creative and human-right-compliant means.[69] These challenges include "tak[ing] measures to improve testing capacities, access to medical supplies, and participation in vaccine and treatment research; enhanc[ing] production and innovation through intra-African collaboration; expand[ing] deployment of community health workers, […]; and boost[ing] medical personnel capacity […]."[70] Consistent with the advice of the UN Economic Commission for Africa (ECA), these initiatives must be "part of a comprehensive effort to improve the resilience and preparedness of healthcare systems" in the region.[71] Ghana's leaders appeared to be following this advice when, in August 2021, President Nana Akufo-Addo commissioned a set of hospitals and related medical facilities to repair disparities in the country's healthcare system that the outbreak of COVID-19 had compounded.[72] He observed that "not only has the pandemic disrupted our daily lives, but it has also exposed the deficiencies with our healthcare system because of the years of under-investment and neglect."[73]

The foregoing events are taking place within the context of the catalyst of a healthcare debate in Africa.[74] It is a debate on health as an economic driver anchored on multiple themes, including efficiency and effectiveness as well as improved communication between finance and health ministries to ensure quality growth in healthcare delivery.[75] At a time when healthcare systems in the region are enduring the "double burden" of noncommunicable diseases like hypertension, stroke, diabetes, and cancer, superimposed on the original communicable category like malaria, tuberculosis, and HIV/AIDS, half of the population across the region still lacks adequate health services.[76] The noncommunicable diseases typify middle-class lifestyles.[77]

To be sure, there is progress in Africa from the application of modern technology in healthcare delivery. For example, technology has afforded more people in the remote corners of the continent increased access to better healthcare hitherto unavailable while, through better access to data, modern technology enables African doctors and policymakers to make more informed decisions about how to improve their healthcare systems.[78] However, across the region, healthcare systems still confront a range of challenges, including adulterated medications, medical clinics in sweltering hot conditions without air-conditioning, and lack of medical equipment like Magnetic Resonance Imaging (MRI) machines, among other problems.[79] Even prior to the outbreak of COVID-19, many Africans ranked their health and healthcare among the lowest in the world.[80]

Organization of This Book

This book has seven chapters, including this introduction as Chapter 1. This sets the tone of the study with a concise statement of the problem, including the argument of the study and animating theme. Chapter 2 sets forth an analytical framework in the form of a self-aware conversation, rather than the usual disquisition on theoretical framework and methodology, on the sources used in developing and supporting the argument of the study. In addition to defining the key terms of the study, the chapter expounds on the method of comparative analysis that informs this work, and the layout of four hallmarks of a good healthcare system as a guide for healthcare reforms in Ghana. Chapter 3 presents the NHIS, the latest incarnation of healthcare reforms in Ghana under the Fourth Republic. In addition to a discussion on healthcare in the country before 2003 when the program was introduced, it provides a critical update on the nearly two-decade operation of the scheme.

Chapter 4 analyzes the politics of health reforms in Ghana, guided by the hallmarks introduced in Chapter 2, while Chapter 5 explores the economics of the reforms. Chapter 6 is devoted to examination of the extent to which healthcare delivery in Ghana under the Fourth Republic meets the standard and stringencies of health as human right. Chapter 7 concludes with a look into the political economy of healthcare reforms in Africa, including the struggle for health as a human right, and the character of Ghana's contributions. Key features, which set this book apart from similar or comparable works, include an increased accent on health as human right, emphasis on comparative analysis in healthcare studies, and the unveiling of a four-hallmark framework embedded in law, politics, economics, and human rights as a guide to healthcare reforms in Ghana.

8 Introduction

Notes

1 See Will Kenton and Michael J. Boyle, "Political Economy," *Investopedia* (Updated Feb. 25, 2021), www.investopedia.com/terms/p/political-economy.asp (defining political economy as "an interdisciplinary branch of the social sciences that focuses on the *interrelationships* among individuals, governments, and public policy"). Emphasis added.
2 Ibid ("Interdisciplinary studies" under "Political Economy in Academia").
3 See "Maps of Ghana," *World Atlas*, www.worldatlas.com/maps/ghana.
4 "Ghana: Republic of Ghana," *Nations Encyclopedia*, www.nationsencyclopedia.com/economies/Africa/Ghana.html; "Ghana: Location and Size," *Photius*, https://photius.com/countries/ghana/geography/ghana_geography_location_and_size.html.
5 See "Maps of Ghana," note 3.
6 "Ghana Population (Live)," *Worldometer*, www.worldometers.info/world-population/ghana-population/.
7 "Ghana Demographics Profile," *Index Mundi* (last updated November 27, 2020), www.indexmundi.com/ghana/demographics_profile.html (citing *CIA World Factbook*).
8 "Ghana," *Nations Online*, www.nationsonline.org/oneworld/ghana.htm.
9 "Ghana," *Infoplease*, www.infoplease.com/country/ghana.html; "Kingdom of Ghana," *USHistory.org*, www.ushistory.org/civ/7a.asp. Colonial authorities in Africa had a knack for assigning bland and uncreative names to their colonial estates. Many names were assigned based on landmarks like rivers or just the natural resources or trade item found there when the affected European colonizers met the society in question. Thus, Ghana was called the Gold Coast to commemorate the trade in gold that was found there in commercial quantities. Similarly, the Ivory Coast (Cote d'Ivoire in French) was so named because of the existence of ivory there and Nigeria at first as Slave Coast because of the enormous slave trade there. Sometimes two countries confusedly got the same name. That was the case with Nigeria and Niger Republic, its neighbor to the North, both of which took their common names from the River Niger that ran through their territories.
10 Ibid.
11 "Ghana," *Worldmark Encyclopedia of Nations* (2007), www.encyclopedia.com/topic/Ghana.aspx.
12 See, for example, Michael D. Callahan, *Mandates and Empire: The League of Nations and Africa, 1914–1931* (Brighton: Sussex Academic Press, 1999); and Quincy Wright, *Mandates Under the League of Nations* (Westport, CT: Greenwood Press, 1968).
13 Callahan, note 12; and Wright, note 12.
14 In addition to Togo and the then Gold Coast, territories in Africa formerly held by Germany included present-day Cameroon, Central African Republic, Chad, Guinea, and Nigeria (German West Africa), as well as Burundi, Kenya, Mozambique, Rwanda, and Tanzania (German East Africa). See *German Imperialism in Africa: From the Beginning Until the Second World War* (translated by Bernd Zöllner), ed. Helmut Stoecker (Atlantic Highlands, NJ: Humanities Press Int'l, 1987).
15 See F.M. Bourret, *Ghana: The Road to Independence, 1919–1957* (Redwood City, CA: Stanford University Press, 1960), 193.
16 Ibid.
17 "Togo," *Infoplease*, www.infoplease.com/country/togo.html.
18 Ghana Independence Act 1957, 1957 CH. 6 (February 7, 1957), www.legislation.gov.uk/ukpga/Eliz2/5-6/6/enacted?view=plain (granting the country "fully responsible status within the British Commonwealth of Nations," effective March 6, 1957, under the name of Ghana). See also A New Nation: Gold Coast Becomes Ghana in Ceremony, 1957/03/07 (July 3, 2006), https://archive.org/details/1957-03-07_A_New_Nation (newsreel video of independence festivities).

Introduction 9

19 See David Owusu-Ansah, *Historical Dictionary of Ghana* (Lanham, MD: Rowman & Littlefield, 2014), 92–93.
20 Otherwise, the tutelage goes deeper. Ghana's first interaction with whites came in 1471 when Portuguese traders landed on the coast in search of gold, ivory, and spices. Kent Mensah, "Ghana's Successful but Unpopular Healthcare," *Al Jazeera* (August 6, 2014), www.aljazeera.com/news/africa/2014/07/ghana-successful-but-unpopular-healthcare-2014722101651828127.html. Portuguese navigators built a fortress at Elmina in 1482, a transit point for slaves exported to the New World that, till today, remains a monument of the slave activities that took place in the area. Subsequently, other Europeans came, including the Dutch, the Danes, the Swedes, the Prussians, and the British. Among these European powers, Britain colonized the Gold Coast. British colonialism in the country lasted from January 1902 when the British government declared Ashanti a British crown colony with the regions further north becoming the Protectorate of the Northern Territories of the Gold Coast. "History of Ghana," *HistoryWorld.net*, www.historyworld.net/wrldhis/PlainTextHistories.asp?historyid=ad43.
21 See Egon Schwelb, "The Republican Constitution of Ghana," *American Journal of Comparative Law*, 9 (1960) (extended commentary on the 1960 Constitution). A famous saying from Kwame Nkrumah, who led the country from 1951 until 1966, was "give us first the political kingdom and all other things would be added unto it." This statement, a parody of Matthew 6:33 of the Christian Bible, underscored Nkrumah's belief in self-rule as the key to Ghana's economic transformation. See Daniel Yergin and Joseph Stanislaw, *Commanding Heights: The Battle Between Government and the Marketplace that is Remaking the Modern World* (New York: Simon & Schuster, 1998), 83–88.
22 Nkrumah led the country from 1951 until 1966, when he was overthrown in a military coup. See "Kwame Nkrumah, President of Ghana," *Encyclopedia Britannica*, www.britannica.com/biography/Kwame-Nkrumah.
23 See "Ghana: Constitution and Politics," *The Commonwealth*, http://thecommonwealth.org/our-member-countries/ghana/constitution-politics. See also "Ghana: The Fourth Republic," *Photius*, www.photius.com/countries/ghana/government/ghana_government_the_fourth_republic.html.
24 See Alexander K.D. Frempong, Constitution-Making and Constitutional Rule in Ghana, Paper Presented at a Colloquium by the Dept. of Political Science, University of Ghana (March 1–2, 2007).
25 Ibid.
26 "Regions of Ghana," *Statoids*, www.statoids.com/ugh.html. The original five were Ashanti, Eastern, Northern, Trans-Volta Togoland, and Western. Ibid. For the identity of some of these districts, see Ghana Statistical Service, *2010 Population and Housing Census: Summary Report of Final Results* (Accra: Sakoa Press Ltd, 2012), 93–103, www.statsghana.gov.gh/docfiles/2010phc/Census2010_Summary_report_of_final_results.pdf.
27 "Ghana," *Worldmark Encyclopedia of Nations*, note 11; see also "Ghana," Travel Documents System, www.traveldocs.com/world-atlas/Ghana-atlas84 ("People of Ghana").
28 "Ghana," Travel Documents System, note 27 ("Economy of Ghana").
29 Ibid.
30 NS Energy Staff Writer, "Top Five Gold Mining Countries of Africa from Ghana to Burkina Faso," NS Energy (August 28, 2020), www.nsenergybusiness.com/news/top-gold-mining-countries-africa/.
31 "The Top Cocoa-Producing Countries," *World Atlas*, www.worldatlas.com/articles/top-10-cocoa-producing-countries.html.
32 "Ghana," Travel Documents System, note 27 ("Economy of Ghana").
33 Ibid.

34 "Crude Oil Production | Africa," *Trading Economics*, https://tradingeconomics.com/country-list/crude-oil-production?continent=africa.
35 Although also a period of democratic experiment, the period 1957 to 1960 when Ghana had a governor-general who represented the Queen of England, is not usually included among these eras of republic.
36 See M. Dee Dubroff, "What is the Difference Between a Parliamentary and Presidential System of Government?" *InfoBloom*, www.infobloom.com/what-is-the-difference-between-a-parliamentary-and-presidential-system-of-government.htm. As this source explains, under a presidential system, the chief executive, often called a president, is separate from the legislature, whereas under a parliamentary system, the chief executive, often called a prime minister, is part of the legislature (usually known as Parliament). Ibid. Under a presidential system, the executive and legislative functions of the government are separated and restraints, called checks and balances, are put in place to limit the powers of both the chief executive and the legislators, whereas under a parliamentary system, the legislature holds the power, and the chief executive is accountable to the legislature. Ibid.
37 See, for example, "Independence, Coups, and the Republic, 1957–Present," in *The Ghana Reader: History, Culture, Politics*, eds. Kwasi Konadu and Clifford C. Campbell (Durham, NC: Duke University Press, 2016), 299–360; and Youry Petchenkine, *Ghana: In Search of Stability, 1957–1992* (Santa Barbara, CA: ABC-CLIO, 1993).
38 "Independence, Coups, and the Republic," note 37.
39 See Noble Kofi Nazzah, "Jerry Rawlings Is Dead, but He Still Looms Large in Ghanaian Politics," *Foreign Policy* (December 30, 2020), https://foreignpolicy.com/2020/12/03/jerry-rawlings-is-dead-but-he-still-looms-large-in-ghana-politics/. See also William Wallis, "Jerry Rawlings, a Showman President of Varied Ideologies," *Financial Times* (November 20, 2020), www.ft.com/content/c23175d4-a39e-4550-bcfd-bc66a2b2a8cf; "Jerry Rawlings: Why He Divided Opinion in Ghana," *BBC News* (November 12, 2020), www.bbc.com/news/world-africa-27193658.
40 See, for example, "Jerry J. Rawlings, Head of State, Ghana," *Encyclopedia Britannica* (last updated June 18, 2021), www.britannica.com/biography/Jerry-J-Rawlings; "Jerry Rawlings, From Coup-Plotter to Ghanaian Statesman," *New York Times* (November 12, 2020), www.nytimes.com/2020/11/12/world/africa/jerry-rawlings-dead-version.html. After he seized power on June 14, 1979, Rawlings ruled for 112 days before handing power to civilians. Matt Schudel, "Jerry Rawlings, Coup Leader Who Ruled Ghana for 20 Years, Dies at 73," *Washington Post* (November 12, 2020), www.washingtonpost.com/local/obituaries/jerry-rawlings-coup-leader-who-ruled-ghana-for-20-years-dies-at-73/2020/11/12/d8453a32-2504-11eb-a688-5298ad5d580a_story.html.
41 Nazzah, "Jerry Rawlings Is Dead," note 39.
42 See, for example, Minion K.C. Morrison, "Political Parties in Ghana through Four Republics: A Path to Democratic Consolidation," *Comparative Politics*, 36(4) (July 2004), 421–442.
43 Ibid.
44 *Achieving a Shared Goal: Free Universal Health Care in Ghana* (Oxford, UK: Oxfam Int'l, March 2011), 10, www.oxfam.org/sites/www.oxfam.org/files/rr-achieving-shared-goal-healthcare-ghana-09033-en.pdf.
45 This notion calls to mind the memorable thoughts of Vaclav Havel (1936–2011), activist and former Czech President, in his address to the US Congress on February 21, 1990, wherein he portrayed democracy as little more than an ideal. Havel stated, "As long as people are people, democracy, in the full sense of the word, will always be no more than an ideal. In this sense, you too are merely approaching democracy. But you have one great advantage: you have been approaching democracy uninterruptedly for more than 200 years." Reprinted in Larry Berman and Bruce Allen

Murphy, *Approaching Democracy*, 8th ed. (Upper Saddle River, NJ: Pearson Education, Inc., 2013), p. 540

46 Anja Rudiger, "Human Rights and the Political Economy of Universal Health Care: Designing Equitable Financing," *Health & Human Rights Journal*, 18 (2016), 67, 69 (observing that "in contrast to the exclusions and inequities entailed in treating health care as a market commodity[,] […] [h]uman rights principles inspire […] the development of a heterodox concept of public goods, defined as the essential goods, services, and infrastructure needed to satisfy human needs and realize human rights"). Rudiger was referring to the US health reform debate. See also Chapter 6, footnotes 7–22 (outlining various reasons which make the human-rights model superior to the traditional economic approach).

47 West Africa is one of six subregions in Africa. The other five, in no particular order, are: Central Africa, Eastern Africa, Northern (Arab) Africa, Southern Africa, and the African Diaspora. See "Subregions," African Center for Strategic Progress, https://acstrap.org/subregions/. See also "The Six Regions of the African Union," West Africa Brief, www.west-africa-brief.org/content/en/six-regions-african-union (with a map showing the subregions). With its 15 countries, all of which are members of the Economic Community of West African States (ECOWAS), West Africa is the subregion with the largest number of states. And with a population estimated at 350 million people, it is also the most populous subregion. Ibid. In 2003, the African Union (which succeeded the Organization of African Unity, OAU) created the African Diaspora as a sixth subregion in an attempt to encourage the participation of people of African descent living outside the continent, irrespective of their citizenship and nationality, who were willing and able to contribute to the development of the continent. Ibid.

48 Emblematic studies include: Hassan Wahab, "The Politics of State Welfare in Africa: Ghana's National Health Insurance Scheme in Comparative Perspective," Ph.D. Dissertation, Indiana University Bloomington (September 2015); and A.B. Assensoh and Hassan Wahab, "A Historical-Cum-Political Overview of Ghana's National Health Insurance Law," *Journal of African and Asian Studies*, 7 (2008), 289–306. Other samples include: Nathan J. Blanchet et al., "The Effect of Ghana's National Health Insurance Scheme on Health Care Utilization," *Ghana Medical Journal*, 46 (June 2012), 76–84; Freeman F.K. Gobah and Zhang Liang, "The National Health Insurance Scheme in Ghana: Prospects and Challenges: A Cross-Sectional Evidence," *Global Journal of Health Science*, 3 (October 2011), 90; *Achieving a Shared Goal*, note 44; Rhodaline Baidoo, "Toward a Comprehensive Healthcare System in Ghana," M.A. Thesis, Center for Int'l Studies, Ohio University (March 2009), https://etd.ohiolink.edu/rws_etd/document/get/ohioou1237304137/inline; Jennifer L. Singleton, "Negotiating Change: An Analysis of the Origins of Ghana's National Health Insurance Act," Honors Project, Paper 4, Macalester College (May 1, 2006), http://digitalcommons.macalester.edu/soci_honors/4; and K.B. Barimah, "Traditional Healers as Service Providers in Ghana's National Health Insurance Scheme: The Way Forward," *Global Public Health*, 8 (2013), 202–208 (focusing on the relationship between the NHIS and traditional medicine in Ghana).

49 Ernest Owusu-Dapaah, "Empowering Patients in Ghana: Is There a Case for a Human Rights-Based Health Care Law?" *Lancaster University Ghana Law Journal*, 1 (2015), 91, www.lancaster.edu.gh/uploads/law/Advisory%20and%20Editorial%20Board.pdf.

50 "Who We Are," Oxfam Int'l, www.oxfam.org/en/about.

51 See Alice Sharman, "Oxfam International to Move Headquarters to Nairobi," Oxfam, www.civilsociety.co.uk/news/oxfam-international-to-move-headquarters-to-nairobi.html.

52 "Who We Are," note 50.

53 "History of Oxfam Int'l," Oxfam Int'l, www.oxfam.org/en/countries/history-oxfam-international.

54 Ibid.
55 Ibid.
56 "Our Commitment to Human Rights," Oxfam Int'l, www.oxfam.org/en/our-commitment-human-rights.
57 See generally Samantha Power and Graham Allison, eds., *Realizing Human Rights: Moving from Inspiration to Impact* (New York: St. Martin's Press, 2000).
58 Ibid., pp. xiii–xiv (emphasis in original).
59 Paul Hunt, "Foreword," in *The Right to Health: A Multi-Country Study of Law, Policy and Practice*, eds., Brigit Toebes et al. (The Hague: T.M.C. Asser Press and Verlag Berlin Heidelberg, Germany: Springer, 2014), v–vi.
60 Ibid., p. vi.
61 See Amartya Sen, "Universal Healthcare: The Affordable Dream," *Vanguard* (London) (January 6, 2015), www.theguardian.com/society/2015/jan/06/-sp-universal-healthcare-the-affordable-dream-amartya-sen.
62 Ibid.
63 Ibid.
64 COVID-19 is a respiratory disease that can result in serious illness or death. It is caused by a new strain of coronavirus not previously identified in humans, which spreads from person-to-person through respiratory droplets produced when an infected person, within close proximity, coughs, or sneezes. There is currently no effective antiviral treatment for the disease, though some vaccines believed to be generally effective have been developed to inoculate against the condition. The World Health Organization (WHO) declared the disease a pandemic on March 11, 2020. See "COVID-19: Frequently Asked Questions: Basics," Centers for Disease Control and Prevention [USA], www.cdc.gov/coronavirus/2019-ncov/faq.html; David J. Cennimo, "What is COVID-19?" *Medscape* (updated January 4, 2021), www.medscape.com/answers/2500114-197401/what-is-covid-19.
65 "Policy Brief: Impact of COVID-19 in Africa," United Nations Economic Commission for Africa (May 28, 2020), 6, www.uneca.org/sites/default/files/PublicationFiles/sg_policy_brief_on_covid-19_impact_on_africa_may_2020.pdf [hereinafter "Impact of COVID-19 in Africa"].
66 Ibid.
67 See "COVID-19 Ghana's Outbreak Response Management Updates," *Ghana Health Service*, www.ghanahealthservice.org/covid19/.
68 See "Impact of COVID-19 in Africa," note 65, p. 1. See also Ahmed Mushfiq Mobarak and Rifaiyat Mahbub, "What the US Can Learn from How African Countries Handled COVID," CNN (November 3, 2020), www.cnn.com/2020/11/03/africa/africa-coronavirus-lessons-opinion-intl/index.html; and Cara Anna, "As US Struggles, Africa's COVID-19 Response is Praised," *AP* (September 22, 2020), https://apnews.com/article/virus-outbreak-ghana-africa-pandemics-donald-trump-0a31db50d816a463a6a29bf86463aaa9?campaign_id=9&emc=edit_nn_20210307&instance_id=27836&nl=the-morning&regi_id=124708682&segment_id=52986&te=1&user_id=3018d6faed4962db07930c7110d6aad4. But this statement risks being overstated, given that there are still some unknowns about this pandemic, especially as virulent strains of the disease emerge in parts of the world, including South Africa. See Patrick Gathara, "Charity Alone Will Not End the Calamity of COVID-19 in Africa," *Al Jazeera* (July 31, 2021), www.aljazeera.com/opinions/2021/7/31/accountability-is-africas-best-route-out-of-the-pandemic (counseling accountability, rather than charity, as Africa's "best route out of the pandemic"); Claire Felter, "How Dangerous Are New COVID-19 Strains?" Council on Foreign Relations (January 7, 2021), www.cfr.org/in-brief/how-dangerous-are-new-covid-19-strains?gclid=Cj0KCQiA1KiBBhCcARIsAPWqoSqLuooY_obXNC_aRxXuELh5kVnMYG8xr-NpA1rHgIvtD8sP0qVZHqwaAnzjEALw_wcB. One of the lessons of COVID-19 is the need to build stronger and more resilient healthcare systems in regions across the globe. See "Lessons from COVID-19: Building a Stronger Global Health System," *Foreign Policy*

(May 26, 2020), https://foreignpolicy.com/events/fp-virtual-dialogue-lessons-from-covid-19/.
69 See "Impact of COVID-19 in Africa," note 65. Instructively, the theme for 2020's Human Rights Day is "Recover Better—Stand Up for Human Rights." As the United Nations elaborates, the theme "relates to the COVID-19 pandemic and focuses on the need to build back better by ensuring Human Rights are central to recovery efforts" in that the world will "reach [its] common global goals only if" communities across the world "create equal opportunities for all, address the failures exposed and exploited by COVID-19, and apply human rights standards to tackle entrenched, systematic, and intergenerational inequalities, exclusion and discrimination." "Human Rights Day 10 December," United Nations, www.un.org/en/observances/human-rights-day#:~:text=2020%20Theme%3A%20Recover%20Better%20%2D%20Stand,are%20central%20to%20recovery%20efforts. The United Nations sets aside December 10 every year for commemoration as Human Rights Day.
70 "Impact of COVID-19 in Africa," note 65, p. 3.
71 Ibid.
72 See "'Agenda 111' to Optimally Advance Ghana's Healthcare Delivery—President," *Ghana Web* (August 18, 2021), www.ghanaweb.com/GhanaHomePage/NewsArchive/Agenda-111-to-optimally-advance-Ghana-s-healthcare-delivery-President-1335367.
73 Quoted in "Akufo-Addo Has Packaged NDC's Idea and Named it Agenda 111—Segbefia," *Ghana Web* (August 19, 2021), www.ghanaweb.com/GhanaHomePage/NewsArchive/Akufo-Addo-has-packaged-NDC-s-idea-and-named-it-Agenda-111-Segbefia-1336129.
74 See, for example, Lily B. Clausen, "Taking on the Challenges of Health Care in Africa," *Stanford Business* (June 16, 2015), www.gsb.stanford.edu/insights/taking-challenges-health-care-africa (synthesizing the views of three health professionals—Abayomi Ajayi, Letitia Adu-Ampoma, and Azure Tariro Makadzange — who discussed the hurdles confronting African healthcare on a panel about healthcare in Africa at the Stanford Africa Business Forum); Anita Powell, "South Africa Debates Bill for National Health Care," *Learning English*, https://learningenglish.voanews.com/a/south-africa-debates-bill-for-national-heath-care/5127964.html (focusing on a proposal by the South African government designed to expand healthcare delivery in the land beyond the current 15 percent of South Africans with private health insurance coverage). Learning English is the Voice of America's (VOA's) multimedia source of news and information for English learners worldwide.
75 "The Great Debate Focuses on How to Fix Africa's Healthcare," ECA (February 12, 2019), https://uneca.org/stories/great-debate-focuses-how-fix-africa%E2%80%99s-healthcare.
76 See Clausen, note 74. The acronym HIV "stands for human immunodeficiency virus, […] the virus that causes HIV infection." The acronym "can refer to the virus or to HIV infection." "HIV/AIDS: The Basics," National Institutes of Health, https://hivinfo.nih.gov/understanding-hiv/fact-sheets/hivaids-basics#:~:text=HIV%20stands%20for%20human%20immunodeficiency,stands%20for%20acquired%20immunodeficiency%20syndrome. The acronym AIDS "stands for acquired immunodeficiency syndrome. AIDS is the most advanced stage of HIV infection." Ibid. Here is the connection between HIV and AIDS. "HIV attacks and destroys the infection-fighting CD4 cells of the immune system. The loss of CD4 cells makes it difficult for the body to fight off infections and certain cancers. Without treatment, HIV can gradually destroy the immune system and advance to AIDS." Ibid.
77 These are so called because these diseases can be prevented through modification of the common lifestyle causes of these conditions, such as unhealthy diet, physical inactivity, tobacco use, and excessive alcohol use. See *Global Action Plan for the*

Prevention and Control of Noncommunicable Diseases 2013–2020 (Geneva, Switzerland: World Health Organization, 2013), 3.
78 Clausen, note 74.
79 Ibid.
80 See, for example, Angus S. Deaton and Robert Tortora, "People in Sub-Saharan Africa Rate Their Health and Healthcare Among the Lowest in the World," *Health Affairs*, 34(3) (March 2015), 3519–3527; and B. Rose Huber, "Sub-Saharan Africans Rate Their Health and Health Care Among the Lowest in the World," Woodrow Wilson School of Public & Int'l Affairs, Princeton University (February 25, 2015) (news story on the Deaton and Tortora research).

2 Analytical Framework

Introduction

This chapter composes and sets forth an analytical framework comprising the package of conceptual materials used in developing and supporting the argument of this book. It consists of three main elements: a set of three key concepts, delineation of the main features of the technique of comparative analysis which informs this work, and four hallmarks of a good healthcare system presented as a guide for healthcare reforms in Ghana. This chapter is not a theoretical or methodological framework in the formal disquisition sense, of which a dissertation readily comes to mind; instead, it is a less extensive, yet self-aware, conversation on the conceptual framework which undergirds the thrust of this book anchored on a critical assessment of healthcare reforms in Ghana under the Fourth Republic.

Key Terms

The beginning of analytical wisdom, as the Chinese thinker Confucius (551–479 B.C.) once famously indicated, is to call things by their proper names through precise definition of key terms.[1] In obedience to this Confucian injunction, three key terms that need a definition here are *healthcare system, universal healthcare,* and *human rights.*

Healthcare System

To define a healthcare system, we need to first explain *health*. The term is "[t]he capacity to live a full, active[,] and breathing life[,]" and a property that ranks "among the most precious treasures" humans have.[2] International human rights instruments define *health* broadly to include conditions of "complete physical, mental, and social well-being, […] not merely the absence of disease or infirmity," whose enjoyment governments must recognize as a fundamental right to be extended to "every human being without distinction of race, religion, political belief, economic or social condition."[3] Building on this proposition, a *healthcare system* comprises any collection of people and material resources of

DOI: 10.4324/9781003264125-2

16 *Analytical Framework*

varying degrees of integration and coordination, including monies, and information technology, designed to maintain or promote health.[4] This composite includes formal healthcare services like the delivery of personal medical attention by a doctor, whether dispenser of traditional or allopathic medicine; taking care of the sick at home; activities designed to prevent diseases and promote good health; and interventions designed to improve good health, such as road safety and environmental safety campaigns.[5] Still other phenomena outside this formal boundary, yet germane to health, are activities like increased school enrollment for girls, and changing the educational curriculum to make students better future caregivers and consumers of healthcare products.[6]

Different scholars identify different markers of a good healthcare system.[7] Suffice it to say that such a system may be a function of five variables: equity, quality, responsiveness, efficiency, and resilience.[8] *Equity* in healthcare means basic fairness in the healthcare burden among healthcare consumers. "Who pays how much for what, when?" is a key element in the design and implementation of any healthcare system.[9] *Quality* in healthcare refers to "the degree to which health services for individuals and populations increase the likelihood of desired health outcomes and are consistent with current professional knowledge."[10] Shortfalls in quality, in terms of safety, effectiveness, patient-centered care, and timeliness, result in avoidable risks for patients and signifies that the healthcare system is under-performing relative to what could potentially be achieved given available resources.[11] *Responsiveness* stands for "the extent to which a health system meets people's expectations and preferences concerning non-health matters," such as respect for the dignity of patients, their sociocultural beliefs and preferences, autonomy, and preserving the confidentiality of their information.[12] It is widely acknowledged as a key dimension of healthcare performance.[13] *Efficiency* in healthcare refers broadly to "the extent to which available inputs [in resources] generate the highest possible level of health outcomes."[14] Shortfalls in efficiency may be due to a range of factors that includes "waste or poor operational performance in the production of health services or outcomes[,]" an occurrence which indicates that the affected healthcare system is performing below expectation.[15] *Resilience* in healthcare means "the capacity of health actors, institutions, and populations to prepare for and effectively respond to crises; maintain core functions when a crisis hits; and, informed by lessons learned during the crisis, reorganize if conditions require it."[16]

"Performance is intrinsic to the vitality of a healthcare system."[17] Accordingly, improved healthcare performance requires action in the three interrelated policy areas of service delivery, healthcare financing, and governance.[18] The first two are self-explanatory. The last, *governance*, refers to "the processes and institutions for collective decision-making," and connotes institutional attributes like transparency, accountability, participation, integrity, and capacity.[19] Multiple features which influence a country's healthcare system include the unique history and culture of its society, priorities accorded to certain ethical values (such as autonomy of patients and healthcare providers), and the level of economic resources available for healthcare.[20] Given the collage of the foregoing factors, even the most dysfunctional or incompetent countries in the world still have a (nominal) healthcare system.[21] The peculiarities also justify the focus on Ghana in this book.

Universal Healthcare

Universal healthcare means healthcare for all.[22] More elaborately, it is affordable healthcare for all, free of all unnecessary impediments by whatever name, whether copays, deductibles, or user fees, capable of leading a patient to medical bankruptcy.[23] "Financial barriers are a key predictor of poor access to and quality of health care."[24] As a UN General Assembly resolution pointed out in 2012, the access involved is "safe, affordable, effective, and quality" healthcare services, whether "promotive, preventive, curative, [or] rehabilitative" that do "not expose the users to financial hardship."[25] The goals of universal healthcare parallel some of the features of a good healthcare system recounted above.[26] These goals, revolved around protecting individuals from impoverishment arising from illness, include equity in access to health services, present when any individual who needs healthcare services gets access to those services, without regard to employment status or ability to pay; and extending healthcare services good enough to improve the health of individuals receiving those services.[27] The main point, as then director-general of the World Health Organization (WHO) succinctly put it, is that "[n]o one in need of health care, whether curative or preventive[,] should risk financial ruin as a result."[28] Though others both within and outside the particular country can help, governments have primary responsibility for transiting their societies toward universal healthcare.[29]

Numerous United Nations instruments, including pronouncements authored or inspired by WHO, espouse the concept of universal healthcare. Besides the WHO's Constitution of 1948,[30] these instruments include the Declaration of Alma Ata of 1978,[31] and Resolution 58.33 adopted by the World Health Assembly in May 2005.[32] The WHO Constitution stipulates that "[t]he enjoyment of the highest attainable standard of health is one of the fundamental rights of every human being without distinction of race, religion, political belief, economic or social condition."[33] Building on this broad definition, the Declaration of Alma-Ata, pronounced that the attainment of good health at "the highest possible level" "is a most important world-wide social goal."[34] The Declaration, a monument of the International Conference on Primary Health Care, is notable for its message of "healthcare for all."[35]

Similarly, Resolution 58.33 urged governments to "develop their health systems, so that all people have access to services and do not suffer financial hardship paying for them."[36] Specifically, in striving for transition to universal coverage for their citizens, governments should work to achieve multiple goals, including "contribut[ing] to meeting the needs of the population for health care and improving its quality, [...] reducing poverty, [...] [and] attaining internationally[-]agreed development goals."[37] Commentators who have joined this wagon on expanded healthcare include the Nobel laureate Amartya Sen who posited that lack of resources at any one time to provide quality medical attention to all should not be an excuse "for eliminating our search for ways of proceeding toward just that, nor a ground for refusing to provide whatever can be easily provided right now for all."[38] Sen reasoned that "[c]laims that we live in an era of limited resources fail to mention that these resources happen to be less limited now than ever before in human history."[39]

Universal healthcare is linked to social health insurance (SHI), a form of financing and managing healthcare based on risk pooling.[40] SHI pools both the health risks of the people on one hand, and the contributions of individuals, households, enterprises, and the government on the other.[41] Tax-funded financing used by some states typifies SHI.[42] Commentators who make this linkage see SHI as a key and necessary mechanism without which it is hard for a country to achieve universal healthcare. Irrespective of how a particular health system chooses to finance its healthcare, these commentators contend, "prepayment and pooling of resources and risks are basic principles" in protecting citizens from financial risk.[43]

Similarly, universal healthcare has been linked to international relations. International and regional organizations which have made that connection include the UN General Assembly, the African Union (AU), and the global health czar WHO. The UN General Assembly advised states to take healthcare into account in formulating foreign policy.[44] In its view, healthcare is "a pressing foreign policy issue of our time,"[45] an "important cross-cutting policy issue,"[46] whose inclusion governments and non-governmental organizations should work hand-in-hand to promote "as an important element on the international development agenda."[47] While commenting on the international influences on healthcare, the UN General Assembly also acknowledged national peculiarities relating to healthcare, including a recognition that "the choice of a health financing system should be made within the particular context of each country."[48] The General Assembly expressed its recognition regarding "the responsibility of Governments to urgently and significantly scale up efforts to accelerate the transition towards universal access to affordable and quality health-care services."[49]

In a subsequent resolution adopted days apart, on December 12, 2012, the General Assembly "invite[d] Member States to adopt a multi-sectoral approach" that, among other things, "tak[es] into consideration the social determinants of health," "recognize[s] the importance of universal coverage in national health systems," and "provide[s] access to health services for all," including poor people.[50] The resolution also "urge[d] Member States to continue to consider health issues in the formulation of foreign policy."[51] In a statement released in September 2016, the AU disclosed the commitment of African leaders to achieve universal healthcare for their citizens by 2030.[52] The AU is an intergovernmental organization comprising the 55 countries in Africa.[53] It was launched in 2002 as a successor to the Organization of African Unity (OAU) in existence from 1963 to 1999.[54] For its part, the WHO set aside December 7, 2016 as "Universal Health Coverage (UHC) Day."[55] This is another way of saying that, in addition to local benefits, universal healthcare also has global benefits as well. As Professor Sen pointed out in his piece on universal healthcare, using the Ebola pandemic as an example, effective universal healthcare in the countries where the disease originated, could have mitigated or completely eliminated the epidemic.[56]

The accent on universal healthcare "capture[s] the degree to which different societies are reaching their ambition to provide equal access to health for all."[57] It is an accent built on the notion that "[a]ll people aspire to receive quality, affordable health care[,]"[58] that has also spawned a movement across 117 countries.[59] Individuals have a right to equal access to public services, next after the right to choose their own governments.[60] The mother of those services, upon which other services rests because of the platform it provides for enjoyment of those other services, is access to healthcare. Little wonder that today many countries of different economic statuses, including low-income states, are either implementing or getting ready to implement programs designed to achieve universal healthcare.[61]

In the 1970s and 1980s, international financial institutions like the World Bank and the International Monetary Fund (IMF) instituted putative "structural adjustment" of many economies in the developing world that mandated cuts in social programs, including healthcare services, in return for international monetary assistance.[62] Part of the sign of the new era is the World Bank's espousal of universal healthcare indicated by more access, improved quality, and affordability,[63] as its "strategic priority."[64] Jim Yong Kim, then president of the Bank, stated, "We can bend the arc of history to ensure that everyone in the world has access to affordable, quality health services in a generation."[65] To be sure, "[t]here is no single formula" to universal healthcare, but rather different states take different routes to this goal.[66] However, states need "to push [themselves] beyond [their] old limits."[67] Kim equally advised that in shooting for the "brighter future" of universal healthcare, states should "not forget the lessons of the past[,]"[68] including best practices from other countries.

The solicitude for expanded healthcare is not academic. Every year, an estimated 250 million people across the world, many of them in Africa, endure financial catastrophe or descent below the poverty line, not to mention penalties like lost income, all due to healthcare beyond their reach.[69] Contrarily, dependable access linked with universal healthcare works. Individuals in households with healthcare coverage utilize healthcare significantly more than those without, and having health insurance coverage is associated with a high degree of insulation from financial risk as well as from the incidence of catastrophic health expenditure, vis-à-vis households with no coverage.[70]

Yet, for Ghana, and for many low-income countries, a practical question is whether universal healthcare is affordable, whether a low-income country can equitably and effectively provide healthcare through universal coverage.[71] The answer is yes for a variety of reasons that Professor Sen eloquently spelled out.[72] The first, notably, is that, basically speaking, healthcare, like education, is labor-intensive. Because wages are low in poor countries, these countries can spend less to provide the same labor-intensive services as richer countries.[73] Second, pooled coverage remedies many of the most easily curable diseases and prevents readily avoidable ailments otherwise left unaddressed under the out-of-pocket system, "because of the inability of the poor to afford even very elementary healthcare and medical attention."[74] What is more, universal healthcare does not rule out private services for individuals with the means to purchase extra services. As the population grows richer, the result of universal healthcare and increased access to education, many people may choose to pay more and have additional private healthcare.[75] Plus, as Sen pointed out, the requirements of universal healthcare does not dictate complete equality—even though reduction of economic and social inequality has instrumental relevance for good health.[76] Third, many medical and health services are shared, rather than exclusive. In other words, "[c]overing more people together can sometimes cost less than covering a small number individually."[77] Fourth, because many diseases are infectious, "[u]niversal coverage prevents their spread and cuts costs through better epidemiological care."[78]

The concept of universal healthcare seems too obvious to form the basis for any extended analysis: isn't healthcare for all what government should be about? However, many governments do a poor job of distributing what scarce resources they have, whether in healthcare or any other field.[79] In some developed countries, such as the US, governments generate plentiful healthcare resources that they distribute inequitably.[80] In contrast, in many developing countries, governments generate non-plentiful healthcare resources that they equally distribute inequitably. The point is that universal healthcare is not so commonsensical as the concept deceitfully connotes. To add to the complexity, there is no one road to universal healthcare; instead, different political systems take different paths to universal healthcare.[81] This reality justifies the comparative analysis this book adopts. "Examining the different national paths taken toward universal health care, can shed light on how those systems work now—and on what steps might be necessary to improve them, so that they can serve as instructive models for other countries[.]"[82]

Human Rights

Human rights are guarantees of freedom, such as life, liberty, security, and subsistence to which people as humans have rights.[83] They are "the rights that distinguish men and women from the other creatures who inhabit the earth, the rights that make for the 'humanness' of human beings."[84] Access to good healthcare occupies a central place among these rights. There are over three-dozen of these rights distilled from the international bill of human rights.[85] The level of a country's development is measured "by the extent to which its citizens enjoy human rights in all their ramifications."[86] The values codified in international human rights instruments "are at the core of what it means to lead a complete and fulfilled human life."[87] Many discussions on human rights echo the tenets of Western liberalism, embedded in John Stuart Mill's famous proposition that "[o]ver himself, over his own body and mind, the individual is sovereign."[88]

However, rather than limited to individual rights, human rights also include collective or group rights.[89]

Comparative Analysis

Comparison is a tool of methodology,[90] that researchers use "to relate the particularities of individual countries to broader trends and processes[,]"[91] in an attempt ultimately designed to learn best-practices from other cultures.[92] Comparative analysis involves "studying and comparing which solutions […] work best for certain types of problems, as well as observing patterns of failure across multiple systems."[93] The technique of comparative analysis enables researchers to "identify and interrogate our own often unarticulated assumptions of the way" things really are.[94] For as the English writer Rudyard Kipling (1865–1936) once famously observed, a person who knows only England knows not England well.[95] Comparative analysis is some mind-travel abroad that "awakens us to the varieties of human experience and shows us that there are different ways of doing things than what we are used to in our own country[,]" such that "[i]n the end we come home with a greater sensitivity to both the positive and negative features of our homeland as well as an enhanced appreciation of why other people do things differently."[96]

Through the comparative method, the researcher "reaches conclusions about cause and effect through structured and systematic comparing and contrasting of cases" that would be hard to achieve otherwise.[97] Unlike physical and biological scientists, who "use laboratories to reproduce experiments in their search for scientific laws and factors," social scientists "cannot conduct such laboratory experiments in their search for generalizations about politics."[98] The closest to lab experiments these social scientists settle for is the comparative method.[99] "Through comparative studies, [these non-physical scientists] can compensate for the lack of laboratory experiments by comparing political experiences and phenomena in one setting with those in other settings."[100] Given these multiple benefits, "[o]ne of the oddities in the contemporary world is [an] astonishing failure to make adequate use of policy lessons that can be drawn from the diversity of experiences that the heterogeneous world already provides."[101]

Healthcare studies are inherently comparative. Primarily, healthcare is a socioeconomic and political issue in many countries across the world and an object of international concern.[102] Thus, as a field, comparative healthcare studies fosters full understanding of the dynamics of healthcare systems, including cross-country learning and cooperation capable of generating evidence-based information that will help policymakers to rationalize the structure and funding of their healthcare systems.[103] Studying the differential healthcare journeys of other states affords the examiner "multiple vantage points from which to gain a fresh perspective on strengths and weaknesses" of one's own healthcare system.[104] Because many of the problems countries confront in delivering quality healthcare to their citizens are similar, "[t]here are lessons to be learned from comparing health-care systems internationally that can only aid in addressing these problems."[105] Again, as the adage goes, truly knowing England means knowing more than just England.[106] In the contemporary period "[h]eightened interest in comparative healthcare studies—the health reform experiences of other countries—coincided with the national debates in the US on healthcare in the early 1990s under William J. Clinton."[107]

The WHO, a global health czar, appears to believe in the comparative method and puts a premium on comparative healthcare studies. In a statement on sustainable health financing that it adopted on May 25, 2005, the World Health Assembly, a WHO agency, urged member states "to share experiences on different methods of health financing, including the development of social health-insurance schemes, and private, public, and mixed schemes."[108] The same document also advised the WHO director-general "to create sustainable and continuing mechanisms, including regular international conferences [...], in order to facilitate the continuous *sharing of experiences and lessons* learnt on social health insurance."[109] The World Bank believes similarly. Hence, then World Bank President Kim advised that in shooting for the "brighter future" of universal healthcare, states should "not forget the lessons of the past[,]"[110] including best practices from other countries.

Introspectively, the species of comparative analysis that informs this study is a mixture of the most-similar-systems design (MSSD), most-different-systems design (MDSD), and within-case comparison (WCC).[111] MSSD is a research technique wherein the researcher compares cases that are similar with respect to a number of factors but with distinct outcomes.[112] It is predicated on the logic that two cases, such as two countries similar in a variety of ways, would have similar political outcomes, and where that is not the case, but, instead, variations in outcome occurred, the researcher will seek explanation regarding the dissimilarity.[113] One concern about this design relates to the premium that it places on identifying the differences between cases, rather than the similarities: "If two cases are most similar, what is remarkable about comparing them?"[114] As Professors J. Tyler Dickovick and Jonathan Eastwood explain, "[w]hat is remarkable is *where* most similar cases differ. Differences in outcomes between similar cases are noteworthy, and differences in possible causes are what will help us explain them."[115]

MDSD is a research technique wherein "the researcher identifies two cases that are different in nearly all aspects yet are similar on a particular outcome."[116] The puzzle then leads the researcher to develop hypotheses to explain the peculiar similarity.[117] "Just as MSS design [...] place[s] a priority on identifying differences between cases, MDS design [...] place[s] a premium on identifying the similarities that can give us analytical leverage."[118] In an MDS design, the variables that are noteworthy and telling are those that are not different.[119]

In contrast to these two interactive comparative techniques, like its very name implies, WCC is an insular technique entailing the study of one country at different points in time and space.[120] Under this one-case technique, "the researcher look[s] more carefully within [his or her] own case(s) to examine the variations there[in]," the logic being that "[l]ooking at different moments in time or in space may allow us to dig deeper into a case to better understand our evidence."[121] WCC is often associated with "process-tracing" by which "the researcher examines histories, archival documents, interview transcripts and other sources to see whether the causal process a theory hypothesizes or implies in a case is in fact evident in the sequence and values of the intervening variable in that case."[122]

Although social science research focuses on "what is and why," it may also legitimately delve into what should be in instances when agreed-upon criteria exist "for deciding what makes one thing better than another."[123] By its nature, this research combines the best of what is and what should be, *describing* healthcare reforms in Ghana as it is now while *prescriptively* incorporating suggestions on the ideal way forward. Given the foregoing, the exploration of healthcare reforms in Ghana under the Fourth Republic that this book conducts can benefit immeasurably from the technique of comparative analysis embedded in comparative healthcare studies.

As Oliver Wendell Holmes (1841–1935), one-time Associate Justice of the US Supreme Court, once observed, "the life of the law" is not embedded in logic but rather in experience, including "[t]he felt necessities of the time," and "intuitions of public policy."[124] Given this reality, Holmes advised that individuals not deal with the law "as if it contained only the axioms and corollaries of a book of mathematics."[125] Instead, most germane to our purpose here, "to know what it is, we must know what it has been, and what it tends to become [,]" with each step "alternately consult[ing] history and existing theories of legislation."[126] Such is what we plan to do in this book, using the past and present to venture predictions on Ghana's future related to healthcare reforms under its Fourth Republic since 1993.

Four Hallmarks of a Good Healthcare System: A Guide for Healthcare Reforms in Ghana

The ensuing discussion sets forth four hallmarks of a good healthcare system: good laws, adequate financing, healthcare as human right rather than alienable privilege, and good politics. The notation "good healthcare system" is a prescriptive usage in sync with the inherent normative tone of comparative healthcare studies.[127] Accordingly, "good" is proxy for optimal-ness or optimality, a heuristic standard in economic theory believed to be reached when resources may not be "reallocated to make one individual better off without making at least one individual worse off."[128] The four hallmarks are presented as a guide for healthcare reforms in Ghana, together with an assessment of the Ghanaian healthcare system's performance on each of the hallmarks. Different studies use different measures for assessing the performance of a healthcare system. In one often-cited measure, Professor Marc J. Roberts and his colleagues explored how to design effective government interventions, to enhance performance and fairness of health systems, focusing on the five areas of financing, payment, organization, regulation, and behavior.[129] In addition to drawing out the multi-disciplinarity in healthcare studies embedded in the combination of international experience with sensitivity to local conditions, the book also elicited the ethical choices inescapably involved in decisions relating to healthcare.[130] The measure used here is a simplified technique that mimics methods in the literature, but departs from those methods in terms of its increased accent on human rights. This is an orientation inherent in the definition of healthcare that slowly but steadily is gaining traction in some sections of the academic literature.[131]

The measures also build on the assessment instrument that the WHO introduced in its seminal report in 2000. The assessment instrument comprised health level and distribution, responsiveness level and distribution, fairness in financial contributions, health expenditure per capita, and level of health performance. All of these measurement tools, excepting responsiveness, are self-explanatory. Responsiveness focuses on the non-healthcare aspects of healthcare delivery, such as the way in which patients are treated, the environment of that treatment, and the overall experience of the patient's contacts with the healthcare system. Key indicators of responsiveness include attention, autonomy, amenities of care, choice, communication, confidentiality, and respect. Table 2.1 applies these concepts in the context of Ghana. For a double function, the diagram complements the recap of Ghana's performance on the four hallmarks introduced in this discussion (see Table 2.2). The next discussion unveils the four hallmarks. The actual assessment of Ghana's performance based on the four hallmarks is saved for the appropriate portions of this book: good laws and good politics in Chapter 4 dealing with the politics of healthcare reforms in Ghana, good funding in Chapter 5 dealing with the economics of healthcare reforms in Ghana, and healthcare as human right in Chapter 6 focusing on this same issue.

Unveiling the Four Hallmarks

The four hallmarks are interwoven. As a socioeconomic human right, what makes healthcare delivery an onerous, but by no means impossible, proposition is that, for a country to achieve a well-functioning healthcare system, all of these factors must be in place. A first factor is good laws. Every country has a domestic legal system that includes its constitution (higher law) and the regional and international treaties relating to healthcare that the country ratified, notably the International Covenant on Economic, Social, and Cultural Rights (ICESCR).

A second hallmark of a good healthcare system is good funding. Money is "the mother's milk of any healthcare system and key to both access in

Analytical Framework 25

Table 2.1 Health system statuses and performances of WHO members in 2000 (estimates for 1997): Juxtaposition of Ghana with 13 neighboring and non-neighboring countries

Country	Health level (DALE)[132]	Health distribution	Responsiveness level	Responsiveness distribution	Fairness in financial distribution	Healthcare expenses per capita in US$	Overall goal status[133]	Level of health performance	Ranking of healthcare system
France	3	12	16–17	3–38	26–29	4	6	4	1
Italy	6	14	22–23	3–38	45–47	11	11	3	2
UK	14	2	26–27	3–38	8–11	26	9	24	18
USA	24	32	1	3–38	54–55	1	15	72	37
Tunisia	90	114	94	60–1	108–11	79	77	46	52
Mauritius	78	77	56	3–38	124	69	90	113	84
Libya	107	102	57–8	76	12–15	84	97	94	87
Ghana	**149**	**149**	**132–35**	**146**	**74–5**	**166**	**139**	**158**	**135**
Botswana	187	146	76–9	111–12	89–95	85	168	188	169
Rwanda	185	185	145–47	143–44	58–60	177	171	181	172
South Africa	160	128	73–4	147	142–43	57	151	182	175
Ethiopia	182	176	179	179–80	138–39	189	186	169	180
Nigeria	163	188	149	177	180	176	184	175	187
Sierra Leone	191	186	173	186	191	183	191	183	192

Source: *The World Health Report 2000: Health Systems: Improving Performance* (Geneva, Switzerland: World Health Organization 2000), 152–155 (Annex. tbl.1).

Table 2.2 Recap of Ghana's performance on the four hallmarks

Item No.	Hallmark	Key elements	Progress status	Bases for assessment
1.	Good laws	Constitutionalization, ratification of multilateral treaty	Suboptimal	The tepid and amorphous provision on the right to health in Ghana's latest constitution
2.	Good funding	Adequate funding, minimizing reliance on direct payments to finance services, increased efficiency, and fairness in healthcare financing	Suboptimal	Ghana has made insufficient progress in meeting the target of 15% of its annual budget to healthcare. Instead, based on World Bank data, as of 2016, the most recent year for which information is available, Ghana spent a pitifully low 4.45% of its GDP on healthcare
3.	Health as human right	Entrenchment of features like expanded access, and equity of a kind that makes healthcare a human right within the law	Suboptimal	Given the various problems that still impede the NHIS 18 years after its adoption, Ghana's fledgling healthcare system does not seem to guarantee access to healthcare as a human right
4.	Good politics	Healthcare-friendly politics designed to produce effective laws and adequate financing that increase the chances of making healthcare a human right under the law	Suboptimal	Neither Act 650 nor Act 852 seriously addressed any of the funding issues that impede healthcare reform in Ghana. Instead, politics was reduced to little more than wrangling between the two major political parties on healthcare matters that did not lead to improved funding

healthcare and health outcomes."[134] Good funding, signified by the allocation of adequate revenue for healthcare services, is the lifeblood of a good healthcare system. The mark of the maturity of a state's healthcare system is the funding that, backed by the masses, its political leaders are willing to devote to healthcare goods. A country can devote a sizable share of its GDP to healthcare and still get suboptimal healthcare delivery, but adequate funding is an important starting point in the journey toward a good healthcare system.

How much a nation is willing to devote to healthcare, along with the level of material sacrifices it is ready to endure to get healthcare for the vast majority of its citizens, "opportunity cost," if we may, speaks to its seriousness about improving healthcare. Because few countries in the world have all the resources that they need to meet their healthcare needs, achieving expanded healthcare requires the use of creative steps in funding, including reducing waste and efficient management of available resources.[135] Adequate funding is important because financial barriers impede access to healthcare services. Governments have an obligation to protect individuals from impoverishment that could arise from illness, whether due to out-of-pocket payments or loss of income when a household member falls sick. Again, as Dr. Margaret Chan, then director-general of the WHO nailed it, "[n]o one in need of health care […] should risk financial ruin as a result."[136]

The human right hallmark stands for the notion of health as right, rather than as a privilege that the government may withdraw when it chooses to. As indicated earlier in this chapter, human rights are guarantees of freedom, such as life, liberty, security, and subsistence to which people as humans have rights.[137] Because it underpins many human rights, including the right to life,[138] healthcare is a, if not *the*, mother of socioeconomic human rights. As elaborated in Chapter 6, bearing on this matter, expanded healthcare embedded in human rights has several benefits that such a benefit not anchored in human right lacks, including an appeal to rights based solely on a person's humanity, and a strategic unity that can force governments to either hold the line on rights or increase those rights, rather than reduce them.

Finally, in regard to good politics as hallmark of a good healthcare system, healthcare is an "intrinsically political" phenomenon "built on principles of fairness and equity that require governments to allocate healthcare benefits according to need, and financial contributions according to ability to pay."[139] Transition to expanded healthcare is "primarily a political negotiation" between contending interest groups and stakeholders with divergent priorities, with the potential to lead to "dysfunctional processes," if not handled well.[140] Accordingly, a government sends an important political message based on the healthcare funding it adopts.[141] Because "[i]n many countries the health care sector wields little political power or influence [over] decisions about the allocation of public funds[,]" "[e]xpenditure on health care has tended to be viewed simply as a drain on scarce resources, rather than as an investment in the nation's future."[142] In a nutshell, the politics of universal healthcare dictate that the state must raise sufficient resources for health, through steps, such as increasing the efficiency of revenue collection, reprioritizing government budgets, innovating financing, and putting developmental assistance when it is available to good use; removing financial risks and barriers to access, and guaranteeing that those barriers are removed by, for example, providing incentives for people to improve their health through preventive measures; improving efficiency and minimizing waste, and promoting equity in access.[143] Good politics has a distinctive characteristic that sets it apart from the other hallmarks: All of the other hallmarks—good laws, adequate funding, and healthcare as a human right—are susceptible to political influence.[144] Put differently, at the risk of oversimplification, good politics may be viewed as a function of the previous three hallmarks, that is, politics designed to produce effective laws and adequate financing that increases the chances of making healthcare a human right rather than a privilege that a regime may withdraw when it chooses.[145]

Conclusion

This chapter was designed to accomplish three goals: identification and definition of the key terms of the book, delineation of the analytic framework that underlies the work, and the layout of four hallmarks of a good healthcare system presented as a guide for healthcare reforms in Ghana. The first two are self-evident, but the last requires some more elaboration here. There is no perfect or error-safe system for assessing the status and performance of healthcare systems. Instead, in its 2000 report, WHO portrayed the wealth of information that it presented as "innovative" materials that "can be refined and improved," and expressed the hope that "careful scrutiny and use of the results will lead to progressively better measurements" in the future.[146] For the measures of responsiveness and equity in financial contributions wherein it used a range, rather than exact figures, WHO explained that "[a]ll the main results are reported with uncertainty intervals in order to communicate to the user the plausible range of estimates for each country on each measure."[147] Worse still, WHO used estimates for 1997, three years behind the publication of its report. Small wonder perhaps that after its ranking in 2000, the global health czar stopped producing these rankings, citing "the complexity of the task."[148]

The same sense of humility informs the hallmarks this book develops. The same sense of humility equally explains the characterization and representation of the hallmarks in the foregoing analysis as a guide. Among other things, the conversation in this chapter was designed as a prelude to the critical assessment of the Ghana healthcare reform initiatives undertaken in Chapters 4–6. Before then, it is necessary that we pause to describe the NHIS, the assignment Chapter 3 grapples with.

Notes

1 "The Rectification of Names," *Cultural China*, www.cultural-china.com/china WH/History/en/165History878.html.
2 Paola Testori Coggi, "Foreword from the European Commission," in *Health System Performance Comparison: An Agenda for Policy Information and Research*, eds. Irene Papanicolas and Peter C. Smith (Maidenhead, UK: Open University Press, 2013), xi.
3 See Constitution of the World Health Organization (1948), www.who.int/gov ernance/eb/who_constitution_en.pdf. The Constitution was adopted by the International Health Conference held in New York June 19–July 22, 1946, signed July 22, 1946, by the representatives of 61 States, and entered into force April 7, 1948. Amendments adopted by the Twenty-Sixth, Twenty-Ninth, Thirty-Ninth, and Fifty-First World Health Assemblies (resolutions WHA26.37, WHA29.38, WHA39.6, and WHA51.23), and incorporated into the initial text,

came into force on February 3, 1977, January 20, 1984, July 11, 1994, and September 15, 2005, respectively.
4 See Philip C. Aka, *Genetic Counseling and Preventive Medicine in Post-War Bosnia* (Gateway East, Singapore: Palgrave Macmillan, 2020), 31–32.
5 Ibid., p. 32.
6 Ibid.
7 See Daniel Dramani Kipo-Sunyehzi et al., "Ghana's Journey towards Universal Health Coverage: The Role of the National Health Insurance Scheme," *European Journal of Investigation in Health, Psychology, and Education*, 10 (October 2019), 94–109, doi:10.3390/ejihpe1001000996–7 (identifying multiple pathways toward universal health coverage that include "fairness and equity").
8 See *Healthy Systems for Universal Health Coverage: A Joint Vision for Healthy Lives* (Geneva, Switzerland, World Health Organization, and Washington, DC: World Bank, 2017), 6.
9 Edward Baker et al., *Managing the Public Health Enterprise* (Burlington, MA: Jones Barlett Learning, 2010), 170.
10 *Healthy Systems for Universal Health Coverage*, note 8, p. 12.
11 Ibid.
12 Ibid.
13 Ibid.
14 Ibid.
15 Ibid.
16 Ibid., citing Margaret E. Kruk et al., "What is a Resilient Health System? Lessons from Ebola," *Lancet* (2015), 1910–1912.
17 Aka, note 4, p. 45.
18 See *Healthy Systems for Universal Health Coverage*, note 8, p. 7.
19 Ibid.
20 Aka, note 4, p. 32.
21 *World Health Report 2000: Health Systems: Improving Performance* (Geneva, Switzerland: World Health Organization, 2000), 11 ("Health systems of some sort have existed for as long as people have tried deliberately to protect their health and treat diseases").
22 See *Universal Health Coverage: Why Health Insurance Schemes are Leaving the Poor Behind* (Oxford, UK: Oxfam Int'l, October 9, 2013), 3, www.oxfam.org/sites/www.oxfam.org/files/bp176-universal-health-coverage-901013-en_pdf. (abstract) (defining universal healthcare to mean that "all people get the treatment they need without fear of falling into poverty," specifically that "everyone has the same financial protection and access to the same range of high[-]quality health services, regardless of their employment status or ability to pay.").
23 Philip C. Aka et al., "Ghana's National Health Insurance Scheme (NHIS) and the Evolution of a Human Right to Healthcare in Africa," *Chicago-Kent J. Int'l & Comp. Law*, 17(2) (2017), 2, 4.
24 Anja Rudiger, "Human Rights and the Political Economy of Universal Health Care: Designing Equitable Financing," *Health & Human Rights Journal*, 18 (2016), 67, 69.
25 "Global Health and Foreign Policy," UN Gen. Assembly, A/67/L.36 (December 6, 2012), 10, https://ncdalliance.org/sites/default/files/resource_files/Global%20Health%20and%20Foreign%20Policy%20resolution%202012_67th%20GA.pdf.
26 See footnotes 8–19 and accompanying text.
27 "What is Universal Coverage?" *World Health Organization*, www.who.int/health_financing/universal_coverage_definition/en/.
28 Dr. Margaret Chan, "Message from the Director-General," in *The World Health Report: Health System Financing: The Path to Universal Coverage* (Geneva, Switzerland: World Health Organization, 2010), vi, vii.

29 "Sustainable Health Financing, Universal Coverage, and Social Health Insurance," Doc. A58/20 (WHA58.33), 58th World Health Assembly (May 25, 2005),1(8), https://cdn.who.int/media/docs/default-source/health-financing/sustainable-health-financing-universal-coverage-and-social-health-insurance.pdf?sfvrsn=f8358323_3 (recognizing "the responsibility of Governments to urgently and significantly scale up efforts to accelerate the transition toward universal access to affordable and quality health-care services"). See also "Global Health and Foreign Policy," note 25, p. 8 (expressing the recognition of the UN Gen. Assembly regarding "the responsibility of Governments to urgently and significantly scale up efforts to accelerate the transition toward universal access to affordable and quality health-care services").

30 See note 3.

31 Declaration of Alma-Ata, Int'l Conference on Primary Health Care, Alma-Ata, USSR. (September 6–12, 1978), www.euro.who.int/_data/assets/pdf_file/0009/113877/E93944.pdf.

32 See "Sustainable Health Financing," note 29, *passim*. The WHA is the WHO's decision-making body. The Assembly meets annually in Geneva, Switzerland, is attended by delegations from all WHO Member States and focuses on a specific health agenda prepared by the Executive Board. "World Health Assembly," WHO, Media Center, www.who.int/mediacentre/events/governance/wha/en/.

33 Constitution of the World Health Organization, note 3, preamble. A state becomes a member of WHO by ratifying the Constitution of the World Health Organization, the equivalent in this instance of a treaty. As of 2021, WHO has 194 member states. "Countries," World Health Organization, www.who.int/countries/en/. All UN members are eligible for WHO membership. The only UN member who is not a member of the WHO is Liechtenstein. WHO member states appoint delegations to the World Health Assembly, WHO's supreme decision-making body. It is headed by a Director-General and usually meets yearly in May in Geneva, Switzerland, the WHO's headquarters. WHO has an Executive Board comprising 34 members, persons technically qualified in the health field, elected by the Assembly for a three-year term, and headed by a chairperson. The major functions of the Board are to carry out the decisions and policies of the Assembly, to advise it and to facilitate its work. Much of the work of the WHO is done by its regional offices. There are six such offices across the world: Africa with headquarters in Brazzaville, Republic of Congo; Europe, with headquarters in Copenhagen, Denmark; South-East Asia with headquarters in New Delhi, India; Eastern Mediterranean with headquarters in Cairo, Egypt; Western Pacific with headquarters in Manilla, Philippines; and The Americas with headquarters in Washington, DC, USA. As of 2012, WHO employed 8,500 people in 147 countries. "Employment: Who We Are," www.who.int/employment/about_who/en/. In obedience to its principle of a tobacco-free work environment, WHO does not recruit cigarette smokers. "Employment: Who We Need," www.who.int/employment/who_we__need/en/. WHO operates "goodwill ambassadors," about five in number, members of the arts, sport or other fields of public life, aimed at drawing attention to the organization's initiatives and projects. WHO derives its revenues from annual contributions by member states and outside donors. In 2018–19, the largest contributors were the US, the UK, the Bill and Melinda Gates Foundation, GAVI (Vaccine) Alliance, Germany, Japan, and the European Commission. "Our Contributors, World Health Organization," www.who.int/about/funding/contributors.

34 Declaration of Alma-Ata, note 31, art. I.

35 See Declaration of Alma-Ata, note 31, preamble (voicing "the need for urgent action by all" stakeholders, including governments, health and development workers, and the world community "to protect and promote the health of all the people of the world [...]"). See also ibid., art. II (indicating that "gross inequality"

36 Quoted in Fernando Montenegro Torres, *UNICO Studies Series 14: Costa Rica Case Study: Primary Health Care Achievements and Challenges Within the Framework of the Social Health Insurance* (Washington, DC: World Bank, January 2013), ii, www.tpg-iha.com/wp-content/uploads/2016/02/TPG-IHA-Costa-Rica-Briefing-Materials.pdf.
37 "Sustainable Health Financing," note 29, 1(4).
38 Amartya Sen, "Universal Healthcare: The Affordable Dream," *Vanguard* (London) (January 6, 2015), www.theguardian.com/society/2015/jan/06/-sp-universal-healthcare-the-affordable-dream-amartya-sen.
39 Ibid.
40 Social Health Insurance Report of a Regional Expert Group Meeting New Delhi, India, 13–15 March 2003, World Health Organization Regional Office for South-East Asia New Delhi (June 2003), 1.
41 Ibid.
42 Ibid.
43 "Sustainable Health Financing," note 29, preamble. See also ibid. 1(1) (urging member states "to ensure that [their] health-financing systems include a method for prepayment of financial contributions for health care, with a view to sharing risk among the population and avoiding catastrophic health-care expenditure and impoverishment of individuals as a result of seeking care").
44 Ibid., 24.
45 "Global Health and Foreign Policy," note 25, preamble.
46 Ibid., 2.
47 Ibid., 15.
48 Ibid., 17. See also "Sustainable Health Financing," note 29, preamble (same language); and ibid., 1(5) (urging member states "to recognize that, when managing the transition to universal coverage, each option will need to be developed within the particular macroeconomic, sociocultural and political context of each country"). Obviously, this is a recognition evident in the reality that different forces, including political, economic, social, epidemiological, and related variables shape the ways different countries approach universal healthcare. See Global Health Program and Rabin Martin, *Universal Health Coverage: An Annotated Bibliography* (Geneva, Switzerland: Graduate Institute, May 2014), 5, http://graduateinstitute.ch/files/live/sites/iheid/files/sites/globalhealth/ghp-new/publications/UHC_Bibliography_v9_web.pdf.
49 "Global Health and Foreign Policy," note 25, 7.
50 UN Gen. Assembly, Resolution on Foreign Policy Resolution, 67th Sess., 53rd Plenary Meeting, Agenda Item 123, U.N. Doc. No. A/RES/67/81 (December 12, 2012), www.un.org/en/ga/search/view_doc.asp?symbol=A/RES/67/81, 4 (preamble).
51 Ibid., 32.
52 "African Union Welcomes Commitments to Achieve Universal Health Coverage by 2030," African Union (September 1, 2016), Press Release, www.au.int/en/pressreleases/31328/african-union-welcomes-commitments-achieve-universal-health-coverage-2030.
53 "About the African Union," African Union, https://au.int/en/overview.
54 Ibid.
55 "Act with Ambition: Universal Health Coverage (UHC) Day 2016," WHO (December 7, 2016), Event Notice, www.who.int/health_financing/events/uhc-day-2016/en/.
56 Sen, note 38.
57 "Act with Ambition: Universal Health Coverage (UHC) Day 2016," note 55.

32 *Analytical Framework*

58 Daniel Cotlear, "The World Bank's Universal Health Coverage Studies Series (UNICO)," in *The Health Extension Program in Ethiopia*, UNICO Studies Series No. 10, eds. Netsanet W. Workie and Gandham NV Ramana (Washington, DC: World Bank, January 2013), http://documents.worldbank.org/curated/en/356621468032070256/pdf/749630NWP0ETHI00Box374316B00PUBLIC0.pdf.
59 "Universal Health Coverage Coalition," http://universalhealthcoverageday.org/welcome/.
60 See Universal Declaration of Human Rights, G.A. Res. 217 A (III), U.N. GAOR, 3d Sess., U.N. Doc. A/810 (1948), art. 21(1) (stating that "[e]veryone has the right to take part in the government of his country, directly or through freely chosen representatives") and art. 21(2) (stating that "[e]veryone has the right to equal access to public service in his country").
61 Cotlear, note 58.
62 See, for example, Asad Ismi, *Impoverishing a Continent: The World Bank and the IMF in Africa* (Ottawa, Canada: Canadian Center for Policy Alternatives, 2004); Robert Lensink, *Structural Adjustment in Sub-Saharan Africa* (New York: Longman, 1996).
63 See Jim Yong Kim, Poverty, Health and the Human Future, Speech at the World Health Assembly (May 21, 2013), www.worldbank.org/en/news/speech/2013/05/21/world-bank-group-president-jim-yong-kim-speech-at-wirkd-health-assembly.
64 Jim Yong Kim, Speech at Conference on Universal Health Coverage in Emerging Economies, Center for Strategic and International Studies, Washington, DC (January 14, 2014).
65 See Kim, Poverty, Health and the Human Future, note 63.
66 Ibid.
67 Kim, Poverty, Health and the Human Future, note 63.
68 Kim, Speech at Conference on Universal Health Coverage in Emerging Economies, note 64.
69 "Executive Summary," in *World Health Report*, note 28, p. x.
70 Priyanka Saksena et al., "Impact of Mutual Health Insurance on Access to Health Care and Financial Risk Protection in Rwanda," in *World Health Report*, note 28 (abstract).
71 Sen, note 38.
72 See ibid.
73 Ibid.
74 Ibid.
75 Ibid., citing the State of Kerala in India.
76 Ibid.
77 Ibid.
78 Ibid.
79 Otherwise, we would not be talking about the "who gets what, when, and how?" that hallmarks politics. See generally Harold D. Lasswell, *Politics: Who Gets What, When, and How?* (Gloucester, MA: Peter Smith Pub. Inc., 1990) (colloquially defining politics as "who gets what, when, and how").
80 See Rudiger, note 24, pp. 67, 69 (with 17 percent of the GDP devoted to health in 2013, "[h]ealth care funding is plentiful" in the land, "yet the mechanism for raising and allocating those funds are deeply inequitable").
81 See Philip Musgrove, "The Five Cs of Universal Health Care: Canada, Chile, Colombia, Costa Rica, and Cuba Take Different Paths to the Same Goal," *Americas Quarterly* (Summer 2010), www.americasquarterly.org/node/1691; see also "The National Health Insurance Scheme Functions," *EHealth Insurance*, www.ehealthinsurance.com.ng/the-national-health-insurance-scheme-functions/ (stating that although healthcare systems share many similarities in functions, their workability "differs from country to country").
82 Musgrove, note 81.

83 See Jack Donnelly, *International Human Rights*, 4th ed. (Boulder, CO: Westview Press, 2013), 19; and R.J. Vincent, *Human Rights and International Relations* (New York: Cambridge University Press, 1986), 9–11 (discussing five features of human rights). The historiography of modern human rights has many sources. See, for example, Paul Gordon Lauren, *The Evolution of International Human Rights: Visions Seen* (Philadelphia, PA: University of Pennsylvania Press, 2011), 5–42.

84 Samuel Edward Corwin and Jack W. Peltason, *Corwin and Peltason's Understanding the Constitution*, 7th ed. (Oak Brook, IL and New York: Dryden Press, 1976), 4. See also Louis Henkin, "Human Rights: Ideology and Aspiration, Reality and Prospect," in *Realizing Human Rights: Moving from Inspiration to Impact*, eds. Samantha Power and Graham Allison (New York: St. Martin's Press, 2000), 3, 5 (calling human rights "claims of rights, not by grace, or love, or charity, or compassion" that "society is morally, politically, even legally obligated to respect, ensure, and realize").

85 Donnelly, note 83, p. 7. Instruments comprising the international bill of human rights are the Universal Declaration of Human Rights, UDHR (1948), the International Covenant on Civil and Political Rights (ICCPR), and the International Covenant on Economic, Social, and Cultural Rights (ICESCR). The last two came into force in 1976. Some commentators include the United Nations Charter (1945), the first instrument ever to use the language of human rights, among the documents of the international bill of human rights. The UDHR sets forth "common standards of achievement for all peoples and all nations" that the two human rights covenants, as binding multilateral treaties, then elaborated. Additionally, over the years, the UDHR garnered such authoritativeness that today some international law scholars appropriately consider it as customary international law. See Henkin, "Human Rights: Ideology and Aspiration, Reality and Prospect," in *Realizing Human Rights*, note 84, p. 12.

86 U. Oji Umozurike, *The African Charter on Human and Peoples' Rights* (Leiden, Netherlands and Boston, MA: Brill, 1997), 5.

87 Kenneth Roth, "Human Rights Organizations: A New Force for Social Change," in *Realizing Human Rights*, note 84, p. 230 (referring to the UDHR).

88 *The Basic Writings of John Stuart Mill: On Liberty, the Subjection of Women and Unilateralism* (New York: Modern Library, 2002), 3–97.

89 See Philip C. Aka, "Analyzing U.S. Commitment to Socioeconomic Human Rights," *Akron Law Review*, 39(2) (2006), 417, 424.

90 For some scholars, the response to argument on methodology in comparative analysis is to let fools contest in that what gets the job of analysis done should suffice. See John Ohnesorge, "Administrative Law in East Asia: A Comparative-Historical Analysis," in *Comparative Administrative Law*, eds. Susan Rose-Ackerman and Peter L. Lindseth (Northampton, MA: Edward Elgar, 2010), 78 (stating that the goal of a research is served if the purpose of the project in question is made so clear that the readers can judge "for themselves what is gained from the comparison," specifically "whether the materials and the argument support the final conclusions," and if, for the researcher, the method used generates useful insights). But such a nondeliberate(d) approach would not do here.

91 Michael J. Sodaro, *Comparative Politics: A Global Introduction*, 3rd ed. (Boston, MA: McGraw-Hill, 2008), 27.

92 See Karen Evans, "Comparative Successes or Failures? Some Methodological Issues in Conducting International Comparative Research Inpost—Secondary Education," Education-Line. Paper Presented at the British Educational Research Association Annual Conference, University of Sussex at Brighton (September 2–5, 1999), www.leeds.ac.uk/educol/documents/00001309.htm (stating that "comparative studies are motivated by the need to borrow, advise, evaluate and the curiosity-motivated need to find out and describe practices from other cultures").

34 *Analytical Framework*

93 Mary Ko Zimmerman, "Comparative Health-Care Systems," *Encyclopedia of Sociology* (updated February 10, 2020), www.encyclopedia.com/social-sciences/encyclopedias-almanacs-transcripts-and-maps/comparative-health-care-systems.
94 Kate O'Regan and Nick Friedman, "Equality," in *Comparative Constitutional Law*, eds. Tom Ginsburg and Rosalind Dixon (Northampton, MA: Edward Elgar Publishing, 2011), 473, 496 (analyzing the concept and practice of equality in comparative constitutional law, focusing on Canada, the UK, the Council of Europe, and South Africa).
95 Rudyard Kipling, "The English Flag," *Bartleby* (1891), bartleby.com/364/122.html ("And what should they know of England who only England know?").
96 Sodaro, note 91, p. 28.
97 Sodaro, note 91, p. 13.
98 Frank L. Wilson, *Concepts and Issues in Comparative Politics: An Introduction to Comparative Analysis* (Upper Saddle River, NJ: Prentice Hall, 1996), 4.
99 Ibid.
100 Ibid.
101 Sen, note 38.
102 See Marie L. Lassey et al., *Health Care Systems Around the World: Characteristics, Issues, Reforms* (New York: Pearson, 1996) (book's back cover).
103 Aka, note 4, p. 109.
104 Zimmerman, note 93.
105 Ibid. ("Review of Selected Health-Care Systems").
106 Kipling, note 95.
107 Aka, note 4, p. 110.
108 "Sustainable Health Financing," note 29, 1(7).
109 Ibid., 2(3).
110 Kim, Speech at Conference on Universal Health Coverage in Emerging Economies, note 64.
111 See J. Tyler Dickovick and Jonathan Eastwood, *Comparative Politics: Integrating Theories, Methods, and Cases* (New York: Oxford University Press, 2013), 13–19 (identifying the features and breaking down the elements of the comparative method).
112 Ibid., p. 14.
113 See ibid., pp. 14–16 (including the illustration with Ghana and Togo).
114 Ibid., p. 16.
115 Ibid.
116 Ibid., p. 17.
117 Ibid.
118 Ibid.
119 Ibid.
120 See ibid., p. 19.
121 Ibid.
122 Alexander L. George and Andrew Bennett, *Case Studies and Theory Development in the Social Sciences* (Cambridge, MA: MIT Press, 2005), 6.
123 See Michael G. Maxfield and Earl R. Babbie, *Research Methods for Criminal Justice and Criminology*, 7th ed. (Stamford, CT: Cengage Learning, 2015), 32–33 (commenting on social scientific theory). See also Jonathan E. Adler and Catherine Z. Elgin, eds., *Philosophical Inquiry: Classic and Contemporary Readings* (Indianapolis, IN: Hackett Publishing Co., Inc., 2007), 449 (contrasting empirical judgments based on description and moral judgments embedded in prescription); and James N. Danziger, *Understanding the Political World: A Comparative Introduction to Political Science*, 11th ed. (New York: Pearson, 2013), 5–7 (including description and prescription, along with an explanation of three types of political knowledge).

Analytical Framework   35

124 Edmund Fuller, "Oliver Wendell Holmes, Jr.—The Common Law," *Encyclopedia Britannica*, www.britannica.com/biography/Oliver-Wendell-Holmes-Jr/The-Common-Law.
125 Ibid.
126 Ibid.
127 Marc J. Roberts et al., *Getting Health Reform Right: A Guide to Improving Performance and Equity* (New York: Oxford University Press, 2008), 40–60 (commenting on the inescapable ethics of *appraising* national performance in healthcare).
128 Jim Chappelow, "Pareto Efficiency," *Investopedia* (updated September 25, 2019), www.investopedia.com/terms/p/pareto.efficiency.asp.
129 Roberts et. al., note 127, *passim*.
130 Ibid.
131 See, for example, José M. Zuniga et al., eds., *Advancing the Human Right to Health* (New York: Oxford University Press, 2013) (among other achievements, this edited volume sought to provide an account of the parameters of the right to health, strategies on ways to achieve this right, and discussion as to why realization of the right is so essential in the twenty-first century).
132 DALE is the acronym for Disability-Adjusted Life Expectancy. It is "health equality in terms of child survival." *World Health Report 2000*, note 21, p. 144. Put differently, the term reports achievement on the average level of population health. Ibid., p. 146. It is "most easily understood as the expectation of life lived in equivalent full health." Ibid.
133 Regarding this information, the WHO explained that "[m]aximum attainable composite goal achievement was estimated using frontier production model relating overall health system achievement to health expenditure and other non-health system determinants represented by educational attainment." *World Health Report 2000*, note 21, p. 150.
134 Aka et al., note 23, p. 23.
135 See "Executive Summary: Why Universal Coverage?" in *The World Health Report: Health Systems Financing: The Path to Universal Coverage* (Geneva, Switzerland: World Health Organization, 2010), ix–xxii.
136 Chan, note 28, pp. vi–vii.
137 See footnotes 83–84 and accompanying text.
138 *Health in All Policies: Helsinki Statement Framework for Country Action* (Geneva, Switzerland: World Health Organization, 2014).
139 David Heymann and Robert Yates, "Embracing the Politic of Universal Health Coverage," *Chatham House: The Royal Institute of International Affairs* (June 25, 2014), https://www.chathamhouse.org/expert/comment/14972.
140 Chan, note 28, p. vii.
141 See Marko Martić and Ognjen Đukić, "Health Care System in BiH: Financing Challenges and Reform Options?" (October 20, 2017, Friedrick Ebert Stiftung, Sarajevo), 22–23 (focusing on Bosnia and Herzegovina).
142 *World Health Report 1995: Bridging the Gap* (Geneva, Switzerland: World Health Organization, 1995), 91.
143 "Executive Summary: Why Universal Coverage?" in *World Health Report: Health Systems Financing: The Path to Universal Coverage*, note 135, pp. xii–xviii.
144 Aka, note 4, p. 48.
145 Ibid.
146 *The World Health Report 2000*, note 21, p. 144.
147 Ibid.
148 "The World Health Organizations Ranking of the World's Health Systems, by Rank," *Countries of the World*, photius.com/rankings/healthranks.html.

3 Ghana's National Health Insurance Scheme (NHIS)

Introduction

To contextualize and properly understand healthcare reforms in Ghana under the Fourth Republic since 1993, it is necessary to explore the National Health Insurance Scheme (NHIS), a program that, more than any other singular social welfare initiative in recent memory, forms the face of those reforms. The ensuing discussion comprises three elements: Healthcare in Ghana *before* the passage of the NHIS in 2003; the nature and shape of the NHIS; and an argument, instructively captioned "Beyond the NHIS," for Ghana to transition to a single-payer, tax-funded, healthcare arrangement. Analysis of the period before 2003 is warranted not just because of the proverbial starting point it affords in a discussion on healthcare reforms in Ghana under the Fourth Republic but also because, although the NHIS takes a center-stage in any examination of those reforms, a robust conversation on the topic must range beyond the singularity and insularity of any one program, no matter how important that program is. This wisdom informs the comprehensive approach this chapter adopts.

Healthcare Reforms in Ghana Before the NHIS

During the pre-colonial and much of the colonial eras, traditional medicine formed "the dominant health care system in Africa."[1] Ghana was no exception to this general trend. During these periods, many residents depended on traditional medicine, rather than Western healthcare, for their physical and mental wellness and integrity.[2] Moreover, for a variety of reasons that includes lack of access to Western medicine, onto the current period, traditional medicine still serves as the sole source of affordable medicine in many rural communities in Ghana and other African countries.[3]

Testament to the continuing vitality of traditional medicine, Ghana, like many other African countries, has traditional healers' associations which aim to preserve the integrity of traditional medicinal practices and enlighten government officials regarding the contributions of traditional medicine to the stock of healthcare delivery in these countries.[4] Ghana's Traditional Healers' Association

DOI: 10.4324/9781003264125-3

was formed back in the 1960s with its headquarters at Nsawam in Greater Accra Region.[5] Although there were user fees associated with traditional medicinal services, those fees were often token and nothing compared to allopathic Western medicine, usually linked with such fees in many African communities. Compared to allopathic medicine, traditional medicine is more within the reach of many poor people; for example, there are no testing and medication fees for patients using this type of medicine.[6]

After the Gold Coast became independent as Ghana in 1957, the new indigenous government under Kwame Nkrumah assumed responsibility for healthcare.[7] The government pursued socialist-oriented policies which viewed expanded healthcare delivery as a trajectory of economic development and integral to the overall process of nation-building.[8] It was a policy of "free health care for all," highly centralized, whose implementation was limited to public health facilities, like hospitals and clinics, with little involvement of the private sector.[9] The orientation meant no user fees. It is possible that "large-scale popular support for free healthcare[,]" most likely inspired by Nkrumah's socialist-oriented programs, "deterred any serious attempt to introduce user fees."[10] Whatever the justification, the outcome remained pretty much the same: Absence of user fees in the sense many analysts understand the term today.

Although Nkrumah's successors did not share his passion for socialism, they unveiled national development plans that included free education and healthcare for the masses of Ghanaian people.[11] So, to this point, user fees did not become much of an issue. The situation changed, beginning in the 1970s, as Ghana came increasingly under economic hard times, leading to severe cuts in government funding for healthcare and other social programs.[12] For example, in the 1990s, per capita health expenditure amounted to between $5 and $6, compared to $10 in 1970.[13] And by 1997, government spending on healthcare reached an all-time low of 1.3 percent.[14]

To stem the decline in its economic fortunes, Ghana, under Jerry J. Rawlings, sought the assistance of the World Bank and the International Monetary Fund (IMF).[15] As a condition for its loan, the IMF placed Ghana's economy under the strictures of its structural adjustment program (SAP).[16] The program mandated recipient countries to recover costs by way of user fees for delivery of social welfare packages, like healthcare and education, to citizens.[17] For example, "[i]n return for its assistance, the World Bank required the [Ghanaian] Ministry of Health to generate at least 15 percent of its recurrent expenditure from such fees."[18] The result was that the full burden for healthcare services fell on Ghanaian citizens who sought these services. Unsurprisingly, this period coincided with "shortages of essential medicines and other supplies, badly paid and demoralized staff, illegal under-the-table payments by patients for care, and an effective freeze on building new [healthcare] facilities for those without access."[19]

Ghanaians reserve the name "cash and carry" for user fees.[20] Cash and carry required potential patients to pay upfront, at the point of service delivery, before they can receive treatment—even when faced with a medical emergency.[21] It benefitted the relatively few well-off individuals who had the means to pay for expensive healthcare services for themselves and their families at the point of service, and disadvantaged poor citizens who lacked the wherewithal for badly-needed medical attention.[22] Under cash and carry, many hospitals and health centers lacked basic medical supplies like bedding and medication such that poorer patients brought these items into centers themselves and where they proceeded to pay for prescriptions that they struggled to afford.[23] Little wonder that in Nigeria, two countries removed from Ghana to the east, many residents pejoratively labelled these putative health centers "consulting rooms."[24] Absent affordable healthcare services, many citizens with health problems did everything but see a real doctor: They resorted to self-medication, turned to traditional healers, or received medical treatment from quack doctors.[25]

User fees had a vastly negative effect on Ghana's healthcare delivery system.[26] Given the fact that many Ghanaians were poor or unemployed, conditioning services upon user fees "further impoverished them[,]" in that "patients were denied treatment because they were unable to pay prior to their treatment," or were subjected to delayed diagnosis and treatment that had the effect of worsening their health conditions.[27] This explains, but not justify why, within nearly three decades after introduction of these fees, more than half of patients turned to traditional medicine or self-medication.[28] This is especially the case with economically-marginal sectors of the Ghanaian population, such as women and children and the rural poor, who bore the brunt of cash and carry.[29]

To ameliorate some of the effects coming from user fees, the Ghanaian government introduced partial exemptions in its healthcare system.[30] However, these exemptions militated against access to healthcare for poor people for a variety of reasons that included "non-uniform application across regions, difficulties in identifying poor people," and problems related to reimbursement of service providers.[31] What is more, these exemptions also remained unworkable because they "went largely unfunded[.]"[32] This was the setting when, in 1996, the New Patriotic Party (NPP), one of Ghana's major political parties, assessed the user fee system as "notoriously callous and inhuman," and pledged to "thoroughly overhaul[]" it to make it "more equitable" if it came to power.[33]

The National Health Insurance Scheme (NHIS)

The NHIS replaced cash and carry.[34] The program emerged within the broader context of "general acknowledgment that the cash and carry system was ineffective and encouraged inequality."[35] As two of these authors noted elsewhere, "Ghana's healthcare delivery system was in a shambles by the time of the 2000 general election. The economic deprivations arising from the implementation of the Structural Adjustment Program in the country helped bring the problems associated with user fees to the fore."[36] Its promise to overhaul the healthcare system, rather than simply mend it, helped the NPP and its flag bearer, John A. Kufuor, to win the parliamentary and presidential elections of 2000.[37] Kufuor was charged with the responsibility to implement the program after he became president from January 2001. The program was enacted in August 2003 and was implemented from the beginning of 2004, but did not become effective until March 2005, when benefits under the scheme kicked in.[38] Based on consultations with the opposition, made up of the National Democratic Congress (NDC) and labor unions, an agreement was reached on a package with multiple features: A centralized single-payer system designed primarily for the organized formal sector, multi-payer semi-autonomous mutual health organizations for the informal sector, and a private commercial health insurance for Ghanaians with the wherewithal to pay for those services.[39]

The NHIS was designed to minimize the financial barriers that impede access to healthcare,[40] via the guarantee of a basic health package for all Ghanaians at the point of service.[41] Through the program, the Ghanaian government sought to realize the vision "of a national health system free at the point of delivery for all—a service based on need and rights and not ability to pay[,]" where "[e]very citizen of Ghana [is] able to access and use the same range of good-quality health services within easy reach of his or her home."[42] Its objectives were manifold, including: Equity, risk equalization, quality of care, solidarity, efficiency, partnership, and sustainability.[43] Arguably, these are the features that add up to give the NHIS its pro-poor, anti-poverty distinction. Due to the plan, Ghana is ranked among countries informed commentators view as leaders in healthcare reforms in Africa,[44] on a list of bellwethers that includes Botswana, Ethiopia, Libya, Mauritius, Rwanda, South Africa, and Tunisia.[45] Four issues, more illustrative than exhaustive, around which this discussion is organized are: The legal framework of the NHIS, quantum of services subscribers or registrants can access under the scheme, the principle of exemptions that hallmark the program, and its location within three models of healthcare financing.

Legal Framework of the NHIS

The legal framework of the NHIS comprises the constitution, Ghana's charter document; the National Health Insurance Act (NHIA); and the National Health Insurance Fund (NHIF). The first is Ghana's 1992 Constitution.[46] Constitutional law is "the process by which people constitute themselves and their values in a binding legal document adaptive to new conditions not present when the document was created."[47] The closest to a right to healthcare in the Ghanaian Constitution is Article 30 which stipulates that

> [a] person who by reason of sickness or any other cause is unable to give his consent shall not be deprived by any other person of medical treatment, education or any other social or economic benefit by reason only of religious or other beliefs.[48]

Instructively, the provision is part of the "fundamental human rights and freedoms" for all Ghanaians under Chapter Five of the Constitution.[49] The document, in pertinent provisions, mandates that these fundamental human rights and freedoms "be respected and upheld by" all government officials and enforced by the courts.[50] These provisions bear comparison with Chapter Six, §34.2, requiring the President to

> report to Parliament at least once a year all the steps taken to ensure the realization of the policy objectives contained in this Chapter; and, in particular, the realization of basic human rights, a healthy economy, the right to work, the *right to good health care* and the right to education.[51]

However, the texture of this right lacks much-needed depth because, unlike Chapter Five, Chapter Six is only a statement of aspiration toward the formation of "a just and free society,"[52] that aggrieved citizens cannot enforce if the guarantee is breached because such a guarantee is non-justiciable.[53]

The NHIA provides access to healthcare for all Ghanaians, irrespective of ability to pay.[54] It was signed into law as Act 650 by John A. Kufuor, President of Ghana from 2001 until 2009. Chapter 4 deals with the politics of healthcare reforms in Ghana. Therefore, suffice it to state here that passage of the law was made possible through the strong support of a legislature dominated by the NPP.[55] The party was founded on a set of beliefs that includes "development in freedom," the duty of the government to provide "affordable, quality healthcare to every citizen," and the responsibility of the government to provide "a level of support, a safety net" for poor citizens who are unable to fend for themselves."[56]

The support for healthcare continued after control of the government shifted to the NDC. Founded by Jerry J. Rawlings, this party made affordable healthcare part of its development plan to transform the country into a middle-income country by 2015.[57] In October 2012, under the NDC administration, Act 650 was replaced with Act 852, in a bid, avowedly, to revamp the NHIS.[58] Among other objectives, the new law aimed to promote accountability, enhance transparency, and increase the effectiveness of the scheme.[59]

This seeming consensus on healthcare indicates a commitment to expanded healthcare among Ghana's major political parties,[60] as Table 3.1 shows. The agreement on healthcare brings to mind the consensus on welfare programs that crystalized among major political parties in the UK after World War II.[61]

Last but not least is the NHIF. It is a central fund into which all monies due to the NHIS goes. The Fund is the tool for subsidizing the District Mutual Insurance (DMI) plans, as mentioned in the next paragraph, for insulating these plans against random fluctuations and shortfalls in financing; covering healthcare costs for all exempt patients; and supporting programs aimed at improving access to health services.[62] The establishment of the NHIF is borne out of the realization by the government that annual premiums by subscribers alone would be insufficient to finance universal healthcare.[63] Contributions to the

Table 3.1 Leaders of Ghana's Fourth Republic since 1993

Item No.	Leader's Name	Political Party	Years in Office	How term ended
1.	Jerry J. Rawlings	NDC	1993–2001	Term limited
2.	John A. Kufuor	NPP	2001–2009	Term limited
3.	John A. Mills	NDC	2009–2012	Died in office
4.	John D. Mahama	NDC	2012–2017	Lost election
5.	Nana Akufo-Addo	NDC	2017–	Still in office

Fund, more formally known as levies, come from four main sources: A 2.5 percent value-added tax (VAT) on goods and services;[64] an earmarked portion of social security taxes (2.5 percent of the 17.5 percent) from workers in the formal sector; premium payments from informal sector adults; and monies from miscellaneous sources, including budgetary allocations, grants, gifts, donations, voluntary contributions, and returns on NHIS investments.[65]

The Ghana Revenue Authority (GRA) collects these levies which, under the applicable law, it must pay directly into the NHIF within 30 days of receipt of each levy.[66] Regrettably, Ghanaian governments do not comply with this regulation. Instead, as two of the authors indicated elsewhere, commenting on the politics of healthcare in Ghana, finance ministers from both the NPP and NDC generally deposit NHIS funds into a general account, the Consolidated Fund, because of the flexibility it affords the government to use that money for other projects.[67] From a hierarchical standpoint, the NHIS is an agency under the Ghana Ministry of Health and the Minister of Health appoints the head of the NHIS.[68] This factor of control injects the possibility of political interference into the operation of the Scheme which, when activated, facilitates the use of NHIS funds for non-NHIS projects. One negative result of this occurrence is that "[m]onies meant for NHIS are sometimes diverted for other activities whilst claims remain unpaid."[69] It goes to the matter of accountability under the NHIS which this book discusses in greater detail in Chapter 6 on health as human right.

The body charged with implementation of the healthcare initiative is the National Health Insurance Authority. The Authority registers, licenses, supervises, accredits providers, and manages the NHIF.[70] To facilitate healthcare delivery, under the NHIS, Ghana operates a five-tiered service system: National, Regional, District, Sub-district, and Community.[71]

Under the NHIS, all residents must join one of three plans: District Mutual Insurance (DMI), Private Mutual Insurance (PMI), or Private Commercial Health Insurance (PCHI).[72] The first, DMI, operates in every administrative district in Ghana.[73] It is a non-commercial program available to every member of the public who registers as a beneficiary. Subscribers can transfer their policy when they move to a new district. The program is available to residents of reduced means unable to afford insurance premiums, such as poor citizens and individuals without a job. In addition to any premium paid by subscribers, the

DMI is funded by the national government, the source of which subsidy is the NHIF, referred to in the preceding two paragraphs, into which every Ghanaian worker pays 2.5 percent of his or her social security contributions. Other sources of funding include value-added tax of the same percentage.[74]

Under the PMI, the second of the three enumerated plans, any group of people, for example, members of a church or any secular group, can come together and make contributions to cater for their health needs, providing such services under the plan that the governing council approves.[75] PMI plans are *not* eligible for subsidy from the government.[76] The third and final plan, the PCHI is, as its name implies, a plan operated by companies approved by the government. Individuals who have the means can purchase these plans for themselves and their dependents, just as they would buy a car. Like PMIs, PCHI plans are not subsidized by the government. Instead, under this category, individuals may be required to pay a security deposit by the approved companies as a condition for registration or enrolment.[77] The co-existence of the latter two plans with the first effectively means that the Ghanaian government unveiled a "model of universal coverage through district mutual schemes from which individuals can opt out so long as they are covered by a private insurer."[78] In other words, membership in the NHIS is voluntary, not mandatory. We will return to this point later in our recommendation on the need for the NHIS to transition to a single-payer, tax-funded system.

Individuals registered under any of these plans are given a card which they then use to seek and access treatment in any hospital or related healthcare facility in the country—without having to pay for anything, unless they ask for extra services, such as a private ward. Following treatment, their bills are sent to their healthcare provider—which then pays the money to their healthcare giver. Individuals can also use their cards to buy prescribed drugs at accredited pharmacies without paying at the point of service delivery. Instead, as with the healthcare giver or hospital, the pharmacy contacts the individual's healthcare provider for payment.[79]

The legal framework of the NHIS also encompasses the relevant treaties Ghana has ratified, such as the International Covenant on Economic, Social, and Cultural Rights (ICESCR),[80] and the African Charter on Human and Peoples' Rights (ACHPR).[81] The ICESCR mandates state parties to create "conditions which would assure to all medical service and medical attention in the event of sickness."[82] Similarly, the ACHPR enjoined state parties to "ensure that [their residents] receive medical attention when they are sick."[83] These and other instruments are elaborated upon in Chapter 6 dealing with health as human right.

Quantum of Services Available to Subscribers under the NHIS

The NHIS entitles subscribers or registrants to a minimum of services. The Scheme covers about 95 percent of common diseases in the country.[84] Therefore, in the NHIS scheme of things, whichever plan an individual signs up for does *not* cover all services. Services covered under the NHIS are:

- *outpatient services*, including consultations, requested investigations, medications, especially drugs on the NHIS drug list, and approved traditional medicines; outpatients/day surgical operations, such as repair of hernia, and outpatient physiotherapy;
- *inpatient services*, including general and specialist inpatient care, requested investigations, medications, especially prescription drugs on the NHIS drug list, cervical and breast cancer treatment, surgical operations, inpatient physiotherapy, general ward accommodation, and feeding, where available;
- *other specific services*, including oral health services, pain relief, and dental restoration;
- *eye care services*, including refraction, visual fields, A-scan, cataract removal, and eyelid surgery;
- *maternity care services*, including antenatal care, normal and assisted deliveries, Caesarean section, and post-natal care;
- *emergencies of every kind*, defined as crisis health situations demanding urgent intervention, whether medical, surgical, pediatric, obstetric and gynecological, road traffic accidents, and dialysis for acute renal (kidney) failure; and
- *public health services*, including immunization, family planning, inpatient and outpatient treatment of mental illness; treatment of tuberculosis and related conditions; and confirmatory HIV test for AIDS patients.[85]

In the same vein, there is a long list of excluded services that beneficiaries are *not* entitled to for which services they must pay more to receive benefits. These excluded services include: Rehabilitation other than physiotherapy; appliances and prostheses, such as optical aids, heart aids, orthopedic aids, and dentures; cosmetic surgeries and aesthetic treatment; anti-retroviral drugs for HIV; and assisted reproduction.[86] Others not covered are: Echocardiography, photography, angiography, dialysis for chronic renal (kidney) failure; organ transplants; all drugs not listed on the NHIS list; heart and brain surgery, other than those resulting from accidents; cancer treatment, other than breast and cervical; mortuary services; diagnosis and treatment abroad; medical examinations for purposes other than treatment in accredited health facilities (e.g., visa application, driving licenses, etc.); and accommodation in Very Important Person (VIP) wards.[87]

NHIS membership is open to all citizens and persons resident in Ghana.[88] In delivering healthcare services to beneficiaries, the National Health Insurance Authority, which runs the program, uses service providers that it credentials. The fee arrangements the Authority applies with these providers have changed over the years: Initially, fee-for-service (FFS), later diagnosis-related grouping (DRG), and most recently, an inclination toward capitation fees.[89] FFS is a payment method where services are unbundled and paid for separately.[90] This fee arrangement went out of vogue when the Authority encountered problems in processing claims expenditure because of increasing utilization, leading to the introduction of the DRG, in an attempt to solve the problem.[91] Under the DRG, service providers are reimbursed at a fixed rate per service based on diagnosis and treatment.[92] Finally, in 2012, the NHIA introduced the capitation system of payment for primary out-patients' services on a pilot basis in the Ashanti Region of Ghana.[93] Under this method, providers are paid a fixed amount of money based on the number of patients for delivering a range of services.[94] Persons well-versed with the operations of the NHIS like this payment method because of its capacity to reduce delay, check fraud, and improve the quality of healthcare for patients, but service providers oppose it.[95] As a result, its implementation has not gone beyond the pilot stage.[96]

Operation through the Principle of Exemptions

Various pilot initiatives, several of them unveiled by the Ministry of Health, preceded the introduction of the NHIS in 2003. One of these was Community Health Insurance (CHI). These schemes are "voluntary health insurance, organized at the level of the community[.]"[97] The first of these pilot schemes by the Ministry of Health was unveiled in 1993.[98] This was followed by another in 1997 in four districts of the Eastern Region of the country which had dire need for healthcare services.[99] None of these efforts metamorphosed into a national plan at this stage because of lack of political will.[100] Another set of initiatives was the Mutual Health Organization (MHO). These are "voluntary organizations[,]" "usually owned, designed, and managed by the communities they service[,]" which "provide health insurance services to their members."[101] They are organizations "based on ethical principles of mutual aid and social solidarity[,]" whose popularity "reflects a need in communities to address the difficulty of paying for health care when care is required."[102] The number of these MHOs grew from just three in 1999 to 258 four years later.[103] However, just like CHI schemes, MHOs were only able to provide healthcare access for a small percentage, not more than 2 percent, of the Ghanaian population.[104]

The NHIS operates through what we might, for lack of a better term, call the principle of exemptions. Workers in the formal sector are, in principle, exempt from paying premiums, since their 2.5 percent contributions into the Social Security and National Insurance Trust (SSNIT) are accepted in lieu of a premium.[105] Other groups exempted from paying premiums under the law include: Self-employed who contribute to the SSNIT;[106] pregnant women (whether in need of antenatal, delivery, or post-natal health care services);[107] persons under 18 years of age whose parents have enrolled in the scheme;[108] persons the Minister for Social Welfare determined to be indigent;[109] persons the Minister for Social Welfare determined to be "differently-abled," meaning disabled;[110] senior citizens aged 70 years and above;[111] pensioners under the Social Security Pension Scheme;[112] persons with mental disorder;[113] and other categories prescribed by the Minister of Social Welfare.[114] In effect, workers in the formal sector (SSNIT contributors) and workers in the informal sector (premium payees) are the main contributors to NHIS funds.[115]

Regarding coverage of persons under 18, during a meeting of world leaders at the UN General Assembly in New York in 2009, then President, John A. Mills (2009–2012), announced his government's commitment to provide free healthcare for all people under 18 years of age, whether or not their parents were enrolled under the scheme.[116] The hard part is implementation, regarding which the British antipoverty conglomerate Oxfam International,[117] observed that "[d]isappointingly[,] the government has been slow to implement the commitment to free care for all people under 18."[118]

Many groups are exempted from paying premiums under the scheme that, as Oxfam International deadpanned in its 2011 report, practically "the only non-exempt group in Ghana required to pay a regular out-of-pocket premium payment are informally employed adults."[119] As of 2011 (the date of the Oxfam report), these workers paid a premium of anywhere from GH₵7.20 (in lay language 7.20 Ghana Cedis, approximately US$4.60 at the time) to GH ₵48.00, assessed based on income and capacity to pay.[120] Initially, the annual premium varied from one district to another. As of 2019, the annual premium is the same everywhere in Ghana and the new registration is GH₵30 (30 Ghana Cedis or about US$5.48592) for persons in the informal sector from 18–69 years old.[121] In contrast, the NHIF paid a flat rate premium into the scheme on behalf of each exempt member which as of 2008 amounted to GH₵14.[122]

On the surface, healthcare by exemptions seems to work all right. With respect to the exemption for pregnant women, introduced in 2008, "[i]n just one year of implementation 433,000 additional women had access to health care."[123] But such increments tell only part of the story that, as Oxfam International advised, "bolder changes are now urgently required to accelerate progress."[124] This is because, in addition to premiums, under the scheme, subscribers must also pay a processing or renewal fee for their identification cards.[125] The only exceptions to this requirement are pregnant women and indigents, who are exempted from this registration fee.[126]

Three Models of Healthcare Financing and the Location of the NHIS Within These Models

Financing is central to the definition of expanded health coverage.[127] Chapter 5 on the economics of healthcare reforms deals with that issue. Accordingly, the following discussion is narrowly focused on the topic at hand revolving around the placement of the NHIS within the three models of healthcare financing surveyed here. Four possibilities of healthcare financing exist: Out-of-pocket, user-fee healthcare arrangement; tax-funded healthcare financing; social health insurance; and a hybrid mixture of the latter two approaches.[128] The first is user fee or out-of-pocket. Because it prevents people from seeking medical attention, and can exacerbate poverty, the user-fee arrangement is the least efficient and most inequitable means of financing healthcare.[129] "Every second, three people are pushed into poverty because they have to pay out-of-pocket for health care."[130]

The pre-2003 experience of Ghana bears this reality out. The NHIS is traceable to experiments with alternative financing models in the 1990s that evolved "against the background of high user fees, inability to pay, and exemptions failure."[131] These are probably among the reasons why, in the finding of one study, "as a share of the total value of global health spending," the out-of-pocket, user fee system "is eclipsed by" the other categories of funding.[132] The occurrence leaves us with the last three options—which categories other studies track—[133] as viable social insurance possibilities for Ghana and other African countries.

Tax-funded healthcare financing involves the use of general tax revenue as the main source of finance for risk pooling. By definition, it is a prepaid financing arrangement in which "more than half of public expenditure is financed through revenues other than earmarked payroll taxes [...] and in which access to publicly-financed services is, at least formally, open to all citizens."[134] It is a widespread approach to healthcare financing for many countries, evident in the fact that, as one source disclosed in 2004, it is "the predominant source for health care expenditure in 106 out of 191 WHO countries."[135] Tax-funded healthcare financing has certain advantages, which rival approaches lack, emanating from their political tax-and-spend nature; these include "[large]-scale economies in administration, risk management, and purchasing power."[136] However, there are also several drawbacks traceable to that tax-and-spend attribute, notably "inefficiencies that emerge from serving multiple objectives, political pressures to serve privileged groups, the normal challenges of effective management in public services, and problems associated with weak accountability and instability."[137]

Under the *social health insurance* (SHI) *model*, specific contributions for health are collected from workers, self-employed people, enterprises, and the government, and then pooled into a single or multiple social health insurance Fund, as the case may be. This model evolved in response to the deficiencies of some political systems lacking in a "robust tax base," marked by "a low institutional capacity to collect taxes and weak tax compliance."[138] Social health insurance may be managed in various ways, including through a single government insurance fund or through multiple non-governmental funds.[139] Whereas under tax-funded healthcare financing, coverage is automatically universal in the sense that all citizens or residents are typically entitled to services, under social health insurance, "entitlement is linked to a contribution made by, or on behalf of, specific individuals in the population" and universality is "achieved only if contributions are made on behalf of each member of the population."[140]

It is for this latter reason that many SHI schemes combine different sources of funds, with the government often contributing on behalf of individuals or groups who cannot afford to pay themselves.[141] The reason that the Ghanaian government has been slow to implement the commitment to free care for persons under 18,[142] could have been for resource constraints, given the budgetary implications of such expansion in a society, like many in Africa, where individuals in this age category form the bulk of the population. We earlier commented on this model in Chapter 2,[143] wherein we portrayed SHI as a form of healthcare financing anchored on the twin pillars of risk pooling and tax-funding.[144]

Last but not least is the *hybrid model* involving a mixture of tax-funded healthcare financing, and social health insurance financing. Each of the last three categories encompasses some of the four key actions for financing universal healthcare that the WHO advises countries pursuing expanded healthcare to prioritize—minimizing direct payments and maximizing mandatory prepayment, establishing large risk pools, and using general government revenue to cover those who cannot afford to contribute.[145] In contrast, user fee arrangements lack all of these four features.

Which of these three categories does Ghana's NHIS scheme fall into? Based on the description of the program's features in the preceding section, Ghana is neither fully tax-funded nor fully social insurance. Instead, it appears to straddle both approaches, an occurrence that makes it a little bit of both or, in the terminology of Floyd and Gross, mixed private/public systems.[146] According to one study, about 70–75 percent of total revenue of the NHIS comes from tax monies, about 20–25 percent from formal sector contributions and about 5 percent from the informal sector.[147] As Oxfam International observed, "[t]he NHIS's heavy reliance on tax funding" contradicts its image "as social health insurance" of a manner that realistically makes it "more akin to a tax-funded national health care system[.]"[148]

Beyond the NHIS

Although seemingly starkly different from the US, Ghana's healthcare system still brings to mind the system in place in the US that, before the Affordable Care Act of 2010, some commentators likened to "a fragmented hodgepodge of private and public plans" that left tens of millions uninsured.[149] The US's healthcare system is "a maze of private and public health insurance [...] which leaves "millions uninsured and millions more underinsured and unable to access healthcare due to high deductibles and co-payment."[150] There are multiple reasons why Ghana should move to a single-payer, tax-funded healthcare system. To use the US again as an example, such a system sounds very much like "Medicare-for-all."[151] Rather than multiple competing health insurance companies, in such a system, a single public or quasi-public agency is charged with responsibility for financing healthcare for all residents, under an arrangement where everyone has health insurance under one health insurance plan that provides access to a range of medical services that includes doctors, hospitals, long-term care, prescription drugs, dentists, and vision care.[152] Under this system, individuals still retain the choice of where they receive care.[153]

Advantages of a single-payer system include the equality of access (equity) that it provides for uninsured and underinsured persons, reduced medical overheads, and an increased incentive to direct healthcare spending toward public health measures (for example, childhood obesity in the US).[154] Possible downsides include lengthy wait times and restricted availability of certain healthcare services, such as elective surgery and cosmetic procedures.[155] However, its advantages arguably outweigh any disadvantages and major obstacles to adopting this system are more political than practical.[156] A way around that politics would be to educate and mobilize the public on the merits of a single-payer system, who then elect politicians into office who in turn work to remove those political barriers.[157]

Applying these concepts to Ghana, the NHIS is a healthcare system that is mostly funded by tax revenues. It is a program built on the principle of exemptions where the only group not exempted from annual premium payments are informally employed adults,[158] one embedded in social insurance "from which individuals can opt out so long as they are covered by a private insurer."[159] And under the NHIS, everyone pays registration fees, except for indigents and pregnant women who are the only groups exempted from payment of these fees.[160] One way to achieve some harmonization of these moving parts would be a single-payer, tax-funded system, based on single lifetime payments of premiums, and free of all registration fees (an accommodation under the NHIS now extended only to indigents and pregnant women).

Ghana's medical system comprises about 1,800 public hospitals and 1,300 private hospitals and medical centers.[161] Of the latter, about 200, located mostly in rural areas, are run by religious institutions, usually Christian or Muslim.[162] The country also has more than 550 pharmacies, some of them open for 24 hours, mostly in urban areas.[163] There are concerns about some pharmacies selling adulterated or low-quality medications.[164] The doctor-patient ratio in Ghana is about one doctor for over 15,000 patients, there is a six-month waiting list under the NHIS for low-income and self-employed persons, and emergency medical services are available only in urban areas, compelling many residents in local communities to fill their treatment needs with traditional medicine.[165] On average, private medical facilities have modern equipment and provide a better quality of treatment, compared to the public medical facilities which are often underfunded and overcrowded and lack the quality expatriates living in Ghana associate with developed countries.[166]

A cornerstone of the NDC campaign in 2008 to overhaul the healthcare system, but one that it did not redeem, was the introduction of a one-time premium payment to facilitate participation of citizens, including the army of workers in the informal economy.[167] Consequently, user fees remain a fact of life in Ghana where, "for example, patients still buy their own drugs, even for common health conditions like headaches and malaria fever, because there are no medications in government pharmacies, while hospitals with dilapidated equipment and few medical supplies hit the headlines of major newspapers."[168] These are recurring problems that the NDC and NPP governments share, rather than issues limited to any one government, which a single-payer system can eliminate or ameliorate.

Although our proposal in this book for a single-payer, tax-funded arrangement may sound a bit sweeping, it does not depart substantially from the present supposedly hybrid system which is mostly funded by tax revenues. In the apt language of Oxfam International, the NHIS's "heavy reliance on tax funding erodes the notion that it can accurately be described as social health insurance and in reality is more akin to a tax-funded national health care system[.]"[169] A single-payer, public-funded system is conducive to "the fundamental role of public financing in" universal healthcare that the NHIS symbolizes,[170] and would resolve the inequities of the current system, retain healthcare workers who otherwise would work in the private sector with the more favorable conditions of service this sector affords,[171] and cut down on administrative overheads.[172]

A single-payer system anchored on general taxation will do away with the current three plans under the NHIS that registrants must join.[173] It will also draw Ghana closer to the imperatives of universal health coverage built around provision of access to the same range of high-quality health services for individuals, regardless of their employment status or ability to pay[174]—in marked contrast to the current system where informal workers, the only group not exempted from payment of premiums under the NHIS, are charged premiums avowedly based on income and capacity to pay.[175] Under this system, access to private health could still be available for individuals who choose that option and are willing to pay for it, but that option should not be part of the public health scheme the way it is now under the NHIS. This proposal is not inconsistent with Oxfam International's recommendation that Ghana "prioritize investment in the expansion of *public* health care services whilst also continuing to improve regulation of the *private* health care sector."[176]

Ghana can adopt this formula while keeping a watchful eye on problems like rationing and long queues associated with single-payer systems, of the kind that occurs in countries like the UK.[177] It can discover more efficient and equitable ways of raising revenue for health from tax reform, while ensuring that adequate proportions of national budgets are allocated to health, in compliance with the target of the Abuja Declaration on commitment to at least 15 per cent of government spending on healthcare.[178] A single-payer, tax-funded healthcare financing is today the arrangement of choice for many WHO members committed to universal health coverage.[179]

Our argument for a single-payer, tax-funded healthcare program in Ghana chimes with the viewpoint of Daniel Dramani Kipo-Sunyehzi and his colleagues related to the role of the NHIS on Ghana's journey toward universal health coverage.[180] These scholars focused on the still low coverage of the NHIS averaging anywhere from 25–40 percent of Ghana's population approaching two decades since the introduction of the program.[181] They blamed the relatively low enrolment on the non-mandatory nature of the program, contrasted, for example, to European countries like Denmark, Finland, France, Germany, Norway, Sweden, and the UK.[182] Unlike the programs in these countries, the NHIS is a voluntary healthcare system "where members must pay an annual premium to register and make efforts to renew their NHIS membership every year."[183] A way around this problem, they advised, is to turn the Scheme into a program of "compulsory membership based on general tax revenue" broad enough to generate money that covers all workers, whether public or private, formal or informal.[184]

Moses Aikins et al. take a more or less similar position, commenting on the financial sustainability of the NHIS, based on interviews with a group of 20 individuals, styled "stakeholders," well versed in the operations of the program.[185] These scholars start with the proposition that "[a]ctive membership [in the NHIS] is low because many enrolled members do not renew their membership when it expires[,]" with the result that the revenue that would have accrued to the program through membership renewal is reduced.[186] Their solution is that every Ghanaian, including those in the informal economy, be registered under the Scheme and "hold an active card at all times."[187] One way to achieve this is to link mandatory membership with access to certain social services.[188] For example, enrolment and active membership in the NHIS could be made "compulsory for people accessing banking services, driver's license, car registration and national identification card" to access these services.[189] Similarly, "[p]eople registering their business must be made to make an undertaking to ensure that all employees are registered and have a valid card."[190]

Conclusion

This chapter provided a description of the NHIS, the program that forms the face of healthcare reforms in Ghana under the Fourth Republic since 1993. However, although unquestionably a centerpiece, the program illustrates, rather than exhausts the struggle for healthcare reforms in Ghana that dates back to the early days of the country's independence in 1957 and before. Even within the Fourth Republic, the NHIS came after one full decade into the life of this latest instalment of democratic rule, during which period Jerry J. Rawlings and the NDC that he founded, held office—and when, instructively, healthcare held a much lower profile as an issue in politics than it subsequently did, beginning with John A. Kufuor and his NPP.

In Chapter 2, we laid down four hallmarks that we proposed as a guide to healthcare reforms in Ghana subsequent chapters in the book must amplify after this survey on the NHIS. With the mission now accomplished, this book shifts its attention and searchlight to the reasoning behind the assessment of Ghana's healthcare initiatives under the Fourth Republic, exemplified by the NHIS, as suboptimal. The next three chapters provide that justification, each focusing on a particular aspect of the broader issue: Chapter 4 on the politics of healthcare reforms in Ghana, Chapter 5 on the economics, and Chapter 6 on health as human right. Individually and collectively, these chapters rank among the centerpiece of this book.

Notes

1 Ali Arazeem Abdullahi, "Trends and Challenges of Traditional Medicine in Africa," *African Journal of Traditional, Complementary, and Alternative Medicine*, 8 (115) (2011), 123, www.ncbi.nlm.nih.gov/pmc/articles/PMC3252714/.
2 Ibid.
3 See, for example, M. Fawzi Mahomoodally, "Traditional Medicines in Africa: An Appraisal of Ten Potent African Medicinal Plants," *Evidence-Based Complementary*

and *Alternative Medicine*, 2013 (art. ID 617459) (2013), https://doi.org/10.1155/2013/617459.
4   "Health and Welfare," in *Ghana: A Country Study*, ed. La Verle Berry (Washington, DC: GPO for the Library of Congress, 1994).
5   Ibid.
6   "Is There a Role for Trado-Medicine in the Nigerian Health Sector?" *Nigeria Health Watch* (October 4, 2018), https://nigeriahealthwatch.medium.com/is-there-a-role-for-trado-medicine-in-the-nigerian-health-sector-d824d13a47e8.
7   See *Ghana: Seven-Year Development Plan 1963/64–1969/70* (Accra, Ghana: Office of Planning Commission, 1964), https://s3-us-west-2.amazonaws.com/new-ndpc-static1/CACHES/PUBLICATIONS/2017/11/03/SevenYearDevtPlan.pdf; "Ghana [Seven]-Year Development Plan Presentation," *GhanaHero* (March 11, 1964), www.ghanahero.com/Visions/Nkrumah_Legacy_Project/documents/deve_plans/7_Year_Dev_Plan-Ghana-v3_marked.pdf.
8   *Achieving a Shared Goal: Free Universal Healthcare in Ghana* (London, UK: Oxfam Int'l, 2011), 17, www.oxfam.org/sites/www.oxfam.org/files/rr-achieving-shared-goal-healthcare-ghana-090311-en.pdf. Nkrumah once stated that Ghana's progress toward economic development will be measured "by the improvement in the health of our people." Quoted in Rhodaline Baidoo, "Toward a Comprehensive Healthcare System in Ghana." M.A. Thesis, Center for Int'l Studies, Ohio University (March 2009), 13, https://etd.ohiolink.edu/!etd.send_file?accession=ohiou1237304137&disposition=inline.
9   Daniel Dramani Kipo-Sunyehzi et al., "Ghana's Journey towards Universal Health Coverage: The Role of the National Health Insurance Scheme." *European Journal of Investigation in Health, Psychology, and Education*, 10 (October 2019), 94–95, doi:10.3390/ejihpe10010009.
10 *Achieving a Shared Goal*, note 8, p. 17.
11 See, for example, Samuel Adu-Gyamfi, "What We Can Learn from the Ghanaian Experience of National Health Insurance," *City Press* (September 4, 2019), www.news24.com/citypress/voices/what-we-can-learn-from-the-ghanaian-experience-of-national-health-insurance-20190904.
12 See, for example, Jeffrey Herbst, *The Politics of Reform: Ghana, 1982–1991* (Berkeley, CA: University of California Press, 1993), esp. pp. 17–37 on "Ghana in Economic Crisis," and pp. 118–137 titled "Ghana, the Multilateral Organizations, and the International Economy."
13 Frank Nyonator and Joseph Kutzin, "Health for Some? The Effects of User Fees in the Volta Region of Ghana," *Health Policy & Planning*, 14 (1999), 330.
14 Kwadwo Konadu-Agyemang, "The Best of Times and the Worst of Times: Structural Adjustment Programs and Uneven Development in Africa: The Case of Ghana," *Professional Geographer*, 52 (2010), 476; Herbst, note 12, pp. 118–137.
15 See Charles A. Anyinam, "The Social Costs of the International Monetary Fund's Adjustment Programs for Poverty: The Case of Health Care Development in Ghana," *Int'l Journal of Health Services*, 19(3) (1989), 531–547. See also Paul Emiljanowicz, "How Jerry Rawlings Used Democratic Structures to Legitimize Military Rule," *Conversation* (May 23, 2021), https://theconversation.com/how-jerry-rawlings-used-democratic-structures-to-legitimise-military-rule-160714.
16 See Anyinam, note 15.
17 Ibid.; Konadu-Agyemang, note 14.
18 *Achieving a Shared Goal*, note 8, p. 17.
19 Konadu-Agyemang, note 14.
20 Abdul-Rahim Mohammed, *"Cash and Carry" or Health Insurance in Ghana?* (Sunnyvale, CA: Lambert Academic Publishing, 2012).

21 See, for example, Hassan Wahab, "The Politics of State Welfare Expansion in Africa: Emergence of National Health Insurance in Ghana, 1993–2004," *Africa Today*, 65(3) (2019), 91–112. doi:10.2979/africatoday.65.3.06.
22 Ibid.
23 W. Asenso-Okyere et al., "Cost Recovery in Ghana: Are There Any Changes in Health Care Seeking Behavior?" *Health & Planning*, 13 (1998).
24 See Emmanuel Nwachukwu, "Health Sector Decay: Nigerians Dying Needlessly," *New Watcher* (September 13, 2021), https://thenewwatcher.com/health-sector-decay-nigerians-dying-needlessly-10119.html ("[M]ost hospitals in Nigeria are no more than mere consulting rooms, lacking in everything").
25 Ibid., p. 188; Konadu-Agyemang, note 14.
26 Wahab, note 21.
27 Baidoo, note 8, p. 28.
28 Konadu-Agyemang, note 14; *Achieving a Shared Goal*, note 8, p. 17.
29 *Achieving a Shared Goal*, note 8, p. 7. Oxfam Int'l poignantly notes that "despite the instrumental role of the World Bank in pushing for cost recovery in the form of user fees in Ghana, its subsequent loans throughout the 1980s and 1990s did nothing to address their catastrophic impact." Ibid., p. 17.
30 Ibid.
31 Ibid.
32 Ibid.
33 New Patriotic Party, "The Manifesto: Development in Freedom, Agenda for Change," *Ghana Web* (September 20, 2005), 36, 37, www.ghanaweb.com/GhanaHomePage/election2004/npp_manifesto.pdf.
34 Mohammed, note 20.
35 Jennifer L. Singleton, "Negotiating Change: An Analysis of the Origins of Ghana's National Health Insurance Act," Honors Project, Paper 4, Macalester College (May 1, 2006), 18, http://digitalcommons.macalester.edu/soci_honors/4.
36 Hassan Wahab and Philip C. Aka, "The Politics of Healthcare Reforms in Ghana under the Fourth Republic since 1993: A Critical Analysis," *Canadian Journal of African Studies*, 55(1) (2021), https://doi.org/10.1080/00083968.2020.1801476.
37 Ibid.
38 Sophie Witter and Bertha Garshong, "Something Old or Something New?: Social Health Insurance in Ghana," *BMC Int'l Health & Hum Rights*, 9 (August 2009), www.ncbi.nlm.nih.gov/pmc/articles/PMC2739838/.
39 Wahab and Aka, note 36.
40 Moses Aikins et al., "Positioning the National Health Insurance for Financial Sustainability and Universal Health Coverage in Ghana: A Qualitative Study among Key Stakeholders," *PloS One* (June 15, 2021), 5, https://doi.org/10.1371/journal.pone.0253109.
41 Hassan Wahab, "Assessing the Implementation of Ghana's NHIS Law," Paper Prepared for Workshop in Political Theory and Policy Analysis Mini-Conference (Spring 2008), 4, http://ostromworkshop.indiana.edu/seminars/papers/wahab_mcpaper08.pdf.
42 *Achieving a Shared Goal*, note 8, p. 8.
43 Wahab, "Assessing the Implementation of Ghana's NHIS Law," note 41, p. 1, citing Kwaku Afriyie, *National Health Insurance Framework for Ghana* (Accra, Ghana: Ministry of Health, August 2004), 7–10.
44 "The State of Healthcare in Africa: Full Sector Report" (Nairobi, Kenya: KPMG Africa Ltd., 2012), 11, www.kpmg.com/Africa/en/IssuesAndInsights/Articles-Publications/Documents/The-State-of-Healthcare-in-Africa.pdf.; "The Future of Healthcare in Africa," *Economist Intelligence Unit* (London) (2014), 10, www.economistinsights.com/sites/default/files/downloads/EIU-Janssen_HealthcareAfrica_Report_Web.pdf.

45 State of Healthcare in Africa, note 44, p. 6 (listing Ghana alongside Botswana, Ethiopia, Libya, Mauritius, Rwanda, and South Africa); "The Future of Healthcare in Africa," note 44 (recognizing Ghana, along with Tunisia, Ethiopia, and South Africa).
46 "*Ghana's Constitution of 1992 with Amendments through 1996*," Constitute Project (April 18, 2016), www.constituteproject.org/constitution/Ghana_1996.pdf?lang= en [hereinafter Ghana's 1992 Constitution]. The constitution came into effect on January 7, 1993. It has 26 chapters and 5 appendices under two "schedules." Ibid. These chapters encompass a variety of topics, including "fundamental human rights and freedom," as well as the power of the courts to protect these rights.
47 Philip C. Aka, *Bosnia as Civic State and Global Citizen: Alternative Futures Outside the EU* (Lanham, Boulder, New York, and London: Rowman & Littlefield, 2021), ix, 200.
48 Ghana's 1992 Constitution, note 46, art. 34.
49 See ibid., Chap. 5, arts. 12–34.
50 Ibid., art. 12(1). See also ibid., art. 33(1) (allowing individuals whose fundamental human rights are violated access to the court to redress the violation).
51 "*Ghana's Constitution of 1992 with Amendments through 1996*," Constitute Project (August 26, 2021) www.constituteproject.org/constitution/Ghana_1996.pdf [hereinafter Ghana's 1992 Constitution, revised 1996], Chap. 6, §34.2.
52 Ghana's 1992 Constitution, revised 1996, note 51. Chap. 6, §34.1.
53 See "Justiciability," Legal Information Institute, Cornell Law School, www.law.cornell.edu/wex/justiciability ("Justiciability refers to the types of matters that a court can adjudicate. If a case is 'nonjusticiable,' then the court cannot hear it").
54 Nat'l Health Insurance Act, Act 650 (August 2003), http://d1020125.u42.pws-servers.com/UploadFiles/Publications/National%20Health%20Insurance%20 Act090407134319.pdf.
55 Founded in 1992, the NPP is a right-of-center conservative party. The party touts itself as a "liberal democratic political party" with "direct links to the oldest democratic traditions of Ghanaian politics." "Who We Are," New Patriotic Party, www.newpatrioticparty.org/index.php/the-party/who-we-are/who-we-are. "Our Creed," official website of the New Patriotic Party, www.newpatrioticparty.org/index.php/who-we-are/what-we-stand-for/our-creed.
56 "Our Creed," note 55.
57 *Achieving a Shared Goal*, note 8, p. 8.
58 Republic of Ghana, Nat'l Health Insurance Act, 2012, Act 852 (October 2012), https://s3.amazonaws.com/ndpc-static/CACHES/NEWS/2015/07/22//NHIS +Act+2012+Act+852.pdf.
59 Ibid.
60 See also *Achieving a Shared Goal*, note 8, p. 33 (observing that the Ghana "health sector enjoys a high level of political commitment.").
61 See Michael J. Sodaro, *Comparative Politics: A Global Introduction*, 3rd ed. (New York: McGraw-Hill, 2008), 408–409 (commenting on the acceptance by Conservative and Liberal politicians of the welfare programs, including health insurance, initiated by the Labour Party after World War II). The consensus is a marked contrast to the entrenched opposition to healthcare reform in the US that dates back a long time. See, for example, Steven Brill, *America's Bitter Pill: Money, Politics, Backroom Deals, and the Fight to Fix Our Broken Healthcare System* (New York: Random House, 2015); Jill Quadagno, *One Nation, Uninsured: Why the U. S. Has no National Health Insurance* (New York: Oxford University Press, 2006); Kenneth Janda et al., *The Challenge of Democracy: Government in America*, 6th ed. (Boston, MA: Houghton Mifflin, 1999), 329 (commenting on how advertising campaigns of interest groups, such as the Health Insurance Association of America, contributed to help defeat President Bill Clinton's healthcare plan); and Monte M.

Poen, *Harry S. Truman Versus the Medical Lobby: The Genesis of Medicare* (Columbia, MO: University of Missouri Press, 1996), 113–114.
62 *Achieving a Shared Goal*, note 8, p. 8.
63 *Ibid.*, note 8, p. 8.
64 VAT is a consumption tax "placed on a product whenever value is added at a stage of production and at final sale." "Value-Added Tax—VAT," *Investopedia*, www.investopedia.com/terms/v/valueaddedtax.asp. Under this arrangement, "[t]he amount of VAT that the user pays is the cost of the product, less any of the costs of materials used in the product that have already been taxed." Ibid.
65 *Achieving a Shared Goal*, note 8, p. 8.
66 Aikins et al., note 40, p. 2.
67 Wahab and Aka, note 36, pp. 216–217, n.20.
68 Aikins et al., note 40, p. 10.
69 Ibid. (citing Stakeholder 2).
70 *Achieving a Shard Goal*, note 8, p. 18.
71 Ibid., p. 3.
72 See "Health Insurance in Ghana," *GhanaWeb*, www.ghanaweb.com/GhanaHomePage/health/national_health_insurance_scheme.php.
73 Ibid.
74 Ibid.
75 Ibid.
76 Ibid.
77 Ibid.
78 Singleton, note 35, p. 17.
79 See generally Sodzi Sodzi-Tettey et al., "Challenges in Provider Payment under the Ghana National Health Insurance Scheme: A Case Study of Claims Management in Two Districts," *Ghana Med Journal*, 46(4) (2012), 189–199, www.ncbi.nlm.nih.gov/pmc/articles/PMC3645172/.
80 International Covenant on Economic, Social and Cultural Rights, G. A. Res. 2200A (XXI), opened for signature December 9, 1966, 993 U.N.T.S. 3, entered into force January 3, 1976. [hereinafter ICESCR].
81 African (Banjul) Charter on Human and Peoples' Rights, OAU Doc. CAB/LEG/67/3 rev. 5, 21 I.L.M. 58 (1982), adopted June 27, 1981, entered into force 21 October, 1986 [hereinafter ACHPR].
82 ICESCR, note 80, art. 12(d).
83 ACHPR, note 81, art. 16(2).
84 Aikins et al., note 40, p. 2
85 Sara Sulzbach et al., *Evaluating the Effects of the National Health Insurance Act in Ghana: Baseline Report* (Bethesda, MD: The Partners for Health Reformplus Project, Abt Associates Inc., December 2005), 63, www.abtassociates.com/files/Insights/reports/2005/national_health_insurance_ghana_1205.pdf.
86 "Health Insurance in Ghana," note 72.
87 Ibid.
88 Kipo-Sunyehzi et al., note 9, p. 97.
89 Aikins et al., note 40, pp. 2–3.
90 Ibid.; "Fee-for-Service," *Health Insurance*, www.healthinsurance.org/glossary/fee-for-service/.
91 Aikins et al., note 40, pp. 2–3.
92 Ibid.; see also Lisa Eramo, "What Is a Medicare Diagnosis Related Group (DRG), and Why Does It Matter for Beneficiaries?" *Medicare Advantage* (April 27, 2021), www.medicareadvantage.com/coverage/diagnosis-related-group (Medicare DRG "is a payment classification system that groups clinically-similar conditions that require similar amounts of inpatient resources. It's a way for Medicare to easily pay your hospital after an inpatient stay.").

93 Aikins et al., note 40, pp. 2–3.
94 Ibid.; see also Julia Kagan and Thomas J. Catalano, "Capitation Payments," *Investopedia* (July 6, 2021), www.investopedia.com/terms/c/capitation-payments.asp.
95 Aikins et al., note 40, pp. 2–3.
96 See ibid.
97 Guy Carrin, *Community-Based Health Insurance Schemes in Developing Countries: Facts, Problems, and Perspectives*, Discussion Paper No. 1 (Geneva, Switzerland: World Health Service, 2003), 3.
98 *Achieving a Shared Goal*, note 8, p. 8.
99 Ibid. In 2004, under the NHIS, the Ghanaian government implemented a free maternal healthcare program in these four most deprived regions. Ibid., p. 17.
100 Ibid., p. 18.
101 Lynne Miller Franco et al., "Effects of Mutual Health Organizations on Use of Priority Health-Care Services in Urban and Rural Mali: A Case-Control Study," *Bulletin of the World Health Organization*, www.who.int/bulletin/volumes/86/11/08-051045/en/.
102 Ibid.
103 *Achieving a Shared Goal*, note 8, p. 18.
104 Ibid.
105 *Achieving a Shared Goal*, note 8, p. 21. The government initially proposed that formal sector workers pay an annual premium, additional to the Social Security and National Insurance Trust contribution, to enroll in the NHIS. However, it backed off when workers and their union threatened a mass protest. Ibid.
106 "About Us," Official Website of the NHIS, www.nhis.gov.gh/about.aspx (last visited April 10, 2017).
107 Ibid.
108 Ibid.
109 Official Website of the NHIS, note 106.
110 Ibid.
111 Ibid.
112 Ibid.
113 Ibid.
114 Ibid.
115 Kipo-Sunyehzi et al., note 9, p. 97.
116 See *Achieving a Shared Goal*, note 8, p. 18.
117 See Chapter 1, notes 56–62, and accompanying texts.
118 *Achieving a Shared Goal*, note 8, p. 18.
119 Ibid., p. 21.
120 *Achieving a Shared Goal*, note 8, p. 21.
121 Kipo-Sunyehzi et al., note 9, pp. 97–98. As of July 2021, one Ghanaian Cedis is equivalent to 0.17 US$ or 17 cents.
122 *Achieving a Shared Goal*, note 8, p. 21.
123 Ibid., p. 8.
124 Ibid.
125 Official Website of the NHIS, note 106.
126 Ibid.
127 "What is Universal Coverage?" *World Health Organization*, www.who.int/health_financing/universal_coverage_definition/en/ (stating that "[a]mong other things, achieving UHC requires a good health financing system.").
128 See Social Health Insurance, World Health Organization, 58th World Health Assembly, Provisional Agenda Item 13.16 (2005), 6, 7.
129 See Peter Waiswa, "The Impact of User fees on Access to Health Services in Low- and Middle-Income Countries," RHL: The WHO Reproductive Health

Library (May 1, 2012), http://apps.who.int/rhl/effective_practice_and_organizing_care/cd009094_waiswaw_com/en/ (finding that "little evidence suggests that introduction of user fees for healthcare has little public benefit, especially with regard to improving access to services in an equitable and efficient way, or to improving healthcare outcomes.") (abstract).
130 *Universal Health Coverage: Why Health Insurance Schemes Are Leaving the Poor Behind* (London, UK: Oxfam Int'l, October 9, 2013), 3, www.oxfam.org/sites/www.oxfam.org/files/bp176-universal-health-coverage-091013-en_.pdf.
131 *Achieving a Shared Goal*, note 8, p. 8.
132 William Savedoff, *Tax-Based Financing for Health Systems: Options and Experiences* (Geneva, Switzerland: World Health Organization, 2004), 2.
133 See, for example, *The Right to Health at the Public/Private Divide: A Global Comparative Study*, eds. Colleen M. Floyd and Aegal Gross (New York: Cambridge University Press, 2014), *passim* (case study of 16 national healthcare systems, excluding Ghana). These three categories were healthcare programs based on: *tax-financed* or national public health systems, exemplified by Canada, Sweden, New Zealand, and the United Kingdom; *social health insurance* systems, exemplified by Israel and the Netherlands among others; and *mixed private/public systems*, exemplified by Brazil, China, India, South Africa, and the United States among others. Ibid.
134 Savedoff, note 132, p. 3.
135 Ibid.
136 Ibid.
137 Ibid., pp. 2–3.
138 Carrin, note 97.
139 Social Health Insurance, note 128, 6.
140 Ibid.
141 Ibid.
142 *Achieving a Shared Goal*, note 8, p. 18.
143 See Chapter 2, notes 40–43, and accompanying texts.
144 Ibid.
145 *Universal Health Coverage*, note 130, p. 3.
146 *Right to Health at the Public/Private Divide*, note 133, p. 128.
147 Witter and Garshong, note 38, p. 4 (based on data for 2008).
148 *Achieving a Shared Goal*, note 8, p. 8.
149 Ruth Rosen, "Time for Single Payer?" *San Francisco Chronicle* (December 29, 2003), www.sfgate.com/opinion/article/Time-for-single-payer-2544505.php.
150 Olga Oksman, "We Need Fundamental Changes: U.S. Doctors Call for Universal Healthcare," *Guardian* (London) (May 5, 2016), www.theguardian.com/us-news/2016/may/05/us-doctors-calling-universal-healthcare-system-affordable-care-act.
151 Andrea S. Christopher, "Single Payer Healthcare: Pluses, Minuses, and What It Means for You," *Harvard Health Blog* (June 27, 2016), www.health.harvard.edu/blog/single-payer-healthcare-pluses-minuses-means-201606279835. Medicare is the federal health insurance program for certain classes of Americans, including persons aged 65 and above and younger people with certain disabilities. It is contrasted with Medicaid, the US's public health insurance program for low-income people. See "What is the Difference between Medicare and Medicaid?" *HHS*, www.hhs.gov/answers/medicare-and-medicaid/what-is-the-difference-between-medicare-medicaid/index.html.
152 Christopher, note 151.
153 Ibid.
154 Ibid.
155 Ibid.
156 Ibid.

157 Ibid.
158 Ibid., p. 21.
159 See Singleton, note 35, p. 17.
160 See Official Website of the NHIS, note 106.
161 "Expat Guide to Health Care in Ghana," AETNA, www.aetnainternational.com/en/individuals/destination-guides/expat-guide-to-health-care-in-ghana.html.
162 Ibid. See also Huihui Wang et al., *Ghana National Health Insurance Scheme: Improving Financial Sustainability Based on Expenditure Review* (Washington, DC: World Bank, 2017), 11, https://openknowledge.worldbank.org/bitstream/handle/10986/27658/9781464811173.pdf (putting the number at about 3,500 healthcare facilities, 57 percent of them public, 33 percent private, and 7 percent faith-based centers).
163 "Expat Guide to Health Care in Ghana," note 161.
164 Ibid.
165 Ibid.
166 Ibid.
167 Wahab and Aka, note 36.
168 Ibid.
169 *Achieving a Shared Goal*, note 8, p. 8.
170 Ibid., p. 18.
171 See "A Background to Health Law and Human Rights in South Africa," *Health and Democracy* (June 1, 2007), 25, www.section27.org.za/wp-content/uploads/2010/04/Chapter1.pdf (commenting on South Africa where, according to the author, "[t]he private system provides better conditions to health workers[,]" resulting in "many doctors and nurses leav[ing] the underfunded public system.").
172 Oksman, note 150.
173 See "Health Insurance in Ghana," note 72.
174 *Universal Health Coverage*, note 130, p. 3.
175 *Achieving a Shared Goal*, note 8, p. 21.
176 Ibid., p. 40 (emphasis added).
177 See Sally C. Pipes, "The Many Failures of Single Payer," *Nat'l Rev* (December 1, 2014), www.nationalreview.com/article/393679/many-failures-single-payer-sally-c-pipes (conversation on the British healthcare system that also integrates discussion on Canada and portions of the United States, such as Vermont).
178 *Universal Health Coverage*, note 130, p. 29.
179 See Savedoff, note 132, p. 3.
180 See generally Kipo-Sunyehzi et al., note 9.
181 Ibid., p. 106.
182 Ibid.
183 Ibid., p. 105.
184 Ibid., p. 106.
185 See generally Moses Aikins et al., note 40. The stakeholders were selected from the Ministry of Health, Ghana Health Services, groups representing health workers, private medical practitioners, members of civil society organizations, and development partners. Ibid. ("Abstract: Method"). They belong in two groups, namely: Those in a position to influence NHIS policy, and actors involved in the implementation of the program. Ibid., p. 4 ("Analytical approach and stakeholders' identification").
186 Ibid., p. 8.
187 Ibid., citing Stakeholder 20.
188 Ibid., citing Stakeholder 3.
189 Ibid.
190 Ibid.

4 The Politics of Healthcare in Ghana

Introduction

Politics is one of the four hallmarks laid out in Chapter 2 as a guide to healthcare reforms in Ghana—and a heuristic tool for gauging the effectiveness of these reforms, exemplified, under the Fourth Republic since 1993, by the NHIS. In addition to embracing "good politics," vis-à-vis economics and health as human right, this hallmark has the particular distinction of subsuming the element of "good laws." Here is why. Under the constitutional scheme of things, the political branch is not the only arm of the government involved in law-making. Instead, as co-branches, the other two arms have some measure of participation, consistent with their nature, in law-making. In a presidential system of government of the type Ghana practices under its Fourth Republic, more often than not, proposals for law-making emanate from executive agencies and the signature of the President complements and completes every law—unless the legislature musters a two-third majority, called veto, in the event of a non-signature.[1] Finally, the courts, symbolizing the judiciary, interpret the law, including the power of judicial review signified by their power to rule any legislative measure which does not conform to the high(er) law unconstitutional, thereby effectively nullifying its quality as law since such a measure cannot be enforced.

However, as popular representatives of their constituents, lawmakers have ultimate responsibility for making laws, all the way to amendment of the constitution, the utmost law of the land. Adding to this advantage of politics as a hallmark is the fact that Ghana's presidential system of government appears to have properties beneficial to healthcare. As two of these authors argued elsewhere, due to the relative paucity of veto points in the operation of Ghana's presidential system of government, the chief executive "looks more like a British prime minister than a United States president."[2] This and factors like the lack of a divided government under the Fourth Republic "create an environment of reduced veto points that facilitates the enactment and implementation of expanded healthcare."[3] A final distinctive characteristic that sets good politics apart from the other hallmarks is that all of the other three—good laws, adequate funding, and healthcare as a human right—are susceptible to political influence.[4]

DOI: 10.4324/9781003264125-4

In other words, good politics may, arguably, be viewed as a function of the previous three hallmarks, namely: Politics designed to produce effective laws and adequate financing that increases the chances of making healthcare a human right rather than a privilege that a regime may withdraw when it chooses.[5]

Chapter 2 sets forth the foundation for the assessment of politics and the three other hallmarks of healthcare in Ghana under the Fourth Republic as suboptimal. There we indicated, with respect to politics, a requisite criterion revolved around "[h]ealthcare-friendly politics designed to produce effective laws and adequate financing that increase the chances of making healthcare a human right under the law."[6] Instead, against this backdrop, "[n]either Act 650 nor Act 852 seriously addressed any of the funding issues that impede healthcare reforms in Ghana."[7] We blamed the occurrence on "wrangling between the two major political parties on healthcare matters that did not lead to improved funding."[8] With respect to good laws which, as explained above, we put on the column of politics, we stated "[c]onstitutionalization, [and] ratification of multilateral treaty[,]" as a requisite element, pointing to, as our justification, "[t]he tepid and amorphous provision on the right to health in Ghana's latest constitution."[9] The task in this chapter is to shed some more light for ranking the politics of healthcare reform as suboptimal. The ensuing discussion breaks down into two interrelated parts: The nature of politics in Ghanaian healthcare reforms under the Fourth Republic, and grounds for adjudging that politics to be suboptimal.

Politics in Ghanaian Healthcare

Politics matters in the origination, design, and implementation of healthcare programs, including the extent to which healthcare is defined as a human right, elaborated in Chapter 6.[10] Dispensing with the culture of silence and related repression that marked the era of military rule preceding the Fourth Republic, Ghanaians expressed a preference for healthcare as a pressing social issue upon the return to democratic-civilian rule in 1993. Public opinion reflected this preference and the major political parties eagerly built this into their platforms.[11] Thus, during the 2000 election campaign, the NPP promised to abolish cash-and-carry and replace it with a universal healthcare program, while, for its part, the NDC pledged a review of the existing system with a view to improving it.[12]

The NPP won the 2000 presidential and parliamentary elections based partly on its promise to revamp the healthcare system. In contrast, the NDC "was slow in fully aligning its agenda to voter preferences," particularly with respect to healthcare, an occurrence which featured as a major factor in its defeat.[13] The NPP won re-election in 2004 by tagging the NDC as the party of cash-and-carry and promising to fully implement healthcare. Linking the NDC with the detested user fees worked, and it was not until 2008, two election seasons later, that the NDC regained power.

To claim credit for healthcare, upon assuming office, each political party chose to enact its own healthcare initiative. On 26 August 2003, the new NPP administration headed by John A. Kufuor as President, enacted Act 650, the National Health Insurance Bill. The measure became law on September 5, 2003, when President Kufuor signed it into law, although it did not come into effect until 2005. Similarly, following its victory in the 2008 presidential and parliamentary elections, on March 22, 2012, months away from the general elections of that year, the NDC introduced its own national health insurance bill in the form of Act 852. It was a bill "almost identical" to Act 650 that it repealed and replaced.[14] "Mending rather than repealing [Act 650] would have kept the narrative that the NPP was the party that brought expanded healthcare to Ghana, something anathema to the NDC."[15] President John Mahama signed the bill into law on October 31, 2012.[16] In a nutshell, politicians from both parties "appreciate[d] the importance and saliency of healthcare reforms."[17] Buoyed by that appreciation, they "portray[ed] themselves and their parties as pro-healthcare reforms, while blaming the opposition for working to undermine healthcare."[18]

Since 2008, a main issue in Ghana's healthcare debate has been a one-time premium payment, in an attempt to deal with the difficulties arising from enrolment into the program, many of which problems Chapter 6 on health as human right touches upon. That year, the NDC made introduction of a one-time premium payment a cornerstone of its campaign. The idea was to implement expanded healthcare by facilitating citizen participation in the NHIS, particularly for the army of workers in the informal economy. In response to NPP criticism, the National Health Insurance Authority, which oversees the NHIS, had produced reports showing that the policy is feasible. One of those reports announced that the policy would become operational in 2011. However, more than a decade later, the proposal remains unimplemented.

In the run-up to the 2012 elections, the NPP heightened its accusations that the NDC had not kept its campaign promise on the one-time premium, but was instead taking detrimental steps capable of bringing about the "collapse" of the healthcare system. For its part, the NDC government stuck to its message that the one-time premium policy would be implemented. Despite its election campaign, the NPP lost. In the aftermath of their defeat, Members of Parliament from the NPP added a new line of attack against the national healthcare plan centered around public distrust of the program, tapping into a public sentiment evidenced in a lack of interest in continued enrolment in the healthcare scheme. Conversely, NDC Members of Parliament encouraged their constituents to enrol in the NHIS because it was a good program; this amounted to a 360-degree reversal of their stance when they were the minority in parliament.

Justifying the Rating of Healthcare Politics in Ghana Under the Fourth Republic as Suboptimal

This section continues the discussion, with particular focus on our justification for rating the politics of the healthcare debate in Ghana, symbolized by the NHIS, as suboptimal. The discussion also restates some of our comments in Chapter 2 on the two hallmarks in question.

Good Politics

Healthcare delivery is a responsibility entrusted to the political leadership of a country, who must not only find creative ways to provide resources for healthcare at home whilst ensuring that external support for healthcare is used for that purpose, rather than used for non-healthcare issues. More elaborately, the journey of universal healthcare of the type Ghana has embarked upon under the Fourth Republic dictates that the government must raise sufficient resources for healthcare. It can do so through steps such as increasing the efficiency of revenue collection, reprioritizing government budgets, innovative financing, and putting developmental assistance, when available, to good use; removing financial risks and barriers to access, and guaranteeing that those barriers are removed by, for example, providing incentives for people to improve their health through preventive measures; as well as by improving efficiency and minimizing waste, and promoting equity in access.

As popular representatives of the people, the legislature, under the auspices of the Ghanaian Parliament, leads this process through its power of *oversight*. In many systems, the responsibility of the legislature breaks down into "passing laws, establishing the government's budget, confirming executive appointments, ratifying treaties, investigating the executive branch, impeaching and removing from office members of the executive and judiciary, and redressing constituents' grievances."[19] These functions track the concept of oversight. Under the US presidential system, which Ghana has followed since 1993, oversight by Congress takes place through various means that include reviewing, monitoring, and supervision of national agencies, programs, activities, and executive branch implementation of public policy.[20] Other avenues the US Congress uses to realize oversight are authorization, appropriations, investigative, and legislative hearings by standing committees; specialized investigations by select committees; and reviews and studies by congressional support agencies and staff.[21]

However, as we observed earlier in this book, in Chapter 2 and the discussion preceding this, little of these oversight functions took place in Ghana. Neither Act 650 nor Act 852 seriously addressed any of the funding issues that confronts the NHIS. Worse still, in the aftermath of the two laws' passage, the two major political parties have discouraged their supporters from enrolling or renewing their membership into the NHIS. This did not promote the financial sustainability of the fledgling program.

A more recent development, indicative of the dysfunctional politics on healthcare reform, was President Nana Akufo-Addo's commission of medical projects to reduce the disparities in healthcare resources that COVID-19 amplified.[22] The initiative began in April 2020 when the president promised, during a televised address, to build 94 new hospitals to be completed within a year.[23] The number breaks down into 88 districts in Ghana without hospitals, and six regional hospitals.[24] Each of them, the President said, "will be a quality, standard design 100-bed hospital with accommodation for doctors, nurses, and other health workers."[25]

In August 2021, more than a year later, the President launched Agenda 111, ostensibly designed to implement the promise he made in April 2020.[26] The locale for the commissioning was Trede in the Atwima Kwanwoma District of the Ashanti Region where, on August 17, 2021, the President performed a ground-breaking ceremony.[27] Agenda 111 comprised district, specialized, and regional hospitals spread across the country, broken down into: 101 district hospitals, six regional hospitals in the newly-created regions, two specialized hospitals in the middle and northern belts, one regional hospital in the Western Region, and renovation of the Effia-Niwanta Regional Hospital.[28] All of the hospitals would have staff accommodation for medical doctors, nurses, and other health workers; and each would be equipped or outfitted with facilities, such as outpatient services, including consultation for medical and surgical cases, ophthalmology, dental and physiotherapy, and imaging services.[29] The President announced that each hospital would be completed within 12 months.[30]

The objectives behind Agenda 111 include the delivery of quality healthcare at the district level, boosting access to healthcare services for all citizens in an attempt to realize Goal Three of the UN Sustainable Development Goals.[31] The project is underlain by the belief that the surest way to improve healthcare delivery in the country is to provide new infrastructure and repair of existing hospitals that have become dilapidated.[32] The government praised the project as "the largest healthcare infrastructure project ever undertaken in the history of Ghana since independence."[33] In announcing the project, the President stated:

> There are 88 districts in our country without district hospitals; we have six (6) new regions without regional hospitals; we do not have five infectious disease control centers dotted across the country; and we do not have enough testing and isolation centers for diseases like COVID-19. We must do something urgently about this. That is why Government has decided to undertake a major investment in our healthcare infrastructure, the largest in our history. We will, this year, begin constructing 88 hospitals in the districts without hospitals.[34]

Tying the commissioning of the project to disparities in healthcare access catalyzed by COVID-19, the President indicated, "[f]or us in Ghana not only has the pandemic disrupted our daily lives, but it has also exposed the deficiencies with our healthcare system because of the years of under investment and neglect."[35] To facilitate construction of the medical facilities, the government secured a US$100 million start-up fund through the Ghana Investment Infrastructure Fund (GIIF).[36]

A leader of the opposition party lambasted the project as 419, advising lawmakers to remove the president from office for dishonesty.[37] He stated, "I think the President should be removed from office as the level of dishonesty of this government should further not be entertained."[38] He elaborated:

> In September 2020, the government cut sod for a district hospital project in Trede in the Atwina Kwanwoma District of Ashanti Region. After a

year of no show, [meaning no actual construction took place] the President carries his Health Minister back to the same town in the same district of Ashanti to cut sod for another hospital project. Our representatives in Parliament must as a matter of urgency initiate processes of impeachment against the President to assuage the anger of Ghanaians.[39]

In Nigeria, three countries east removed from Ghana geographically, 419 refers to Section 419 of Nigeria's Criminal Code which provides:

> Any person who by any false pretense, and with intent to defraud, obtains from any other person anything capable of being stolen, or induces any other person to deliver to any person anything capable of being stolen, is guilty of a felony, and is liable to imprisonment for three years.[40]

Americans are familiar with this provision through the 419 scam. A 419 is a scam perpetrated from Nigeria in which a letter, fax, or email is sent to someone in the United States (or other countries, usually in Europe). The person who receives the letter is informed that he or she could receive a significant sum of money for "helping" someone to get funds out of Nigeria. There are different possible scenarios that explain why the letter recipient needs to help. For example, the recipient of the letter may be told:

- There is unclaimed money or gold that the letter sender needs help accessing.
- A stolen fortune has been amassed and the sender of the letter needs help getting it out of the country.
- A corporate or government official has embezzled funds and must get the money out of the country.
- Money has been won or inherited, but the letter sender needs help getting it out of the country.

> In virtually every case, the person who receives the letter is promised they will be handsomely rewarded for helping the sender to move large sums of money—which does not actually exist. The recipient of the letter may be asked to pay fees in advance (usually referred to as taxes on the money or bribes to foreign officials) or may be asked to provide bank and financial information, which can then be used in identity theft. The recipient may even be forwarded a fraudulent check and asked to deposit it and then forward some of the funds, keeping the rest for himself. The money that is to be forwarded is wired before it becomes clear that the initial check was not a legitimate one.[41]

Under the Fourth Republic, politics arguably gave birth to healthcare. But *good* politics, as we define it in this book, is necessary to take healthcare reforms to the next level beyond the NHIS. However, over the years, much of what has passed as good politics is undiluted partisan bickering between the two major political parties with little regard for improved healthcare funding.

Good Laws

While Ghana appears to have made progress with respect to good laws, there are unresolved issues bearing on constitutional amendment. Elsewhere, we commented on the solecism signified by the entrenchment of a nominal "right" to healthcare as a "fundamental human right" in Ghana's Fourth Republic Constitution. Particularly, we worried about the tepidness and amorphousness of the provision which reads:

> [a] person who by reason of sickness or any other cause is unable to give his consent shall not be deprived by any other person of medical treatment, education or any other social or economic benefit by reason only of religious or other beliefs.[42]

The reference to fundamental human rights lacks needed punch because, as we indicated in Chapter 3, healthcare guarantee under the Ghanaian constitution is non-justiciable.[43] We advised that the way to correct this anomaly would be a constitutional amendment which guarantees, free of vagueness or tentativeness, the right to healthcare. We cited the language of the ICESCR provision as a good template for such a change. This multilateral treaty, which Ghana ratified in 2000, mandated state parties to create "conditions which would assure to all medical service and medical attention in the event of sickness," among other obligations.

From the standpoint of international law, some parting statement is warranted regarding our point about constitutionalizing the right to healthcare to solidify it. The ICESCR permits progressive realization of the right, which arguably justifies a tepid provision. The multilateral treaty allows state parties to take steps, within the limit of their national resources, to secure progressive realization of the socioeconomic rights recognized in the instrument.[44] An explanatory statement, Comment 3 to the treaty published in 1990, echoes the same progressive realization notion.[45]

However, close reading of these very provisions does not justify a tepid constitutionalization. The provisions stipulate a minimum obligation that a state may, in its discretion, choose to exceed. The ICESCR advises that a step within "the maximum of [a state's] available resources," should be "by all appropriate means," all the way to legislative measures.[46] Similarly, Comment 3 specified that any step toward the progressive realization—"deliberate, concrete, and targeted as clearly as possible toward the obligations recognized in the Covenant"—should be "taken within a reasonably short time after the Covenant" enters into effect for the state in question.[47] After all, the ICESCR stipulates that "[n]othing in the [...] Covenant shall be interpreted as impairing the inherent right of all peoples to enjoy and utilize fully and freely their natural wealth and resources."[48] One of those resources needing to be fully utilized is good health.

Conclusion

This chapter provides justification for the assessment of good politics, as we define it in this work, on healthcare reforms in Ghana under the Fourth Republic, epitomized by the NHIS, over and above the sketch laid out in Chapter 2. Because of its overriding influence over the other two hallmarks, galvanized by the power of legislative oversight, good politics has the potential to give Ghana the traction on the ground that it needs in its journey toward the service haven of health as human right. Regrettably, the accumulated evidence, after nearly three decades under the Fourth Republic, nearly two decades of those being expended in experimentation with the NHIS, is that Ghanaian lawmakers—as vectors of good politics and good laws under our formulation in this book—have yet to meet this expectation.

Notes

1. Text of Ghana's 1992 Constitution, *reprinted* in Ghana's Constitution of 1992 with Amendments through 1996, Constitute Project (August 26, 2021), § 106.10, www.constituteproject.org/constitution/Ghana_1996.pdf [hereinafter Ghana's 1992 Constitution]. Ghana has a unicameral (single chamber) legislature, Ghana's 1992 Constitution, § 4.1, denominated Parliament, made up of 275 members, elected for a four-year term in office with no term limit. "Parliament of Ghana," *Parliament of Ghana*, www.parliament.gh/mps; Ernest Darfour, "The Parliament of Ghana: A Countervailing Force in the Governance Process?" www.psa.ac.uk/sites/default/files/Ghana%20-
2. Hassan Wahab and Philip C. Aka, "The Politics of Healthcare Reforms in Ghana under the Fourth Republic since 1993: A Critical Analysis," *Canadian Journal of African Studies*, 55(1) (2021), 203, https://doi.org/10.1080/00083968.2020.1801476
3. Ibid.
4. Philip C. Aka, *Genetic Counseling and Preventive Medicine in Post-War Bosnia* (Gateway East, Singapore: Palgrave Macmillan, 2020), 48.
5. Ibid.
6. See Chapter 2, tbl. 2.2.
7. Ibid.
8. Ibid.
9. Ibid.
10. Except where indicated otherwise, the discussion in this section and the next draws largely from Wahab and Aka, note 2.
11. Afrobarometer, "Parliament of the Fourth Republic of Ghana—Views from the Grassroots," CDD-Ghana (November 2005), www.afrobarometer.org/files/documents/briefing_papers/AfrobriefNo20.pdf
12. Hassan Wahab, "Are Members of Parliament in Ghana Responsive to their Constituents? Evidence from Parliamentary Debates on Health Care," in *Ghanaian Politics and Political Communication*, eds. Samuel Gyasi Obeng and Emmanuel Debrah (London: Roman and Littlefield, 2019), 99, 103.
13. Wahab and Aka, note 2, p. 220.
14. Ibid.

15 Ibid.
16 Ibid.
17 Ibid.
18 Ibid.
19 "Legislature," *Encyclopedia Britannica*, www.britannica.com/topic/legislature.
20 Frederick M. Kaiser, *Congressional Oversight*, CRS Report for Congress, 97–936 GOV (updated January 2, 2001), http://156.33.195.33/artandhistory/history/resources/pdf/CRS.Oversight.pdf.
21 Ibid.
22 See "'Agenda 111' to Optimally Advance Ghana's Healthcare Delivery– President," *Ghana Web* (August 18, 2021), www.ghanaweb.com/GhanaHomePage/NewsArchive/Agenda-111-to-optimally-advance-Ghana-s-healthcare-delivery-President-1335367.
23 Maxwell Suuk, "Ghanaians Question President's Promise of New Hospitals," *DW* (April 29, 2020), www.dw.com/en/ghanaians-question-presidents-promise-of-new-hospitals/a-53282310. DW is the acronym for Deutsche Welle, a public state-owned broadcasting service, located in Bonn, Germany, which incarnated as a radio station.
24 Ibid.
25 Ibid.
26 "'Agenda 111' to Optimally Advance Ghana's Healthcare Delivery– President," note 22.
27 Ibid.
28 Ibid. Based on the recommendation of a Project Implementation Committee, the government secured land titles for 88 out of the 101 district hospitals. Each unit measuring 15 acres would cost US$17 million. "Agenda 111 is Ghana's Biggest Ever Investment in Healthcare–Akufo-Addo," *Modern Ghana* (August 17, 2021), www.modernghana.com/news/1098624/agenda-111-is-ghanas-biggest-ever-investment-in.html.
29 "'Agenda 111' to Optimally Advance Ghana's Healthcare Delivery– President," note 22.
30 Ibid.
31 Ibid., citing Information Minister Oppong Nkrumah.
32 "Agenda 111 is Ghana's Biggest Ever Investment in Healthcare–Akufo-Addo," note 28 (citing Health Minister Kwaku Agyeman-Manu).
33 Ibid., (statement of Information Minister Oppong Nkrumah).
34 "COVID-19: Government to Begin Construction of 88 District Hospitals This Year–Nana Addo," Ministry of Health, Republic of Ghana [no date specified, but most likely August 18, 2021], www.moh.gov.gh/covid-19-government-to-begin-construction-of-88-district-hospitals-this-year-nana-addo/.
35 "Agenda 111 is Ghana's Biggest Ever Investment in Healthcare—Akufo-Addo," note 28.
36 "Government Secures US$100 Million Start-up Fund for 'Agenda 111' Hospital Project," Ministry of Health, Republic of Ghana (August 17, 2021), www.moh.gov.gh/agenda-111-construction-of-largest-number-of-hospital-projects/.
37 See "Akufo-Addo Should Be Removed from Office; Agenda 111 Is a 419 Project— Brogya Genfi," *PeaceFMOnline* (August 18, 2021), www.peacefmonline.com/pages/politics/politics/202108/450318.php; "Agenda 111: Impeach President Akufo-Addo for Dishonesty—NDC's Brogya Genfi," *MyNewsGH* (August 18, 2021), www.mynewsgh.com/agenda-111-impeach-president-akufo-addo-for-dishonesty-ndcs-brogya-genfi. See also "Akufo-Addo Has Packaged NDC's Idea and Named it Agenda 111—Segbefia," *Ghana Web* (August 19, 2021), www.ghanaweb.com/GhanaHomePage/NewsArchive/Akufo-Addo-has-packaged-NDC-s-idea-and-named-it-Agenda-111-Segbefia-1336129. Brogya Genfi was identified as a former Youth Organizer of the NDC in the Ashanti Region.

38 "Agenda 111: Impeach President Akufo-Addo for Dishonesty—NDC's Brogya Genti," note 37.
39 Ibid.
40 "419 Fraud Explained by a Criminal Defense Lawyer in NY," Bukh Law Firm, P. C., https://nyccriminallawyer.com/fraud-charge/cross-border-fraud/419-fraud/.
41 Ibid. ("What is a 419 Scam?").
42 Philip C. Aka et al., "Ghana's National Health Insurance Scheme (NHIS) and the Evolution of a Human Right to Healthcare in Africa," *Chicago-Kent Journal of International & Comparative Law*, 17(2) (2017), 1, 61–62.
43 See Chapter 3, notes 52–53, and accompanying texts.
44 International Covenant on Economic, Social, and Cultural Rights (ICESCR), G. A. Res. 2200A (XXI), 993 U.N.T.S. 3, Opened for signature December 9; entered into force January 3, 1976 [hereinafter ICESCR], art. 2.1.
45 See CESCR General Comment No. 3: The Nature of States Parties' Obligations, Doc. E/1991/23 (December 14, 1990), esp. 2, Office of the UN High Commissioner for Human Rights, www.refworld.org/pdfid/4538838e10.pdf.
46 ICESCR, note 44, art. 2.1.
47 CESCR General Comment No. 3, note 45, 2.
48 ICESCR, note 44, art. 25.

5 The Economics of Healthcare in Ghana

Introduction

Good economics, translatable into adequate funding, is among the hallmarks we laid down in Chapter 2 as a guide to healthcare reforms in Ghana and a heuristic tool of choice for assessing those reforms. Along with politics, analyzed in Chapter 4, and health as human right, covered in Chapter 6, our rating of Ghana on this hallmark was suboptimal. The key element we isolated for the hallmark was "[a]dequate funding, minimizing reliance on direct payments to finance services, increased efficiency, and fairness in healthcare financing."[1] And with respect to the basis for that assessment, we stated: "Ghana has made insufficient progress in meeting the target of 15 percent of its annual budget to healthcare [,]" but, instead, as of 2016, quoting the World Bank "spent a pitifully low 4.45 percent of its GDP on healthcare."[2]

Prior to the passage of the NHIS in 2003, studies showed that, from a cost-reduction or cost-recovery standpoint, a risk-pooling program, such as the NHIS, offers a better alternative than the user fee, out-of-pocket, arrangement.[3] The purpose of this chapter is to shed more light on our rating of the economics of healthcare under the Fourth Republic as suboptimal. Just as in Chapter 4, the discussion in this chapter breaks down into two main parts: Influence of economics in Ghanaian healthcare, followed by justification of the suboptimal rating of the economics of healthcare in Ghana.

Economics in Ghanaian Healthcare

Problems bearing on the economics of healthcare are issues many other countries in Africa share with Ghana. Accordingly, the ensuing discussion is a conversation on Africa generally that is not limited to Ghana per se. During a meeting in Abuja in spring 2001, Ghana and other African countries pledged to earmark 15 percent of their annual budgets toward healthcare services for citizens of their respective countries.[4] The pledge is famed as "the Abuja Declaration."[5] However, by April 2011, ten years later, few of these countries met this self-imposed, non-obligatory, revenue target necessitated by the dire state of healthcare delivery in their countries in the lead up to the Declaration. Two notable exceptions were

Tanzania and Liberia which, respectively, devoted 18.4 percent and 16.6 percent of their budgets to healthcare.[6]

Ghana was not on the list, although at 14.6 percent in 2009,[7] it came close to meeting the pledge. In the 20-year period from 1995 until 2014, government spending on healthcare in Ghana averaged a lowly US$58 per person.[8] For some countries in the region, the only way around this inadequate funding is external assistance, elaborated in the next section below with respect to Ghana. As Oxfam International, the British antipoverty conglomerate, recounts, in a seminal report in 2011 that it published on healthcare in Ghana, because of a shortfall in funding, "[f]acilities became increasingly indebted and many reverted to charging" fees.[9]

Many European countries devote an average of 10 percent of their GDP to healthcare,[10] and the World Health Organization (WHO), a global health czar, recommends about 6 percent as ideal.[11] Therefore, the figure of 15 percent in the Abuja Declaration ranges beyond these numbers by 5–9 percentage points. However, the number is a reflection of the depth of underinvestment in healthcare in many African countries that dates back to when these countries gained independence. Historically, "government spending on healthcare in many African countries [is] inadequate to scratch the surface of healthcare delivery, a situation then compounded by corruption which leaves even less money available for health services."[12] In 2015, per capita, Africa spent one-tenth on healthcare compared to the rest of the world.[13] More elaborately, although the region comprised 16 percent of the world's population and carried 23 percent of the burden of global disease, that year it accounted for just 1 percent of total global spending on healthcare.[14]

A brief history on the leadup to the Abuja Declaration sheds much-needed light on its 15 percent-of-the-GDP commitment. In September 2000, 189 heads of state, including those from Africa, met and adopted the United Nations Millennium Development Goals (MDGs), eight targets UN member states committed themselves to achieve by 2015.[15] Three of the eight goals—reducing child mortality rates, improving maternal health, as well as combating HIV/AIDS, malaria, and other diseases—relate to healthcare. To make progress on the MDGs, African leaders met in April 2001 in Nigeria's capital city Abuja. Such was the setting in which the Declaration took place.

Ghana is a state party to the International Covenant on Economic, Social, and Cultural Rights (ICESCR).[16] Ghana ratified this instrument on September 7, 2000,[17] three years before the inauguration of the NHIS. Chapter 6 discusses this multilateral treaty in the context of health as human right. Therefore, the comments here are limited to the economics of healthcare. The ICESCR guarantees citizens of state parties the right to healthcare.[18] It enjoins state parties to "recognize the right of everyone" within their jurisdictions "to the enjoyment of the highest attainable standard of physical and mental health."[19] The guarantee solidifies the language in the Universal Declaration of Human Rights (1948) to the effect that "[e]veryone has the right to a standard of living adequate for the health and well-being of himself and of his family, including food, clothing, housing and medical care and necessary social services [....]."[20]

Going further, the Declaration of Alma-Ata, adopted by the WHO in 1978, stipulates that "[g]overnments have a responsibility for the health of their people which can be fulfilled only by the provision of adequate health and social measures."[21] The Declaration envisaged a "comprehensive national health[care] system" which national leaders strive to create by exercising political will, mobilizing resources, and making rational use of external resources.[22] As we elaborate in the next section, none of these commitments to healthcare stands any chance of realization without adequate funding.

Justifying the Rating of Healthcare Economics in Ghana Under the Fourth Republic as Suboptimal

The discussion in this section continues and builds upon the preceding comments. Two interrelated issues explored here are inadequate funding and excessive dependence on external assistance. These two issues are listed in Chapter 6, among the reasons why healthcare reforms in Ghana, as embodied in the NHIS, does not rise to health as human right. In other words, the discussion here is phrased around that notion.

Inadequate Funding

The NHIS is inadequately funded. As Daniel Dramani Kipo-Sunyehzi and his colleagues aptly posit, "[t]he biggest challenge for the implementation of NHIS from the perspectives of health insurance officials is inadequate funding."[23] The NHIS performs better at enrolling groups that are exempted from payment of annual premiums under the program than it does in enrolling all Ghanaians. Yet beneficiaries who relayed their views in opinion surveys "complained of delays during registrations and renewals[,]" as well as about "poor attitude of some health insurance officials and health workers at facilities."[24] Insufficient funding has a hand in this denouement.

Recognizing access to healthcare as a human right means little if not backed with the funding to realize it.[25] Health is wealth, as one famous saying goes. Although money is not everything, as rich countries like the US who still face intractable problems in their healthcare systems despite high rates of budgetary allocation to the health sector demonstrate,[26] a robust health system is not built on a shoestring budget. This matter of financing is obviously one reason why, while acknowledging the important advances in expanded healthcare the NHIS embodied, Oxfam International nevertheless posited that holding Ghana up as a model "is misleading."[27] Given the importance of financing, it is not surprising that the bulk of the suggestions Oxfam proffered for strengthening the NHIS focused largely on financing: What it will cost to finance the vision;[28] and how to pay for financing the vision within a given time frame.[29]

Oxfam International estimated that "under the current financing arrangements, the NHIS would enter into a deficit situation within the first 4 to 5 years of scheme operation, and especially as population coverage rises beyond a certain point."[30] To get around this problem, three sources for financing universal healthcare in Ghana that it suggested were: "savings generated from reduced inefficiencies in the health sector, additional revenue from improved economic growth and progressive taxation, and improved external development aid."[31] The matter of external assistance is discussed below. The other legitimate issue revolved around the possibility of the NHIS running out of money, "especially as population coverage rises beyond a certain point," is one that we address in Chapter 6 within the context of Ghana's rapid population growth vis-à-vis provision of health and other social services.

Excessive Dependence on External Assistance

In addition to being inadequately funded, Ghana's healthcare program, exemplified in the NHIS, is also dependent on foreign aid to a degree that is inconsistent with the pursuit of health as human right, as we argue in Chapter 6. To be sure, there are legitimate grounds for external assistance in the realm of healthcare. The world became a global village a long time ago and pollutants like acid rain respect no national boundaries.[32] Moreover, in the interdependent world in which we live, humans can be vectors of communicable diseases that they carry with them across national boundaries.[33] As one analyst aptly noted, reflecting on the ramifications of modern-day travel,

> The current volume, speed, and reach of travel are unprecedented. The consequences of travel extend beyond the traveler to the population visited and the ecosystem. When they travel, humans carry their genetic makeup, immunologic sequelae of past infections, cultural preferences, customs, and behavioral patterns. Microbes, animals, and other biologic life also accompany them.[34]

This reality of global interdependence explains the linkage of healthcare to international relations by various entities, including intergovernmental organizations, as discussed in Chapter 2.[35] Because of this reality of a global village or in spite of it, in 2008, external aid played a critical role in the implementation of the pregnancy exemption in the NHIS.[36] Specifically, the successful implementation of the exemption was made possible only with debt relief from external sources, including financial support from the British government, without which that expansion of access would have been difficult if not impossible.[37]

However, too much of a good thing can sometimes be a problem for various reasons. First, "[h]ealth systems are one of the core areas of national responsibility."[38] Thus, as the Director-General of the WHO advised in 2010, "any effective strategy for health financing needs to be home-grown."[39] Second, excessive dependence on foreign aid constrains the decision-making options of an aid-dependent state and leaves it vulnerable to fits of withdrawal symptoms when external aid is withdrawn.[40] Third, related to the above and building on it, foreign aid is not sustainable as a funding method.[41] Because they are often dependent on the vagaries of economic fortunes, political goodwill, and related idiosyncrasies of donor countries, rather than on altruism or philanthropy as such, receipt of foreign assistance is unpredictable.[42] It could be if, as one perceptive analyst indicated, offered over extended periods for, say, 20–30 years.[43] However, such flexible grants are a rarity among donors. Fourth, "[i]ncreased donor funds will not be enough to close" the health financing gap in Africa, given that "[e]xternal support for health is a tiny share of global health spending," and also because in the wake of the global financial crisis of 2008, "[d]evelopment assistance for health has been more or less stagnant."[44] These uncertainties counsel that donor-dependent countries "prepare for this eventuality by weaning themselves off aid voluntarily and gradually."[45]

There is no attempt made to disparage or discredit external assistance, as it can play an important complementary role in healthcare delivery, under certain circumstances, as it did for Ghana in 2008 with the pregnancy exemption.[46] In the final analysis though, as one African adage goes, no serious traveler depends wholly or even largely on the legs of another person for his or her own journey.[47] Depending on the legs of another person for one's own journey engenders vulnerabilities inconsistent with a good travel. For a country like Ghana, dependence on foreign assistance would not be a viable way to run a signature program like the NHIS that many countries in Africa consider as a model they could emulate. Consistent with this wisdom, since 2020, Ghana has started weaning itself from reliance on external assistance for its healthcare program.[48] It is a process that it needs to accelerate, taking advantage of revenue from oil production, to which we return shortly. Transition away from external assistance can initially create vulnerability, but can also be "an opportunity to celebrate growth."[49]

In 2007, Ghana struck oil in commercial quantity[50] and started exporting this mineral to the world market in 2010.[51] Because of this economic good fortune, Ghana posted double digit economic growth in 2011.[52] As indicated in Chapter 1, the country is rich in other agricultural and natural resources, top of which are cocoa and gold.[53] Therefore, well managed, Ghana can garner more revenue from oil that could minimize dependence on foreign aid or make that dependence completely unnecessary—provided, of course, that such monies are channelled into healthcare rather than diverted into non-healthcare uses, and there is the political will to achieve that independence. This is especially crucial now that foreign assistance is drying up.[54]

Although it suffers less from issues of corruption and accountability than many African countries, Ghana's record in managing mineral revenues after 100 years of gold mining was not flawless.[55] Therefore, to ensure transparency and proper management of oil revenues, Ghana's leaders passed the Petroleum Revenue Management Act (PRMA), Act 815, of 2011.[56] Among other things, the legislation sets forth mechanisms for collecting and distributing petroleum revenue.[57]

The law established a Public Interest and Accountability Committee (PIAC), made up of thirteen members drawn from organized professional bodies, think tanks, pressure groups, and traditional institutions, among others.[58] The PIAC monitors and evaluates compliance with the law by the government and other institutions, provides an independent assessment of petroleum production and receipts, and publishes its findings in half-yearly and annual reports.[59] It also provides a platform for public debate on how petroleum revenues are spent.[60] A report issued in May 2012 covering oil production in 2011 found that oil revenues provided the government with considerable fiscal relief, thereby enabling it to shift more funds into development programs.[61]

However, there is no indication that these development programs include healthcare. The law was amended in 2015 to include provision for infrastructure.[62] Again, like with the main law, healthcare did not feature on the list. In a nutshell, oil revenue should make it easier for Ghana to wean itself from dependence on external assistance to fund healthcare—provided the government sets aside money for healthcare from those revenues.

Conclusion

Good funding mandates the outlay of adequate funding for healthcare, achieved through various means, including diversification of funding sources to avert the vulnerability and uncertainty that can arise from overdependence on one or a few sources. This is particularly the case given the vast informal sector of the Ghanaian economy. Adequate healthcare funding is funding that completes the job with budgetary provision that speaks to the preciousness a country assigns to the health of its citizens. The Abuja Declaration pegged that level at 15 percent, taking into account the disinvestment in the health sector in many countries on the continent that predates the achievement of independence in these countries compounded by bad governance since that time.

Adequate funding for healthcare may be present when a state succeeds in minimizing cost recovery, symbolized by reliance on direct payments, to finance health services. While, under the NHIS, perceptible minimization has occurred, much room for improvement remains. Through the instrumentality of the NHIS, exercising political will, Ghanaian leaders created an integrated national healthcare system of the type the UN envisaged in 1978 in the Declaration of Alma-Ata.[63] What is missing is mobilization of adequate resources for healthcare work, including rational use of any external resources.

Notes

1 Chapter 2, tbl. 2.2.
2 Ibid.
3 See W.K. Asenso-Okyere, "Financial Health Care in Ghana," *World Health Forum*, 16(1) (1995), 86–91, https://pubmed.ncbi.nlm.nih.gov/7873037.
4 See "The Abuja Declaration: Ten Years On," World Health Organization (2011), 4, www.who.int/healthsystems/publications/abuja_declaration/en/.

5 Ibid.
6 Ibid., p. 3. See also *The World Health Report: Health System Financing: The Path to Universal Coverage* (Geneva, Switzerland: World Health Organization, 2010), xii [hereinafter *World Health Report 2010*]
7 *Achieving a Shared Goal: Free Universal Health Care in Ghana* (Oxford, UK: Oxfam International, March 2011), 33, www.oxfam.org/sites/www.oxfam.org/files/rr-achieving-shared-goal-healthcare-ghana-09033-en.pdf.
8 World Health Organization, *Public Financing for Health in Africa: From Abuja to the SDGs* (Geneva, Switzerland: World Health Organization, 2016).
9 Ibid., p. 18.
10 See Philip C. Aka, *Genetic Counseling and Preventive Medicine in Post-War Bosnia* (Gateway East, Singapore: Palgrave Macmillan, 2020), 52.
11 *World Health Report 2010*, note 6, p. xv. According to this report, this level of spending on health will limit out-of-pocket payments to an amount that makes the incidence of financial catastrophe negligible.
12 Philip C. Aka et al., "Ghana's National Health Insurance Scheme (NHIS) and the Evolution of a Human Right to Healthcare in Africa," *Chicago-Kent Journal of International & Comparative Law*, 17(2) (2017), 1, 47.
13 Osondi Ogbuoji et al., "Closing Africa's Health Financing Gap," *Brookings* (March 1, 2019), www.brookings.edu/blog/future-development/2019/03/01/closing-africas-health-financing-gap/
14 Ibid.
15 See United Nations Millennium Declaration, Doc. A/RES/55/2, UN General Assembly (September 18, 2000), www.un.org/en/development/desa/population/migration/generalassembly/docs/globalcompact/A_RES_55_2.pdf. The eight goals were to: (i) eradicate extreme poverty and hunger; (ii) achieve universal primary education; (iii) promote gender equality and empower women; (iv) reduce child mortality; (v) improve maternal health; (vi) combat HIV/AIDS, malaria, and other diseases; (vii) ensure environmental sustainability; and (viii) develop a global partnership for development. Ibid. Following its expiration in 2015, a new program, the Sustainable Development Goals (SDGs) succeeded the MDGs. See "From MDGs to SDGs," SDGF: Sustainable Development Goals Fund, www.sdgfund.org/mdgs-sdgs.
16 See International Covenant on Economic, Social and Cultural Rights, General Assembly Resolution 2200A (XXI) (adopted and opened for signature, ratification, and accession December 16, 1966, entry into force, January 3, 1976) [hereinafter ICESCR].
17 See "Ratification Status for Ghana," United Nations Human Rights Treaty Bodies: UN Treaty Body Database, https://tbinternet.ohchr.org/_layouts/15/TreatyBodyExternal/Treaty.aspx?CountryID=67&Lang=EN; "Claiming Human Rights—in Ghana," Claiming Human Rights, www.claiminghumanrights.org/ghana.html.
18 See generally ICESCR, note 16.
19 ICESCR, note 16, art. 12.1.
20 Universal Declaration of Human Rights, G.A. Res. 217A, art. 25(1) (December 10, 1948).
21 World Health Organization, Declaration of Alma-Ata, International Conference on Primary Health Care, Alma-Ata, USSR (September 6–12, 1978), www.who.int/publications/almaata_declaration_en.pdf, art. V.
22 Ibid., art. VIII.
23 Daniel Dramani Kipo-Sunyehzi et al., "Ghana's Journey towards Universal Health Coverage: The Role of the National Health Insurance Scheme," *European Journal of Investigation in Health, Psychology, and Education*, 10, 94–109 (October 2019), 94–109, doi:10.3390/ejihpe10010009 (abstract).
24 Ibid.

25 Charles Ngwena, "The Recognition of Access to Health Care as a Human Right in South Africa: Is it Enough," *Health & Human Rights*, 5(1) (2000), 22–44.
26 See Irene Papanicolas et al., "Health Care Spending in the United States and Other High-Income Countries," *Journal of the American Medical Association*, 319(10) (March 13, 2018), 1024–1039, doi:10.1001/jama.2018.1150.
27 *Achieving a Shared Goal*, note 7, p. 15.
28 Ibid., p. 45.
29 Ibid., pp. 45–47.
30 Ibid., p. 45.
31 Ibid., p. 46.
32 See George P. Smith II, "Acid Rain: A Transnational Perspective," *New York Law School Journal of Int'l & Comp. Law*, 4 (1983), 459–502.
33 See, for example, Mary E. Wilson, "Travel and the Emergence of Infectious Diseases," *Emerging Infectious Diseases*, 1(2) (1995), 39–46, doi:10.3201/eid0102.950201; and William H. McNeill, *Plagues and Peoples* (Garden City, NY: Anchor Press/Doubleday, 1976).
34 Wilson, note 33, 39–46 (abstract). Two issues on which the Wilson paper focused are: The role of global travel and movement of biologic life in the emergence of infectious diseases, and the ways in which travel and movement are inextricably tied at multiple levels to other processes that influence the emergence of disease. Ibid.
35 See Chapter 2, notes 44–56, and accompanying texts.
36 *Achieving a Shared Goal*, note 7, p. 18.
37 Ibid.
38 Nick Fahy, "Commentary on International Health System Performance Information," in *Health System Performance Comparison: An Agenda for Policy, Information and Research*, eds. Irene Papanicolas and Peter C. Smith (Maidenhead, England: Open University Press, 2013), 313–314.
39 Margaret Chan, "Message from the Director-General," in *The World Health Report: Health System Financing: The Path to Universal Coverage* (Geneva, Switzerland: World Health Organization, 2010), vii.
40 "The Future of Healthcare in Africa," Economist Intelligence Unit (London) (2014), 29, www.economistinsights.com/sites/default/files/downloads/EIU-Janssen_HealthcareAfrica_Report_Web.pdf.
41 In the language of international development, these measures of foreign assistance go by the name "overseas development assistance" (ODA). The Organization for Economic Cooperation and Development (OECD) defines ODA as government assistance that targets and promotes the economic development and welfare of developing countries. *Official Development Assistance (ODA)* (Paris, France: OECD), www.oecd.org/dac/financing-sustainable-development/development-finance-standards/official-development-assistance.htm. In 1969, the Development Assistance Committee of the OECD adopted ODA as the "gold standard" of foreign aid and to date ODA remains the main source of financing for development aid. Ibid.
42 See Philip C. Aka, "Bridging the Gap Between Theory and Practice in Humanitarian Action: Eight Steps to Humanitarian Wellness in Nigeria," *Willamette Journal of International Law & Dispute Resolution* 24(1) (2016): 1, 48–49 ("External Support or Assistance") (statement within the context of humanitarian assistance that ranked external assistance as secondary); and Thierry Kangoye, "Does Aid Unpredictability Weaken Governance? Evidence from Developing Countries," *Developing Economies*, 51(2) (June 2013): 121–144 (answering the question in the affirmative).
43 Ola Brown, *Fixing Healthcare in Nigeria: A Guide to Some of the Key Policy Decisions That Will Provide Better Healthcare to All Nigerians* (self-published, 2018), 24, www.dropbox.com/s/g8a2m2n49wlavui/Fixing%20Nigeria%20(2).pdf?dl=0.
44 Ogbuoji et al., note 13.
45 Ibid.

46 See notes 36–37, and accompanying texts.
47 See "Africa: The Struggle for Development," in *Global Studies: Africa*, eds. R.C. Grote et al., 8th ed. (New York: McGraw-Hill, 1999), 3, 9
48 Mary-Russell Roberson, "Ghana: Healthcare for a Country in Transition," Duke Global Health Institute (March 15, 2020), https://globalhealth.duke.edu/news/ghana-healthcare-country-transition.
49 Ibid.
50 Francis Kokutse, "Ghana Leader: Oil Reserves at 3b Barrels," Associated Press (Internet Archives) (December 22, 2007) http://web.archive.org/web/20071226200944/http://news.yahoo.com/s/ap/20071222/ap_on_re_af/ghana_oil_discovery_3
51 Jason McLure, "Ghana Oil Reserves to be 5 Billion Barrels in 5 Years," *Bloomberg* (December 1, 2010), www.bloomberg.com/news/articles/2010-12-01/ghana-oil-reserves-to-be-5-billion-barrels-in-5-years-as-fields-develop; Chuck Neubauer, "Ghana Discovery Sparks Fight Over Oil," *Washington Times* (March 26, 2010), www.washingtontimes.com/news/2010/mar/26/ghana-discovery-sparks-fight-over-oil/?page=all.
52 "Ghana Swears in Mahama as New President," *Al Jazeera* (July 25, 2012), www.aljazeera.com/news/africa/2012/07/20127259518486684.html.
53 Chapter 1, notes 28–33, and accompanying texts.
54 See Roberson, note 48.
55 Efam Dovi, "Ghana's 'New Path' for Handling Oil Revenue," *Africa Renewal* (January 2013), www.un.org/africarenewal/magazine/january-2013/ghana%E2%80%99s-%E2%80%98new-path%E2%80%99-handling-oil-revenue#:~:text=Petroleum%20revenue%20contributed%204%20per,most%20notably%20for%20fertilizer%20subsidies.
56 See Pauline Anaman and John Darko, *Is Ghana's Petroleum Revenue Management Act (PRMA), 2011 (Act 815) an Effective Public Financial Tool for Public Investment and Consumption Smoothing?* (2018), www.bsg.ox.ac.uk/sites/default/files/2018-12/Anaman_Petroleum%20Revenue%20Management.pdf.
57 Dovi, note 55.
58 Ibid.
59 Ibid.
60 Ibid.
61 Ibid.
62 See Petroleum Revenue Management (Amendment) Act, Act 893 (2015), www.mofep.gov.gh/sites/default/files/reports/petroleum/PRMA-Amendment-2015.pdf (amending the 2001 law "to provide for the allocation of funds to the Ghana Infrastructure Investment Fund for the purpose of infrastructure development [...] and for related matters").
63 See notes 21–22, and accompanying texts.

6 Health as Human Right in Ghana

Introduction

Health as human right is one of four hallmarks we laid out in Chapter 2 as a guide to healthcare reforms in Ghana, and a key element in the toolbox for assessing these reforms. The other hallmarks covered in the preceding two chapters, respectively, are politics and economics. This chapter critically assesses the extent to which healthcare delivery in Ghana, under the country's Fourth Republic, symbolized in the NHIS, meets the strictures of health as human right. Given the message of this book embedded in human rights, this presentation has a measure of cruciality that its two counterparts—the discussion in Chapter 4 on the politics of healthcare reforms, and the analysis in Chapter 5 on the economics of these reforms—lack. It is an added importance that also explains the more comprehensive tone of the material here.

Like the politics and economics of healthcare in Ghana, we ranked health as human right as suboptimal. We indicated that this condition comes into view when there is an "[e]ntrenchment of features like expanded access, and equity of a kind that makes healthcare a human right within the law."[1] We reasoned that "[g]iven the various problems that still impede the NHIS 18 years after its adoption, Ghana's fledgling healthcare system does not seem to guarantee access to healthcare as a human right."[2] This chapter elaborates our justification beyond the sketch we provided in Chapter 2. The following discussion breaks down into two main parts: Multiple benefits of a human right approach to healthcare in Ghana, and equally multiple reasons why healthcare delivery in Ghana under the NHIS falls below the standard of health as human right. Key highlights of the presentation include the right to healthcare as a tool of social struggle, and the negative impacts of rapid population growth on the provision of social welfare goods, including healthcare services.

DOI: 10.4324/9781003264125-6

Multiple Benefits of a Human Right Approach to Healthcare in Ghana

In Chapter 2, we defined human rights as rights persons have because they are human beings, claims against society recognized as of right, *not* a privilege that the government grants out of grace, love, charity, or compassion.[3] We also indicated that access to good healthcare occupies a central place among these rights. The task here is to explain why that is the case. There are three interrelated aspects to the conversation in this section: The right to healthcare as a tool of social struggle in Ghana and other African countries alike, human rights instruments on the right to healthcare Ghana is linked with, and social determinants of good health.

Right to Healthcare as a Tool of Social Struggle in Ghana and Other African Countries Alike

Healthcare as a tool of social struggle occurs when ordinary citizens frame or lace their political and economic aspirations using the human rights framework.[4] Although "global institutions and norms" recognize and support increased access to social welfare benefits as a human right,[5] individuals and groups still have to act to claim this right. Regrettably, as the Nigerian human rights scholar and activist, Chidi Odinkalu, once observed, many Africans shy away from using the language of human rights in their social struggle.[6] But they must resist that shyness, Ghanaians no less.

First, framing healthcare as a human right (or public good) can provide an alternative to the dominant economics-based discourse. The human rights approach gets "people to think about economic inequality differently, in terms of rights."[7] It "act[s] as a counter to society's unceasing attempt to make poor people think it's their fault that they can't make it."[8] Legislators can internalize human rights principles as part of their democratic principles of governance, as they did in Vermont in the US.[9] There, in 2010, lawmakers adopted a new law which embraced human rights principles as guidelines for healthcare reform.[10] So, while economics can continue to dominate discussions among political leaders, legislative committees on healthcare can use human rights principles as guiding norms for healthcare reform.[11]

Second, building on the first point, because it incorporates an appeal to rights based solely on a person's humanity, the human rights approach is superior.[12] Placing economic and social needs, such as access to life-sustaining healthcare "within an international human-rights framework would allow them to be seen [...] as falling squarely within the categories of rights."[13] More specifically, phrasing one's work in human rights terms "takes you back to the primacy of equality and dignity[,] no matter what the circumstance."[14] And because it is embedded in international law, the human rights approach affords a custom-made "another place to go" outside "the chokehold of domestic law."[15]

Third, the human rights approach has a *strategic* utility that a system not based on human rights lacks. "You cannot reduce rights. You either have to hold the line or increase them."[16]

There is also evidence that "a human rights framework changes the discussion [...] and opens the door to different outcomes. 'A human rights framework helps us see and think about issues in a new light, *helps us to determine what is ours by right*. And when we talk in those terms, the discussion changes.'"[17] By contrast, "[k]eeping a human rights awareness out of public discussion can make it easier for governments to deny responsibilities and evade accountability."[18] Who knows, in Ghana, like in the US, political leaders probably "don't want [people] to know this stuff, for fear that [they] might use it."[19]

Fourth, human rights principles can empower the citizenry by giving them more voice in policymaking.[20] Specifically, framing healthcare as a human right empowers citizens as right holders to demand accountability from their government.[21] As one writer perceptively noted, drawing on a study of South Africa, "[r]arely do public servants and governments welcome being held to account—after all, who would want to be viewed as a human rights violator?"[22]

In sum, a human rights approach to healthcare embodies a potential for social transformation that an approach not based on this orientation lacks. Given the generally poor state of health and healthcare in Africa,[23] applying human rights principles to healthcare has many benefits that the traditional economic approach lacks. Human rights can serve as a tool to mobilize communities to demand healthcare for all. Many Ghanaians are still unaware of their rights to healthcare. Instead, many patients, especially beneficiaries of plans subsidized by the government "tend to see such institutions as doing them a favor and are thus reluctant to complain about any disregard for their rights during their clinical encounters."[24] Given this occurrence, the Ghanaian scholar Owusu-Dapaah makes several recommendations for promoting the development of a human right-based healthcare law to empower patients in Ghana, including creation of a patient rights ombudsman; and integrating healthcare law into the curriculum of law, medical, and nursing schools.[25]

Use of certain activist groups as examples in the discussion of some of the four categories of the application of human rights in social struggle, can leave the appearance that these groups use one of these approaches rather than the others. Such an interpretation would be erroneous since nothing prevents these groups from using *all* those instances in their advocacy work. The story is similar with an entity like Oxfam International. As indicated in Chapter 1, the antipoverty conglomerate takes an approach to combating poverty that is embedded in human rights, one borne out of its belief that "respect for human rights will help lift people out of poverty and injustice."[26] Surely, the orientation is a child of strategy, but it is also simultaneously an alternative to the dominant economics-based discourse, an appeal to rights based solely on a person's humanity, and a tool of empowerment that gives citizens more voice in policymaking.

Global and Regional Human Rights Instruments on the Right to Healthcare Linked to Ghana

All along in this book, we have commented somewhat abstractly on human rights without pinpointing global and regional human rights instruments on the right to healthcare linked to Ghana. This section fills that gap. Four human rights instruments recognizing the right to healthcare that Ghana is associated with are the Universal Declaration of Human Rights (UDHR);[27] the International Covenant on Economic, Social, and Cultural Rights (ICESCR);[28] the African Charter on Human and Peoples' Rights (ACHPR);[29] and the African Charter on the Rights and Welfare of the Child (ACRWC).[30] The first two are global instruments, while the last two are regional instruments. The UDHR proclaims that "[a]ll human beings are born free and equal in dignity and rights."[31] Good health and equal access to healthcare services are essential for the consummation of the "dignity and worth of the human person[.]"[32] More specifically, the UDHR stipulates that "[e]veryone has the right to a standard of living adequate for the *health* and well-being of himself and of his family, including food, clothing, housing and *medical care* and necessary social services."[33] The UDHR is *not* a multilateral treaty. Nevertheless, it is a foundational instrument, exemplifying a "common standard of achievement" in human rights,[34] that the major human rights treaties, such as the ICESCR, subsequently elaborated.[35] Moreover, some human rights experts take the position that the UDHR has risen to the status of customary international law binding on all states.[36]

As indicated in Chapter 5 on the economics of healthcare, Ghana became a state party to the ICESCR on September 7, 2000.[37] The multilateral treaty enjoins state parties to "recognize the right of everyone" within their jurisdictions "to the enjoyment of the highest attainable standard of *physical and mental health*."[38] To minimize the chance of ambiguity, the ICESCR lays down several specific steps these state parties could use "to achieve the full realization of this right."[39] These include providing for the reduction of the stillbirth-rate and of infant mortality and for the healthy development of the child; improving "all aspects of environmental and industrial hygiene"; preventing, treating, and controlling epidemic, endemic, occupational, and other diseases; and creating "conditions which would assure to all medical service and medical attention in the event of sickness."[40] It does not stop there. Instead, it goes as far as to place individuals "under a responsibility to strive for the promotion and observance of" these rights.[41] The guarantee of the right to healthcare elaborates and solidifies the language in the UDHR referred to previously, to the effect that individuals have the right to a standard of living adequate for their health that includes medical care.[42]

The ACHPR stipulates that "[e]very individual shall have the right to enjoy the best attainable state of physical and mental health."[43] Going further, the Charter enjoined state parties to "take the necessary measures to protect the health of their people and to ensure that they receive medical attention when they are sick."[44] Ghana ratified the Banjul Charter in January 1989.[45] The ACRWC provides that "[e]very child shall have the right to enjoy the best attainable state of physical, mental, and spiritual health."[46] It also specifies ten measures that state parties to the treaty could undertake to realize this right, including: Reducing the infant and child mortality rate; providing adequate nutrition and safe drinking water; ensuring appropriate health care for expectant and nursing mothers; and integrating basic health service programs in national development plans, among others.[47] Ghana ratified this instrument in June 2005.[48]

Social Determinants of Health in Ghana

In life, few things stand in isolation all by themselves. Similarly, good health spells more than the mere absence of illness or infirmity.[49] Instead, it is dependent on a number of social determinants not on the surface linked to health but without which good health is hard to realize. These social determinants include the rights to life, food, housing, education, work, human dignity, equality and non-discrimination, access to information and privacy, freedom from torture, as well as the freedoms of association, assembly, and movement.[50] And to be meaningful, the right to health requires that medical products and services be available, accessible, acceptable (i.e., respectful of medical ethics and culturally appropriate), and of good quality.[51]

The conditioning of good health upon these social determinants syncs with the definition of *health* by the WHO as "[a] state of complete physical, mental and social well-being" that must be extended to all equally without discrimination of any kind.[52] Put differently, individuals exposed to physical, mental, and social conditions that minimize their wellbeing *lack* good health.[53] To elaborate on the WHO definition, persons vulnerable to communicable or non-communicable diseases, or exposed to injury or related risks, lack *physical wellbeing*.[54] Similarly, persons with mental illness or who live in poverty or in fear of crime, sexual abuse, or victimization, lack *mental wellbeing*.[55] Finally, persons who lack access to healthcare services, water, sufficient food or jobs, lack *social wellbeing*.[56]

Living with dignity, having the right to make choices, and the ability to control our own bodies may on the surface seem like factors unconnected to health, but can have a big impact on good health. Good health and access to good healthcare services are essential for people's right to dignity.[57] Admittedly, health is also influenced by the choices we make about how persons live their lives, such as whether to engage in antisocial behaviors like smoking tobacco or drinking alcohol excessively.[58] Nevertheless, more often than not, these choices are influenced by whether people have access to education or information.[59]

Applying the WHO's holistic concept of health to Ghana, the "broad range of [social] factors [which] determine good health" in the land "include infrastructure, especially roads, water[,] and sanitation, working and living conditions, nutrition and education[,] as well as the overall distribution of money, power[,] and resources."⁶⁰ Stated differently, "[l]ow levels of literacy, gender inequality, poor sanitation, under-nutrition, alcohol abuse, sedentary life styles and unhealthy diets also contribute to ill health and high mortality rates."⁶¹ Using access to healthcare services for pregnant women under the NHIS as an example, Oxfam International noted that "[u]nfortunately, the impact on assisted deliveries has been less than expected[,]" for a variety of non-financial reasons that includes "distant health facilities, poor road conditions, lack of easily available transport, some social traditions" and even the role of skilled traditional birth attendants, access to whose services are "most unevenly distributed across regions and ethnicities" in the country.⁶² Many of these social determinants which impede healthcare in Ghana fall outside the direct management of the Ministry of Health or other health sector actors.⁶³ Therefore, it stands to reason that "[t]he Ministry of Health acting alone cannot" all by itself remove these impediments.⁶⁴ Instead, "[a] coordinated approach" by all government agencies is needed to promote healthcare in Ghana.⁶⁵

Multiple Reasons Why Healthcare Delivery in Ghana Under the NHIS Falls Below the Standard of Health as Human Right

Ghana's healthcare program marks a refreshing departure from the "cash and carry," user fee arrangement, that preceded it. The scheme's introduction in 2003 symbolized "a bold progressive step that recognized the detrimental impact of user fees, the limitations and low coverage of" the incomprehensive pilot initiatives that preceded it, and "the fundamental role of public financing in" achieving universal healthcare.⁶⁶ Findings credit the NHIS with "an increase in access to formal care amongst members, as well as a significant decrease in out-of-pocket expenditures[,]"⁶⁷ such that, "[w]hile user fees only constituted around 12–14 [percent] of the overall resource envelope in the first half of the decade," as of 2009, the NHIS contributed about 41 percent of overall revenue.⁶⁸ The NHIS garnered increased access to healthcare in Ghana and is credited with covering 95 percent of the burden of disease, including treatment for malaria, respiratory diseases, and diarrhea,⁶⁹ with an overall enrolment of over 12 million people as of 2019.⁷⁰

Moreover, "average OPD [out-patient department] attendance […] increased considerably from 0.49 in 2000 to 0.81 in 2009[,]"⁷¹ and between 2006 and 2009, the proportion of the population enrolled in the NHIS increased by 44 percent.⁷² Other achievements include the growth of government spending on healthcare from one to two digits;⁷³ reckonable advances in the number and distribution of medical personnel, particularly nurses, across the country;⁷⁴ commendable gains in health outcomes;⁷⁵ and the emergence of universal healthcare as "a shared vision across civil society and government" in Ghana.⁷⁶ Last but not least, the impact goes beyond Ghana: The program arguably serves as a model for developing countries in Africa and beyond.⁷⁷

That said, the Ghanaian government still has a long way to go in access and health outcomes to realize its touted vision of "health care for all, free at the point of use."[78] For example, the country lags behind the UN Millennium Development Goals (MDGs) targets in health;[79] despite improvement in outpatient department attendance, averages lag behind the "generally accepted minimum of 3 per person per year for basic universal coverage";[80] and there is little progress registered in family planning,[81] among other downsides. The net result is that many years after implementation of the NHIS, many Ghanaians still rely on the cash and carry user fee system for their healthcare needs, "or resort to unqualified drug peddlers and home treatment due to lack of funds."[82]

In sum, regarding the right to healthcare in Ghana, it is not yet *uhuru* (freedom as East Africans would put it in Swahili).[83] Instead, for Ghana and other healthcare bellwether countries in Africa, little evidence exists regarding the argument that social health insurance "increases the responsiveness of services," supposedly due to the "stronger entitlement" rising beyond the status of "tax-paying consumers" this model of healthcare financing symbolizes.[84] Some of the numerous interconnected factors analyzed in this section which add up to place Ghana's otherwise commendable healthcare initiative below the standard of a health as human right, arrayed in no particular order, include that it is less than free, less than comprehensive, inefficient, lacking in accountability, inequitable, and privileges curative medicine over preventive care. Factors relating to financing, including dependence on external assistance, have been covered already in Chapter 5. These various factors, including the economic suboptimalities, are then compounded by a rapid population growth out of sync with the relatively slow pace of healthcare production. The variables are interlinked. For example, the inadequate financing of the program examined in Chapter 5 is connected to the incomprehensive character of the program this chapter comments on below. The ensuing discussion takes these factors in turn. These reasons are illustrative, rather than exhaustive of all possibilities. Table 6.1 encapsulates these factors.

Not Really Free

In unveiling the NHIS, the Ghanaian government promised the country's citizens and residents free healthcare for all at the point of access that the NHIS, in its current denouement, does not meet.[85] To the contrary, the program is less than free. At issue here would be what exactly we mean by unfree healthcare. There is a popular saying in the US to the effect that there's no free lunch in the sense that everything costs something, even if indirectly or hidden.[86]

This is a viewpoint the WHO itself seems to share regarding healthcare. Elaborating on the concept of Universal Health Coverage (UHC), the WHO indicated that protection against financial risk is not absolute. This is because "[n]o health system meets the full cost of health services out of the prepaid and pooled funds collected by tax or insurance contributions."[87] Instead, many health systems "require some form of co-payment, sometimes of an informal nature, at the time of use[,]" aimed at "restrain[ing] demand and/or limit[ing] the cost to the government or insurance fund."[88] Consequently for the WHO, insulation against financial risk or hardship is still met if "the relative contribution made by out-of-

Table 6.1 Ghana under the NHIS: Recap of health as human right

Item No.	Factor or Variable	Indicators
1.	Not really free	• User fee exists in parallel system • Program does not cover many drugs and services
2.	Not really comprehensive	• Program does not cover many Ghanaians who patronize the private sector • Program does not adequately cover mental health services • The program does not cover services like dialysis for chronic kidney issues
3.	Inefficient	• Arduously slow registration process • Delay in reimbursing healthcare providers • Cost escalation which arises when healthcare providers seek illegally to maximize reimbursement payments • Waste emanating from the NHIA itself, which operates the scheme
4.	Insufficiently accountable	• Lack of transparency indicated by a failure to publish (timely) reports informing Ghanaians on the performance of the scheme • Opinion polls unearthing perception of corrupt practices under the scheme, including illegal charges for services whether in enrolling or receiving services under the program
5.	Inequitable	• Benefits relatively few people at the expense of the many (i.e., everybody pays for healthcare, but only a minority benefits) • The program discriminates against abjectly poor people, as well as workers in the informal sector of the economy • Reimbursement payments favor high-level healthcare facilities like hospitals and jurisdictions with better infrastructure
6.	Privileging curative medicine over preventive care	• Failure to address social determinants of health like bad roads, inadequate drinking water, poor sanitation, low literacy levels, and gender inequality • Claim processing anchored on reimbursement of curative care at the expense of investments that keep people healthy

Item No.	Factor or Variable	Indicators
7.	Rapid population growth out of sync with production of healthcare goods	• From about 6 million persons in 1957, Ghana's population has ballooned to nearly 28 million people as of May 2016 • In contrast, economic growth averaged 2.05% in the 10-year period from 2006–2016 • To the detriment of social programs like healthcare services, Ghana's leaders, like many in other African countries, do not take population control seriously
8.	Inadequate funding	• Covered in Chapter 5 on the economics of healthcare
9.	Dependence on external assistance	• Covered in Chapter 5 on the economics of healthcare

pocket payments from patients at the time of service provision is not so high that it reduces access to care."[89] A rule of thumb is that user fee is all right "if it is administratively more accessible than general government allocations[,]" but becomes a problem when "revenue collection becomes a disproportionately important evaluative criterion in a system which is, after all, ultimately intended to improve health status."[90] Put simply, the litmus test is whether cost recovery features disproportionately in an affected healthcare system.

That said, the NHIS in its present form is not free. There are still medications and services even within the 95 percent of common diseases for which NHIS subscribers, many of whom are low-income earners, pay out of their pockets.[91] That means that, indirectly, cost recovery still looms large in a healthcare arrangement designed ultimately to improve health status. Thus, as Oxfam International advised, to make the program freer and stronger the Ghanaian government may have to take a number of possible proactive steps ranging from introducing a single lifetime payment in place of regular premium payments all the way to abolishing user fees in the parallel system.[92]

Not Really Comprehensive

In addition to not being really free, as currently designed and implemented, the NHIS is less comprehensive than it appears on the surface. Into the second decade of its operation, only about 40 percent or two-fifths of Ghana's population is enrolled in the plan.[93] Due to a range of problems that include long hours spent on "unmoving queues," as of 2014, about 15 million Ghanaians have not registered to use the benefits of the NHIS.[94] This is especially the case with richer citizens who can afford service in the private, user-fee system. In 2018, the National Health Insurance Authority, the agency which oversees the NHIS, promulgated elaborate guidelines governing the operation of private insurance in Ghana.[95] And while one study of the Ashanti region in 2020 unearthed impressive coverage, when disaggregated, the truer picture revealed that about "81.4 [percent] of the population had access to general primary health care, 61.4 [percent] to secondary-level health care and, only 14.3 [percent] to tertiary health care."[96]

Even with the seemingly "high levels of accessibility to general primary health care, accessibility remains poor in some selected districts, especially rural districts in the region[,]" where "[a]bout 30 [percent] of the population [...] travel long distances to access healthcare, particularly specialist services which are available only at secondary and tertiary centers."[97] To correct these access problems, in June 2020, the Ghanaian government announced its intention to build 88 more district hospitals.[98] However, the government did not redeem this promise until August 2021 when President Nana Akufo-Addo commissioned a set of hospitals and related medical facilities that he christened "Agenda 111."[99] Harking back to the observation about the interconnection of these factors, the accessibility issue here is a matter of inequity discussed below.

In no area is this lack of comprehensiveness more evident than in mental health services. In June 2012, the Ghanaian national government unveiled a mental health program under the Mental Health Act, designed to complement the NHIS.[100] Among other features, the law allows people with mental disabilities to challenge their detention in psychiatric hospitals.[101] Before the law, the "practice is that family members deliver individuals to a psychiatric hospital or prayer camp, or police remove individuals off the street when they exhibit confused or aggressive behavior."[102] Not so any longer, thanks to the Mental Health Act. However, an early assessment of the law published on October 2, 2012 by Human Rights Watch revealed that many mental patients hospitalized under the program faced physical and verbal abuse, including being chained to trees.[103]

Accordingly, administrators of the NHIS still have a long way to go to promote improved mental health services. Mental wellness and integrity are critical to the WHO's definition of good health; therefore, people without access to proper mental health treatment lack the mental wellbeing and integrity that epitomize good health. We are aware that the National Health Insurance Act exempts persons with mental disorders from paying premiums.[104] But, by itself, this does not resolve the problem of inadequate access to healthcare services under the NHIS.

In an age when diseases morph from infectious status to chronic life-style categories,[105] the NHIS's common-disease classification needs to be expanded to include more services or conditions. One such service that comes to mind is dialysis for *chronic* kidney failure, even though the scheme covers *acute* kidney failure.[106] Because the line dividing the two illnesses is not too obvious to the naked eye, it would be a good idea for the National Health Insurance Authority to cover both. Another is cancer in both adults and children. Individuals versed in NHIS operation contend that the growing incidence of cancer in Ghana nowadays brings it within the rubric of common diseases that the NHIS should cover.[107] As we indicated in Chapter 3, Ghana's healthcare program is built rather heavily on the principle of exemptions.[108] Such arrangements create invidious distinctions and inequities inconsistent with health as human right. Finally, in this age of pandemics, the list of NHIS services should embrace telemedical services,[109] elaborated below under inefficiency.

Inefficient

In addition to the two factors highlighted above, the NHIS is inefficient. *Efficiency* stands for the relationship between input and output, specifically "the ability to do something or produce something without wasting materials, time, or energy."[110] Inefficiency is a problem of execution, rather than design, that afflicts many healthcare systems, rather than being unique to Ghana.[111] Oxfam International estimates that about 36 percent of healthcare spending in Ghana is wasted due to inefficiencies and poor investment.[112] Collectively, these inefficiencies cost the Ghanaian government millions of Cedis each year,[113] impeding the sustainability of the still fledgling system. On the other hand, plugging these holes of inefficiency "will bring significant gains […] by generating savings that can be ploughed back into improving and expanding service delivery" in the country.[114] According to Oxfam International, a revamp of health insurance administration alone could save the country US$83 million a year, an amount enough to pay for approximately 23,000 more nurses.[115]

One feature which notably makes the NHIS inefficient is registration. To access supposedly free healthcare under the system, beneficiaries need a card which they do not get unless they register. However, the registration process can be arduously slow, leaving individuals to stand in line for many hours in long queues that sometimes barely move.[116] According to one news report, in the capital city of Accra, "people queue as early as 3 a.m. at the National Health Insurance office to register."[117] Add to this, "[m]any Ghanaians simply do not have access to an NHIS agent near where they live."[118] Individuals who manage to register can wait for a long time, in some cases from three to six months, for their membership cards to arrive before they can access the healthcare system.[119]

A second marker of inefficiency in the NHIS arises from major delays in reimbursing hospitals, pharmacists, and other healthcare providers for services, sometimes running into millions of US dollars.[120] It takes three to four months on average for the government to reimburse health facilities within which time some health facilities reportedly turn away insured patients or demand payment before rendering services.[121] A third marker of inefficiency, related to reimbursement, is cost escalation which occurs when healthcare providers "gam[e] the system to maximize reimbursement payments."[122] This escalation arises when NHIS officials set the price levels for provider reimbursement "too high so providers can make profits by procuring medicines at lower prices[,]"[123] rather than pay them the same rate as public providers.[124] For this reason, or in spite of it, many healthcare provides see the NHIS "as a provider's dream: 95 [percent] of health conditions covered with payment methods that offer few or no incentives to contain costs."[125] Nearly 20 years since the inauguration of the NHIS, fraud indicated by cost escalation remains a major challenge to the financial sustainability of the program.[126]

Several sources of savings for Ghana's healthcare system include: A shift away from annual premium payments that eliminates the need for much of the current insurance bureaucracy, slimming down the National Health Insurance Authority and incorporating relevant portions of its responsibility to the Ministry of Health, plugging avenues for fraud and leakages in the healthcare system, and reducing the cost of medicines through better negotiations with suppliers and reducing unnecessary cost escalation along the supply chain.[127] Others are: Paying private providers at the same rate as public providers; incorporating family planning services as part of the current package of benefits under the NHIS; and investing in preventive measures, such as increased bed net distribution to prevent malaria, as well as potable water and increased sanitation to reduce diarrhea and typhoid.[128]

Inefficiency in the Ghanaian healthcare system is compounded by inadequate Information and Communication Technology (ICT), a key tool nowadays for improving the performance of health systems, especially in developing countries like Ghana with fledgling infrastructure.[129] Despite efforts made by the government to improve ICT,[130] its application remains poor.[131] Instead, patient-care processes in Ghanaian hospitals, are still conducted manually rather than electronically and remotely, with no system for the generation of electronic medical records, with negative ramification for referrals.[132] Multiple challenges to health informatics in Ghana include insufficient electric power supply, insufficient Internet connectivity, resistance to new technology by healthcare personnel who fear that new technology will threaten their jobs, and government agencies who lack the skills to maintain ICT equipment.[133] Ghana's ICT application situation has changed little since the appearance of the Achampong article nearly a decade ago.[134]

Moving forward, the outbreak of COVID-19 in 2020 triggered the advent of the age of telemedicine.[135] The pandemic accelerated a rapid integration of telemedicine into healthcare systems across the world as patients "opt for care that mitigates risk and reduces unnecessary interactions."[136] Through the medium of ICT, telemedicine "connect[s] community health workers to medical specialists via [twenty-four]-hour teleconsultation centers," wherein doctors and other medical personnel "coach community health workers and advise on the treatment of their patients[.]"[137] However, there is limited application of telemedicine in Ghanaian healthcare delivery, especially in rural communities.[138] This is an orientation, inconsistent with health as human right, that, in this age of pandemics, needs to change.

Insufficiently Accountable

Adding to the problems highlighted above, the NHIS is insufficiently accountable. Accountability is a cardinal principle of democracy and a concept inescapably tied to transparency.[139] It stands for the proposition that government officials, elected or appointed, "are responsible to the citizenry for their decisions and actions."[140] *Transparency* mandates "that the decisions and actions of those in government are open to public scrutiny and that the public has a right to access such information."[141] Both concepts are so central to the "very idea of democratic governance that" without them, "democracy is impossible."[142] Without them, "elections and the notion of the will of the people have no meaning, and government has the potential to become arbitrary and self-serving."[143] Though less obvious, accountability and transparency are also an issue of human rights. Under international law, individuals have the right to take part in the government of their country and the will of the people, expressed in free and fair elections, forms the basis for the authority of government.[144]

What makes poor accountability troubling is its association with (political) corruption. Political corruption takes place when an office holder uses his or her public office to pursue private ends and gains.[145] Although compared to its counterparts in West Africa like Nigeria and elsewhere in Africa like Kenya and the Democratic Republic of the Congo (Congo Kinshasa), Ghana is mildly corrupt,[146] the incidence of corrupt practices in the Ghanaian healthcare system is large-scale and pervasive.[147] Opinion polls unearth a high perception of corruption in healthcare in all regions of Ghana, with more than half of all respondents indicating that, due to corrupt practices from officials associated with the NHIS, they spent up to 30 percent of their disposable income on excess payments in accessing healthcare services.[148] Practices within the healthcare system that many patients and respondents in opinion surveys legitimately perceive as corrupt include: Sharp practices in medical procurement, diversion of budgeted funds by health administrators, healthcare workers stealing time by not coming to work or doing private practice during work hours, doctors prescribing medications that patients do not need, doctors issuing forged sick leaves and medical reports, failure by healthcare workers to return to patients unused drugs that they have been billed for; as well as illegal charges for services rendered in accessing healthcare under the NHIS, whether related to enrolment in the program, accessing drugs, creation and retrieval of medical records, allocation of hospital beds, or ambulance services.[149]

The emergence of accountability as an issue in the Ghanaian healthcare debate coincides with the publication of Oxfam's report on the NHIS in 2011 which criticized operators of the program for their lack of accountability.[150] As of that date, the NHIS failed to publish reports regarding the performance of healthcare in the country that would help Ghanaians and non-government groups to hold their government and officials of agencies charged with implementing the NHIS, including the Ministry of Health and the Ministry of Finance, accountable for their decisions and actions.[151] Thus, in its report, Oxfam International made suggestions on steps the Ghanaian authorities could take to promote accountability and transparency with respect to the NHIS. These include: Placing the management of the National Health Insurance Fund (NHIF) under the jurisdiction of the Ministry of Health "with a clear legal responsibility to publish timely and comprehensive accounts of both income and expenditure, including regular tracking surveys to monitor spending at all levels of the system";[152] and enforcing regular published accounts from the Ministry of Finance, "indicating disbursements to the health sector against commitments made."[153] Act 852 of 2012, revamping the NHIS, instructively included promoting accountability and transparency among its objectives. The law was enacted in the aftermath of the Oxfam report. However, as indicated in Chapter 3, activities of the government which allows for the conversion of monies meant for the NHIS into non-NHIS uses,[154] work against this objective.

Inequitable

In addition to the four "lacks" discussed above (not really free, not really comprehensive, inefficient, and insufficiently accountable), in its current shape, the NHIS is inequitable. *Inequity* refers to lack of basic fairness or justice. "Who pays how much for what, when?" is a major element in the design and implementation of any healthcare system.[155] The NHIS is inequitable in both access and financing, two features that at times overlap as the ensuing discussion makes clear.

One element, out of several, which makes the NHIS inequitable is that it limits healthcare benefits funded mostly from tax revenue to a small section of the public. As Oxfam International colloquially puts it in its seminal report, practically everybody pays for healthcare but only a minority benefits.[156] To put things in a more practical perspective, about 70 percent of the NHIS's funding, representing more than two-thirds, comes from tax revenue made up of a 2.5 percent health insurance levy plus a sales value-added tax that every Ghanaian citizen pays each time he or she buys goods and services.[157] Given this funding reality, "all Ghanaians, rich and poor, are contributing financially to the health system[.]"[158] However, according to Oxfam International's estimate, only about 18 percent benefits from the scheme.[159] The antipoverty group reached this number through its assessment that "[c]overage of the [scheme] has been hugely exaggerated, and could be as low as 18 [percent]," an occurrence that leaves about 82 percent excluded.[160] Given this number, Oxfam International maintains, the NHIS delivers healthcare for a "lucky few at the expense of the many[,]"[161] and it pinpoints "[t]his large-scale exclusion" to be the most damning flaw of the NHIS.[162]

Besides benefitting a relatively few people at the expense of the many, another feature which makes the NHIS inequitable is that it discriminates against abjectly poor persons.[163] These are persons defined by the World Bank as living on less than one US dollar per day.[164] Despite their material poverty, based on Oxfam International's estimate, 20 percent of this group "pay[s] 6 [percent] of their expenditure as tax and of this nearly 15 [percent] goes into the government health budget."[165] Though the matter of financial inequity is so obvious, like the first feature (benefitting the few at the expense of the many), this problem is also equally an issue of access, given that under the scheme, 64 percent of the richest are registered, compared to 29 percent of the poorest.[166] The progressive nature of taxation in Ghana, meaning that "the rich pay a higher proportion of their expenditure as tax than the poor," minimizes but does not take away this badge of inequity.[167] The result is that "[p]oor people are left with no choice but to resort to home treatment[,]" including "risk[ing] childbirth at home without qualified care."[168]

Just like abjectly poor individuals, the NHIS discriminates against workers in the informal sector. The informal sector consists of economic activities outside the formal economy that elude or are not amenable to government regulation.[169] It is a sector "characterized by underemployment, bad working conditions, uncertain work relationship, and low wages,"[170] where about eight out of every ten workers in Ghana derive their source of income.[171] Informal sector workers, most of whom "liv[e] with high income insecurity," include "self-employed persons, such as farmers, traders, food processors, artisans, and craft-workers," among numerous occupations in rural and urban areas.[172] Where the discrimination against this large group of workers comes in is that under the NHIS marked by the "principle of exemptions,"[173] they "are the only population group required to pay premiums individually and in cash to benefit from the" scheme.[174] It is an inequity rooted in funding given that, "despite their low incomes, informal economy workers are unfairly paying significantly more per head than any other members [under] the scheme."[175] The inequity is equally embedded in access given that it "leads to the large-scale exclusion of informally employed adults and their children."[176] To get a sense of the magnitude of this exclusion, based on the estimates of Oxfam International, "[a]s of June 2010, only 29 [percent] of those registered for NHIS were employed in the informal economy."[177]

A fourth and final characteristic building on and reinforcing the previous three elements of inequity is insurance financing, particularly reimbursement payments, which favor high-level facilities, such as hospitals and jurisdictions with higher levels of infrastructure to facilitate access. It is in light of the foregoing problems of inequity that Oxfam International predicted that the NHIS, as currently implemented, "fail[s] to deliver the scale of change promised"[178] and advised the Ghanaian government to enact "bolder changes," including "overhaul[ing] the health insurance bureaucracy."[179] These characteristics of inefficiency lend credence to our argument in Chapter 3 for the transition of the NHIS to a single-payer, tax-funded system.

Privileging Curative Medicine over Preventive Healthcare

In addition to all of the problems highlighted above, NHIS operations appear to privilege curative medicine over preventive healthcare. "An ounce of prevention is better than a pound of cure," as one famed adage goes.[180] Based on this wisdom, preventive healthcare is quality medical attention short of complex diagnoses and treatment, actuated by the need to remove the causes of ill-health, rather than addressing their symptoms.[181] Preventive medicine encompasses well-targeted education designed "to prevent [people] from developing chronic diseases in the first place[,]" while providing patients with chronic conditions effective techniques for "manag[ing] their health[.]"[182] Progressive healthcare systems stress primary healthcare, anchored on keeping people healthy. They "make disease unacceptable instead of building ever larger infrastructure to accommodate it."[183] In the US, the Affordable Care Act (ACA) under then-president Barack Obama was predicated largely on preventive medicine.[184]

Regrettably, this preventive approach to medicine has yet to reach the shores of many African countries, including Ghana, as we will show shortly.[185] To compound an already bad situation, foreign donors also unwittingly promote this curative approach with their assistance. The lesson here for Ghana and other African countries is wariness regarding excessive dependence on external funding or even uncalibrated public-private partnership with donors, given the tendency toward curative medicine when the donor private-sector agenda drives such partnership.[186] Two indicators illustrate the NHIS's privilege of curative medicine over preventive care. The first is the failure of successive Ghanaian governments to address many of the social determinants of health discussed in the previous section, such as bad roads, inadequate access to clean water, poor sanitation, low literacy levels, and gender inequality, among other problems. The second indication results from the processing of claims in a manner that shifts resources away from preventive to curative care. As Oxfam International points out, "[f]rom 2006 to 2008, while claims payments for curative health were sky-rocketing, the government subsidy to the District Health Administration responsible for preventative health levelled off in real terms in 2006 and 2007 and fell in 2008."[187] However, "[b]y only reimbursing curative care," at the expense of investments that keep people healthy, "the NHIS presents no incentive to facilities to incorporate preventative health into their services."[188]

In its 2011 report, referred to repeatedly in this book, Oxfam International proposed capitation payments, discussed in Chapter 3,[189] as a possible tool for promoting preventive medicine in Ghana's healthcare system because of the "inherent incentive" this payment method gives to providers "to invest in preventative health."[190] As of 2021, ten years later, this issue remains unresolved. Preventive services not covered but that stakeholders, individuals versed with NHIS operations, advise be included on the NHIS roster of services include medical exams biannually for routine screening, health education, and telemedicine.[191] Continued lack of attention to preventive medicine, one stakeholder warned, could "collapse [Ghana's] primary health care system."[192]

Rapid Population Growth Inconsonant with Supply of Healthcare Services

Compounding the preceding six factors plus the issues of inadequate funding along with dependence on external funding as discussed in Chapter 5, is the matter of rapid population growth. Ghana's annual birth rate is estimated at 2.19 percent.[193] This means that the country's population is projected to double approximately every 32 years.[194] Testimony to this rapid growth in population, from about 6 million persons in 1957, Ghana's population has ballooned to nearly 28 million people as of May 2016 with a landmass that remains unchanged at 92,456 square miles.[195] To use a US state for comparison, Ghana is about the size of Oregon, but with a much larger population compared to Oregon's less than 4 million people as of 2014.[196] To use Norway as another example, at independence in 1957, Ghana had a population "about the same as [the country]."[197] Fifty-eight years later, "Norway still has a population of just over five million," while Ghana's has jumped to "almost 28 million."[198]

The high fertility rate is out of sync with the rate of economic growth averaging 2.05 percent in the past 10 years from 2006–2016.[199] If unchecked, Ghana's fertility rate vis-à-vis economic growth rate could pose problem for any socioeconomic venture like expanded healthcare. To be sure, only humans develop an economy. Therefore, a healthy population is the greatest resource of Ghana or any other country.[200] But too much of a good thing can sometimes be a problem. As one Nigerian demographer stated, commenting on Nigeria in a wisdom that also applies here, "[p]opulation is key. If you don't take care of population, schools can't cope, hospitals can't cope, there's not enough housing—there's nothing you can do to have economic development."[201]

Given a choice between population control and achievement of high economic growth, population control seems less arduous and more easily achievable. However, Ghana's leaders appear not to take population control seriously. In its 2011 report, Oxfam International observed that "[f]amily planning coverage is [...] unacceptably low at 31 [percentage]."[202] It advised operators of the NHIS to incorporate family planning services as part of the package of benefits under the program.[203] Finally, unchecked population growth could have negative consequences for food production.[204] In a nutshell, not only does rapid population growth undermine efforts "to increase food production," "lower birth rates, along with better management of land and water resources, are necessary to avert chronic food shortages."[205] However, this is a counsel that Ghanaian leaders have yet to heed.

Conclusion

Market forces fail to adequately address the healthcare needs of populations, leaving governments with obligations for healthcare development.[206] Given the failures of market forces, "governments have an obligation to intervene in order to improve both equity and efficiency, to carry out important public health functions and to produce vital public goods which have a lot of bearing on health development."[207] This is the sense in which, citing the international bill of human rights, some human rights non-governmental organizations insist on the adoption of a human right approach to the advocacy for social welfare programs, including the right to healthcare.[208]

Universal healthcare is not just the flipside of low or targeted coverage;[209] on the contrary, it is a much richer idea with ingredients that include needful concern for human rights. Expanded healthcare embedded in human rights is the only lasting inoculation against the hypothesis of "inverse equity" where "new public-health interventions and programs initially reach those of higher socioeconomic status" before trickling down to the poor.[210] Using the US health reform debate as example, "in contrast to the exclusions and inequities entailed in treating health care as a market commodity[,]" "[h]uman rights principles inspire[…] the development of a heterodox concept of public goods, defined as the essential goods, services, and infrastructure needed to satisfy human needs and realize human rights[.]"[211]

The idea that drives this whole book is how to go beyond the NHIS while standing on it. The lesson of this chapter is that it is difficult to get into Stage 3 of Ghana's healthcare debate, health as human right, without first resolving the complex issues of access and sustainability regarding the NHIS, the latest phase in Ghana's healthcare reforms. Put differently, to stand a chance at health as human right, Ghana's leaders must first get the politics, law, and economics of healthcare delivery in the country right. The aim of this chapter was to explain this proposition.

Notes

1. Chapter 2, tbl. 2.2. ("Key elements").
2. Ibid. ("Bases for assessment").
3. Chapter 2, notes 82–87, and accompanying texts. See also Jack Donnelly, "An Overview," in *Human Rights and Comparative Foreign Policy*, ed. David P. Forsythe (Tokyo, Japan: United Nations University Press, 2000), 310, 315 (stating that "[h]uman rights are held by all human beings, regardless of who or where they are" and that, consequently, "[t]o identify with human rights is to identify with all human beings, regardless of nationality or other status") (internal parentheses omitted).
4. Donnelly, note 3, p. 314.
5. Paul Hunt et al., "Editorial: Making the Case: What Is the Evidence of Impact of Applying Human Rights-Based Approaches to Health," *Health & Human Rights Journal*, 17(2) (November 2, 2015), www.hhrjournal.org/2015/11/editorial-making-the-case-what-is-the-evidence-of-impact-of-applying-human-rights-based-approaches-to-health/.
6. Chidi A. Odinkalu, "Why More Africans Don't Use Human Rights Language," Carnegie Council for Ethics in International Affairs (December 5, 1999), www.carnegiecouncil.org/publications/archive/dialogue/2_01/articles/602.html ("While Africa's human rights problems are immense […], most of [its] people do not describe these problems in human rights terms").
7. Philip C. Aka, "Analyzing U.S. Commitment to Socioeconomic Human Rights," *Akron Law Review*, 39(2) (2006), 417, 431.
8. Ibid., p. 431 (quoting Ethel Long-Scott of the Women's Economic Agenda Project in Oakland, California).
9. Gillian MacNaughton et al., "The Impact of Human Rights on Universalizing Health Care in Vermont, USA," *Health & Human Rights Journal*, 17(2) (December 2015), 83.
10. Ibid.

11 See ibid.
12 Aka, note 7, p. 425.
13 Ibid.
14 Ibid., p. 426 (citing *Close to Home: Case Studies of Human Rights Work in the United States* (Washington, DC: Ford Foundation, 2004), 9.
15 Cited in Aka, note 7, p. 431.
16 Ibid., p. 431.
17 Ibid., p. 432. Emphasis added. Little wonder that US "activists dealing with issues relating to immigrants, prisoners, the poor, and other minorities are now increasingly using human rights as a tool of advocacy[,]" steeped in the belief that "[h]uman rights as a framework has the power to transform [their] activism[.]" Ibid., pp. 431–432.
18 Ibid., pp. 432–433 (quoting Loretta Ross, a human rights administrator and veteran activist).
19 Ibid.
20 Ibid.
21 Ernest Owusu-Dapaah, "Empowering Patients in Ghana: Is There a Case for a Human Rights-Based Health Care Law?" *Lancaster University Ghana Law Journal*, 1 (2015), 91, https://papers.ssrn.com/sol3/papers.cfm?abstract_id=2821895.
22 Leslie London, "What is a Human-Rights Based Approach to Health and Does it Matter?" *Health & Human Rights Journal*, 10(1) (June 2008), www.hhrjournal.org/2013/09/what-is-a-human-rights-based-approach-to-health-and-does-it-matter/.
23 See Chapter 1, note 59 and accompanying text.
24 Owusu-Dapaah, note 21, p. 92.
25 Ibid.
26 Chapter 1, note 50, and accompanying text.
27 Universal Declaration of Human Rights, G.A. Res. 217 A (III), U.N. GAOR, 3d Sess., U.N. Doc. A/810 (1948) [hereinafter UDHR].
28 International Covenant on Economic, Social, and Cultural Rights, G.A. Res. 2200, U.N. GAOR, 21st Sess., Supp. No. 16, U.N. Doc. A16316, 993 U.N.T.S. 3, 6 I.L.M. 360 (1966) [hereinafter ICESCR].
29 African Charter on Human and Peoples Rights (Banjul Charter), June 27, 1981, OAU Doc. CAB/LEG/67/3/Rev. 5, 21 I.L.M. 58 (entered into force October 21, 1986) [hereinafter ACHPR]. The document is sometimes referred to as the Banjul Charter, after the city in The Gambia where it was adopted. The body charged with oversight and interpretation of the ACHPR is the African Commission on Human and Peoples' Rights, set up in 1987 and headquartered in Banjul. In 1998, the OAU adopted a protocol to the ACHPR creating an African Court on Human and Peoples' Rights. See Protocol to the African Charter on Human and Peoples' Rights on the Establishment of an African Court on Human and Peoples' Rights (1998), OAU Doc. OAU/LEG/EXP/AFCHPR/PROT (III) (June 9, 1998) (entered into force January 25, 2004). The Court complements the protective mandate of the African Commission on Human and Peoples' Rights. See ibid., art. 2 (explaining the relationship between the court and the commission). Its power includes the authority to issue advisory opinion "on any legal matter relating to the Charter or any other relevant human rights instruments." Ibid., art. 4.
30 African Charter on the Rights and Welfare of the Child, OAU Doc. CAB/LEG/24.9/49 (1990) (entered into force November 29, 1999) [hereinafter ACRWC].
31 UDHR, note 27, art. 1.
32 UDHR, note 27, preamble.
33 Ibid., art. 25.1. Emphasis added.
34 UDHR, note 27, preamble.

35 Another major human rights instrument which warrants a mention here is the International Covenant on Civil and Political Rights (ICCRP). See ICCPR, G.A. Res. 2200A (XXI), U.N. GAOR, Supp. No. 16, U.N. Doc. A/6316, 999 U.N. T.S. 171 (1966), 6 I.L.M. 368 (1967). It is an instrument, complementary to the ICESCR, that, like the ICESCR, the UN General Assembly adopted in 1966, but came into effect in 1976. Ghana became a State Party to this multilateral treaty on September 7, 2000, the same date it ratified the ICESCR. "United Nations Human Rights Treaty Bodies," UN Treaty Body Database, https://tbinternet.ohchr.org/_layouts/15/TreatyBodyExternal/Treaty.aspx?CountryID=67&Lang=EN.

36 See Hurst Hannum, "The Status of the Universal Declaration of Human Rights in National and International Law," *Georgia Journal of Int'l & Comp. Law*, 25 (1996), 287, 317–354. Customary international law is the branch of international law which deals with norms of international obligations arising from established international practices. Customary international law results from a general and consistent practice of states that they follow from a sense of legal obligation and is contrasted from state obligations that arise from formal written treaties or conventions. "Customary International Law," Legal Information Institute, Cornell Law School, www.law.cornell.edu/wex/customary_international_law.

37 See Chapter 5, note 18, and accompanying text.
38 ICESCR, note 28, art. 12.1.
39 Ibid., art. 12.2.
40 Ibid., art. 12.2(a)–(d).
41 Ibid., preamble. See also "General Comments No. 14 on the Right to the Highest Attainable Standard of Health," Committee on Economic, Social, and Cultural Rights, E/C.12/2000/4 (August 11, 2000), 63–65, www.nesri.org/sites/default/files/Right_to_health_Comment_14.pdf. (assigning responsibility for realizing the right to good health to non-state actors like the WHO, the UN International Children's Fund, the ILO, the IMF, the World Bank, and the International Committee of the Red Cross/Red Crescent).
42 See note 33 and accompanying text.
43 ACHPR, note 29, art. 16(1).
44 Ibid., art. 16(2).
45 "Ratification Table: African Charter on Human and Peoples' Rights," African Commission on Human and Peoples' Rights, www.achpr.org/instruments/achpr/ratification/.
46 ACRWC, note 30, art. 14.
47 Ibid., art. 14, 2 a–j.
48 "Ratification Table: African Charter on the Rights and Welfare of the Child," African Commission on Human and Peoples' Rights, www.achpr.org/instruments/child/ratification/.
49 See Chapter 2, note 3, and accompanying text.
50 See "General Comments No. 14 on the Right to the Highest Attainable Standard of Health," note 41, 3.
51 Ibid., 12.
52 See Chapter 2, note 3, and accompanying text.
53 "A Background to Health Law and Human Rights in South Africa," *Health and Democracy* (June 1, 2007), www.section27.org.za/wp-content/uploads/2010/04/Chapter1.pdf.
54 Ibid.
55 Ibid.
56 Ibid.
57 Ibid.

58 Ibid.
59 Ibid.
60 *Achieving a Shared Goal: Free Universal Healthcare in Ghana* (London, UK: Oxfam International, 2011), 42, www.oxfam.org/sites/www.oxfam.org/files/rr-achieving-shared-goal-healthcare-ghana-090311-en.pdf.
61 Ibid.
62 Ibid.
63 Ibid.
64 Ibid.
65 Ibid.
66 *Achieving a Shared Goal*, note 60, p. 18.
67 Sophie Witter and Bertha Garshong, "Something Old or Something New?: Social Health Insurance in Ghana," *BMC Int'l Health & Hum. Rights*, 9 (August 2009), 6, www.ncbi.nlm.nih.gov/pmc/articles/PMC2739838/.
68 *Achieving a Shared Goal*, note 60, p. 9.
69 Sarah Kirchner, "[Four] Facts about Healthcare," *The Borgen Project* (February 25, 2021), https://borgenproject.org/facts-about-healthcare-in-ghana/. See also Chapter 3, note 79.
70 "NHIS Active Membership Soars," NHIS: National Health Insurance Scheme (July 2, 2020), www.nhis.gov.gh/News/nhis-active-membership-soars-5282.
71 *Achieving a Shared Goal*, note 60, p. 8.
72 Kirchner, note 69.
73 According to Oxfam International's estimate, government spending on healthcare in the country rose from 8.2 percent in 2004 to 14.6 percent in 2009. *Achieving a Shared Goal*, note 60, p. 33.
74 Ibid.
75 For example, between 2002 and 2009, death from malaria reduced by 50 percent for children under five, treatment success rate for tuberculosis reached 85 percent in 2009, child mortality declined by 27 percent by 2009, and infant mortality by 32 percent by 2009. Ibid., p. 33.
76 Ibid., p. 34. See also Chapter 3, notes 57–59, and accompanying texts (commenting on a commitment to expanded healthcare among Ghana's major political parties).
77 *Achieving a Shared Goal*, note 60, p. 18. The range of countries from Africa and abroad understudying the program for its supposed cost-effectiveness include Bangladesh, Benin, Democratic Republic of Congo, Ethiopia, Liberia, Mali, and Senegal. Kent Mensah, "Ghana's Successful but Unpopular Healthcare," *Al Jazeera* (August 6, 2014), www.aljazeera.com/news/africa/2014/07/ghana-successful-but-unpopular-healthcare2014722101651828127.html. The attention was probably spurred by the NHIS's winning of a UN award in 2010. The prize in question was the South-South Cooperation Excellence Award, issued by the UN Development Program and the WHO. See "Ghana's NHIS Wins Major World Award," *Modern Ghana* (March 22, 2011), www.modernghana.com/news/321345/ghanas-nhis-wins-major-world-award.html.
78 *Achieving a Shared Goal*, note 60, p. 8.
79 Ibid., p. 33. For example, there is slow progress on communicable diseases (such as malaria, HIV and AIDS, tuberculosis, meningitis, cholera, and guinea worm) as it faces new challenges in non-communicable illnesses, such as diabetes, cancers, and heart diseases. Ibid., pp. 33–34.
80 Ibid., p. 34.
81 Ibid.
82 Ibid., p. 8.
83 Swahili, short for Kiswahili, is a language widely spoken in East Africa. Broadly speaking, the idea for this statement was inspired by Oginga Odinga, *Not Yet*

Uhuru: The Autobiography of Oginda Odinga (New York: Heinemann, 1968) (drawing from his personal experiences of persecution, Odinga, a former vice president of Kenya, indicates that the freedom in Kenya was a mere appearance with little basis in reality).

84 Witter and Garshong, note 67, p. 12.
85 See Chapter 3, notes 40–42, and accompanying texts.
86 "There Ain't No Such Thing as a Free Lunch—TANSTAAFL," *Investopedia*, www.investopedia.com/terms/t/tanstaafl.asp (explaining that the saying "expresses the idea that even if something seems like it is free, there is always a cost, no matter how indirect or hidden"). The phrase is believed to have originated from the practice of some saloons in the US who provided free lunches to their patrons but required them to purchase drinks in order to get those lunches. Ibid.
87 Social Health Insurance: Report by the Secretariat, World Health Organization, Executive Board, 115th Session, Provisional Agenda Item 4.5, EB115/8 (December 2004), 8.
88 Ibid.
89 Ibid.
90 C.J. Waddington and K.A. Enyimayew, "A Price to Pay, Part 2: The Impact of User Charges in the Volta Region of Ghana," *Int'l Journal of Health Planning & Management*, 5 (1990), 287.
91 See Chapter 3 commenting on the NHIS, specifically the second section which enumerated the quantum of services available to subscribers under the program.
92 *Achieving a Shared Goal*, note 60, pp. 34–35.
93 Chapter 3, note 176, and accompanying text. See also Doris Dokua Sasu, "Share of Population with National Health Insurance Scheme (NHIS) Membership in Ghana from 2014 to 2017," *Statista* (February 9, 2021), www.statista.com/statistics/1172722/share-of-people-with-active-national-health-insurance-membership-in-ghana/ (putting the figure at little over 35 percent as of 2017).
94 Mensah, note 77.
95 See *Guidelines for Private Health Insurance Schemes in Ghana* (Accra, Ghana: National Health Insurance Authority, July 2018), nhis.gov.gh/files/PHISGUIDELINES.pdf.
96 George Ashiagbora et al., "Measures of Geographic Accessibility to Health Care in the Ashanti Region of Ghana," *Scientific African*, 9 (September 2020), https://doi.org/10.1016/j.sciaf.2020.e00453.
97 Ibid.
98 Kirchner, note 69.
99 See "'Agenda 111' to Optimally Advance Ghana's Healthcare Delivery—President," *Ghana Web* (August 18, 2021), www.ghanaweb.com/GhanaHomePage/NewsArchive/Agenda-111-to-optimally-advance-Ghana-s-healthcare-delivery-President-1335367.
100 Mental Health Act (Act 846) (2012), https://ijmhs.biomedcentral.com/articles/10.1186/1752-4458-8-16. For an analysis on the law, see Mark Roberts et al., "An Overview of Ghana's Mental System: Results from an Assessment Using the World Health Organization's Assessment Instrument for Mental Health Systems (WHO-AIMS)," *Int'l Journal of Mental Health Systems*, 8(16) (May 4, 2014), https://ijmhs.biomedcentral.com/articles/10.1186/1752-4458-8-16.
101 Human Rights Watch, *Ghana: People with Mental Disabilities Face Serious Abuse* (October 2, 2012), www.hrw.org/news/2012/10/02/ghana-people-mental-disabilities-face-serious-abuse.
102 Juan E. Méndez, Report of the Special Rapporteur on Torture and Other Cruel, Inhuman or Degrading Treatment or Punishment, Human Rights Council Twenty-Fifth Session, Agenda item 3, A/HRC/25/60/Add.1 (March 5, 2014).
103 Human Rights Watch, *Ghana*, note 101; Méndez, note 102, *passim*.

104 See Chapter 3 commenting on the NHIS, specifically the second section which enumerated the quantum of services available to subscribers under the program.
105 See Philip C. Aka, *Genetic Counseling and Preventive Medicine in Post-War Bosnia* (Gateway East, Singapore: Palgrave Macmillan, 2020), 108.
106 See Chapter 3 commenting on the NHIS, specifically the second section which enumerated the quantum of services available to subscribers under the program.
107 Moses Aikins et al., "Positioning the National Health Insurance for Financial Sustainability and Universal Health Coverage in Ghana: A Qualitative Study among Key Stakeholders," *PloS One* (June 15, 2021), 6–7, https://doi.org/10.1371/journal.pone.0253109.
108 See Chapter 3, notes 92–121, and accompanying texts.
109 See Aikins et al., note 107, p. 7 (citing Stakeholder 7).
110 "Efficiency," *Merriam-Webster Dictionary*, www.merriam-webster.com/dictionary/efficiency.
111 *Achieving a Shared Goal*, note 60, p. 46. For example, Oxfam International cites a WHO report which estimates that "between 20% and 30% of existing health resources are being wasted due to inefficient and inequitable use." Ibid.
112 *Achieving a Shared Goal*, note 60, p. 8.
113 See ibid., pp. 30, 46.
114 Ibid., p. 46.
115 Ibid., p. 7.
116 Mensah, note 77.
117 Ibid. Given this occurrence, as his news report deadpanned, "beneficiaries must meet one unofficial requirement—be physically fit or forget about it." Ibid.
118 *Achieving a Shared Goal*, note 60, p. 29.
119 Ibid.; Hassan Wahab, "Universal Healthcare Coverage: Assessing the Implementation of Ghana's NHIS Law," in *Intellectual Agent, Mediator, and Interlocuter: A.B. Assensoh and African Politics in Transition*, eds. Toyin Falọla and Emmanuel M. Mbah (Newcastle, UK: Cambridge Scholars Publishing, 2014), 188, 198.
120 *Achieving a Shared Goal*, note 60, p. 29 (stating that the Ghanaian government owed health facilities about US$34 million as of the end of 2008). See also National Development Planning Commission, *2008 Citizens' Assessment of the National Health Insurance Scheme: Toward a Sustainable Health Care Financing Arrangement that Protects the Poor* (Accra, Ghana: National Development Planning Commission, 2009); and Afisah Zakariah et al., *Holistic Assessment of the Health Sector Program of Work 2013* (Accra, Ghana: Ministry of Health, 2014).
121 *Achieving a Shared Goal*, note 60, p. 29.
122 Ibid.
123 Ibid.
124 On this, Oxfam International determined, based on an analysis of NHIS data, that "the average reimbursement rate per health facility attendance claim for insured patients is 50 percent higher than non-insured patients paying for themselves in the cash and carry system." Ibid., p. 30.
125 Ibid.
126 See Aikins et al., note 107, p. 7.
127 *Achieving a Shared Goal*, note 60, p. 47 (distilled from tbl. 5, "potential savings that could contribute toward financing universal health care.").
128 Ibid.
129 See "Information Communication Technology in Health[c]are," *Front Enders* (Blog) (November 6, 2016), www.frontenders.in/blog/information-communication-technology-healthcare.html.
130 Emmanuel Kusi Achampong, "The State of Information and Communication Technology and Health Information in Ghana," *Online Journal of Public Health*

Informatics, 4(2) (2012), 4191, doi:10.5210/ojphi.v4i2.4191 ("ICT Policies in Ghana").
131 Ibid. ("Health Management Information Systems") (stating that "[t]he use of health management information system is not widespread").
132 Ibid.
133 Ibid. ("Challenges to Health Informatics in Ghana").
134 Agyenna Kesse-Tachi et al., "Factors Influencing Adoption of eHealth Technologies in Ghana," *Digital Health* (September 5, 2019), 5:2055207619871425, doi:10.1177/2055207619871425; and Ebenezer Afarikumah, "Electronic Health in Ghana: Current Status and Future Prospects," *Online Journal of Public Health Informatics* 5(3) (2014), 230, doi:10.5210/ojphi.v5i3.4943.
135 Elena Muller, "COVID-19 Ushering in the Age of Telehealth," *Health Recovery Solution*, www.healthrecoverysolutions.com/blog/covid-19-ushering-in-the-age-of-telehealth; "Ghana Telemedicine," Novartis Foundation, www.novartisfoundation.org/past-programs/digital-health/ghana-telemedicine. See also Brookings Institution, "Telehealth Before and After COVID-19," Webinar (May 7, 2020), www.youtube.com/watch?v=_T-fUjYDfqc; Patient-Centered Outcomes Research Institute (PCORI), "Confronting COVID-19: The Changing Role of Telehealth," Webinar (May 5, 2020), www.pcori.org/events/2020/part-6-changing-role-telehealth.
136 Muller, note 135; "Ghana Telemedicine," note 135.
137 "Ghana Telemedicine," note 135.
138 See, for example, Victoria Colbert, "Telemedicine Plays a Bigger Role in Healthcare in Ghana," *Borgen Project* (Blog), https://borgenproject.org/telemedicine-plays-a-big-role-in-ghana/ ("Managing Expectations") (commenting on various factors that impede "the ability of telemedicine to improve healthcare in Ghana"); Osei Darkwa, "An Exploratory Survey of the Applications of Telemedicine in Ghana," *Journal of Telemedicine and Telecare*, 6(3) (June 1, 2000), 177–183, https://doi.org/10.1258/1357633001935185 ("Staff in the urban hospital were more likely to be familiar with telemedicine and more likely to have access to information technology than those in the rural hospital") (abstract).
139 "Accountability and Transparency: Essential Principles," *Democracy Web: Comparative Studies in Freedom*, http://democracyweb.org/node/42.
140 Ibid.
141 Ibid.
142 Ibid.
143 Ibid.
144 UDHR, note 27, art. 21(1) and (3). For an extensive analysis on this right, see Thomas M. Franck, "The Emerging Right to Democratic Governance," *American Journal of Int'l Law*, 86 (January 1992), 46.
145 See *What Is Corruption?* Transparency International, www.transparency.org/en/what-is-corruption.
146 In December 2020, Ghana ranked 11th among African countries in a corruption index, compared to Kenya 26, Nigeria 41, and Democratic Republic of the Congo 49. See "Corruption Rank | Africa," *Trading Economics*, https://tradingeconomics.com/country-list/corruption-rank?continent=africa.
147 See generally *Cost and Impact of Corruption on Education and Health Sectors in Ghana* (Accra, Ghana: Ghana Integrity Initiative (GII) Consortium, 2018).
148 Ibid., p. 2.
149 Ibid., p. 2, 48 (tbl. 14); see also Witter and Garshong, note 67 (commenting on the surges in informal payments, such as charges for out-of-hours services and advisement for patients to pay for drugs supposedly out of stock, that take away from the otherwise noticeable decrease in out-of-pocket expenses under the NHIS).

150 See generally *Achieving a Shared Goal*, note 60.
151 See *Achieving a Shared Goal*, note 60, p. 36.
152 It is not clear whether the structure Oxfam International is proposing here, see ibid., p. 36 (under the heading 4.1.2 titled "Establish a National Health Fund,") is a new one, given that the NHIS already has a Fund that we described in Chapter 3, particularly the material dealing with the legal framework of the program.
153 *Achieving a Shared Goal*, note 60, p. 36 (4.1.3 "transparency and accountability").
154 See Chapter 3, statements in-between the texts of notes 68–69.
155 See Edward Baker et al., *Managing the Public Health Enterprise* (Burlington, MA: Jones Barlett Learning, 2010), 170.
156 See *Achieving a Shared Goal*, note 60, pp. 7, 26.
157 Ibid., p. 26. The figure of 70 percent is based on available data for 2008 provided by Oxfam International.
158 Ibid., p. 26.
159 Ibid., pp. 7, 26.
160 Ibid., p. 7.
161 *Achieving a Shared Goal*, note 60, p. 7. See also ibid., p. 8 (positing that the design in the funding of the NIHS rooted largely on tax funding "is flawed and unfair—every citizen pays for the NHIS but only some get to join.").
162 Ibid., p. 26.
163 Ibid., p. 8.
164 Ibid.
165 Ibid., p. 26.
166 Ibid., p. 8.
167 Ibid. (stating that despite the progressive nature of Ghana's tax system, "financial contribution from the poor could well be diverting already scarce resources away from other goods and services essential for their health and well-being.").
168 Ibid., p. 28. Vis-à-vis richer persons, abjectly poor women in Ghana "are more than three times more likely to deliver at home," often the only "private" health services available to these poor women. *Id*.
169 See Clara Osei-Boateng and Edward Ampratwun, "The Informal Sector in Ghana," *Friedrick Ebert Stiftung* (October 2011), 4, http://library.fes.de/pdf-files/bueros/ghana/10496.pdf (reviewing definitions of the term).
170 Ibid., p. 5.
171 Ibid. (abstract)
172 Ibid.
173 See Chapter 3 commenting on the NHIS, specifically the third section which enumerated the principle of exemption under the program.
174 *Achieving a Shared Goal*, note 60, p. 29.
175 Ibid.
176 Ibid.
177 Ibid.
178 Ibid., p. 15.
179 Ibid.
180 The saying is attributed to US founding father, Benjamin Franklin (1705/6–1790).
181 See Philip C. Aka, *Genetic Counseling and Preventive Medicine in Post-War Bosnia* (Gateway East, Singapore: Palgrave Macmillan, 2020), vii, 3–5.
182 "The Future of Healthcare in Africa," *Economist Intelligence Unit* (London) (2014), 17, www.economistinsights.com/sites/default/files/downloads/EIU-Janssen_HealthcareAfrica_Report_Web.pdf (quoting Dr. Ernest Darkoh, founding partner of Broad-Reach Healthcare, a healthcare services company). According to Dr. Darkoh, the most successful outcome for a healthcare system in Africa should be defined as never

needing to see the inside of a hospital. For him, the continuous need to build more hospitals and clinics should be considered a sign of failure. Ibid.
183 "The Future of Healthcare in Africa," note 182.
184 See Aka, note 181, p. 108.
185 See, for example, Netsanet Fetene Wendimagegn and Marthie C. Bezuidenhout, "Integrating Promotive, Preventive, and Curative Health Care Services at Hospitals and Health Centers in Addis Ababa, Ethiopia," *Journal of Multidisciplinary Healthcare*, 12 (April 5, 2019), 243–255, doi:10.2147/JMDH.S193370; Subhojit Goswami, "Africa Needs Preventive Approach to Health Care Instead of a Curative One: Experts," *Down to Earth*, www.downtoearth.org.in/news/health/africa-needs-preventive-approach-to-health-care-instead-of-a-curative-one-experts-59807.
186 Ibid., quoting Githinji Gitahi, Head of Amref Health Africa, a healthcare NGO headquartered in Nairobi, Kenya, with a branch office in New York.
187 *Achieving a Shared Goal*, note 60, p. 30.
188 Ibid.
189 Chapter 3, notes 88–91, and accompanying texts.
190 *Achieving a Shared Goal*, note 60, p. 30.
191 Aikins et al., note 107, pp. 5–6.
192 Ibid., p. 6 (Stakeholder 4).
193 "Ghana," in *CIA Factbook* (2014) (estimate as of 2014).
194 This doubling period is arrived at by taking the number 70 and dividing it by the country's population growth rate, here 2.19, consistent with the formula in determining doubling time. See "Population Growth: Friend or Foe?" *Econedlink*, www.econedlink.org/lessons/projector.php?lid=32&type=educator.
195 "Ghana Population (Live)," *Worldometers*, www.worldometers.info/world-population/ghana-population/. See also Ken Ntiamoa, "Ghana Needs a Population Control Policy," *Modern Ghana* (January 18, 2005), www.modernghana.com/news/116094/1/ghana-needs-a-population-control-policy.html; and Arjun Adlakha, "Population Trends: Ghana," US Bureau of the Census, International Brief No. 96-01 (July 1996), www.census.gov/population/international/files/ib96_01.pdf (providing country data that include the country's 1957 population).
196 "Oregon," *QuickFacts* (US Census Bureau), http://quickfacts.census.gov/qfd/states/41000.html.
197 Elizabeth Ohene, "Letters from Africa: What Can Ghana Learn from Norway," *BBC News* (December 22, 2015), www.bbc.com/news/world-africa-34710175.
198 Ibid.
199 "Ghana GDP Growth Rate 2006–2016," *Trading Economics*, www.tradingeconomics.com/ghana/gdp-growth. Over this period, GDP growth rate in the country reached an all-time high of 8.10% in the first quarter of 2012 and a record low of -2.20% in the fourth quarter of 2008. Ibid.
200 See Nkrumah's statement, Chapter 1, note 18, and accompanying text, directly tying economic development in Ghana to improvement in the health of the people.
201 Quoted in Elisabeth Rosenthal, "Nigeria Tested by Rapid Rise in Population," *New York Times* (April 14, 2012), www.nytimes.com/2012/04/15/world/africa/in-nigeria-a-preview-of-an-overcrowded-planet.html?pagewanted=all&_r=0.
202 *Achieving a Shared Goal*, note 60, p. 34.
203 Ibid.
204 Nafis Sadik, "Population Growth and the Food Crisis," FAO Corporate Doc. Repository, www.fao.org/docrep/U3550t/u3550t02.htm.
205 Ibid.
206 See World Health Organization, Regional Office for the Eastern Mediterranean, *The Role of Government in Health Development* (July 2006), *passim*, http://applications.emro.who.int/docs/em_rc53_tech.disc.1_en.pdf.
207 Ibid., p. 1.

208 See this chapter, notes 1–24, and accompanying texts, commenting on the right to health as a tool of social struggle.
209 See generally Obinna Onwujekwe, Moving Nigeria from Low Coverage to Universal Health Coverage: Health System Challenges, Equity[,] and the Evidence-Base, 74th Inaugural Lecture, University of Nigeria, Enugu Campus (April 2013), www.researchgate.net/publication/317267470_Moving_Nigeria_from_low_coverage_to_universal_health_coverage_national_health_system_challenges_equity_and_the_evidence-base.
210 Cesar G. Victora et al., "Explaining Trends in Inequities: Evidence from Brazilian Child Health Studies," *Lancet* (September 23, 2000), www.thelancet.com/pdfs/journals/lancet/PIIS0140-6736(00)02741-0.pdf.
211 Anja Rudiger, "Human Rights and the Political Economy of Universal Health Care: Designing Equitable Financing," *Health & Human Rights Journal*, 18 (2016), 67, 69, www.hhrjournal.org/2016/12/human-rights-and-the-political-economy-of-universal-health-care-designing-equitable-financing/.

7 Conclusion and Prospects for the Future

Stage 2½?

"If the introduction of 'Cash and Carry' health care was stage one, and the NHIS stage two, it is now time for stage three[.]"[1] So Oxfam International, the UK-based antipoverty conglomerate wrote in its seminal study on the NHIS referenced time and again in this work. We pinpoint stage three to be health as human right.[2] Therein lies the argument and central message of this book. Our option for human right is in due cognizance of the transformational advantage that, as a reform tool, this model has over the traditional economic approach of venture capitalism embedded in supply and demand.

In support of our option for health as human right, we laid out four hallmarks—good laws, good politics, adequate funding, and health as human right—which collectively we propose as a guide to assessment of healthcare reforms in Ghana. Using this heuristic tool of measurement, we assessed the Ghana healthcare initiative anchored in the NHIS as suboptimal. We devoted three chapters of this book—4 to 6—in support of that proposition. In seeking to understand healthcare reforms in Ghana under the Fourth Republic, we looked at the period before 1993 up to the early days of independence under Dr. Kwame Nkrumah.[3] There are some advantages in including the pre-1993 period. First, doing so starts the story of healthcare reforms in Ghana from its proverbial beginning and provides useful insights related to the topic. Second, such inclusion comports with the methodology of this work, broached in Chapter 2 on our analytical framework, anchored in within-case comparison (WCC).[4] WCC involves the study of one country at different points in time and space, in an attempt to unearth variations that will help the researcher better understand their evidence.[5] Including the period before 1993 affords more canvas in time duration for comparative analysis.

Without detracting from the allure that the NHIS deservedly holds for many admirers in Africa, ten years after Oxfam's message and two decades after conscientious experimentation, the program is riddled with numerous problems of access and funding redolent of insufficient progress toward health as human right that this book systematically unearths. If cash and carry is stage one in healthcare reforms in Ghana and the NHIS stage two, in the fateful journey to health as human right, Ghana's healthcare reform initiative under the Fourth

DOI: 10.4324/9781003264125-7

Republic, is probably somewhere around Stage 2½. This speaks to a huge amount of unfinished business. The scenario brings to mind the interminable struggle of Sisyphus in Greek mythology. For the sin of stealing the secret of the gods, Sisyphus was condemned in Hades to repeatedly roll a heavy rock up a hill only to have it roll down again as it nears the top. Less extremely, the situation speaks to the dilemma of realizing human rights in a world where, despite a flurry of domestic and international activities aimed at protecting and promoting these rights, atrocities stubbornly remain.[6] As indicated in Chapter 1, this points up the challenge of translating a cache of human rights laws, domestic, regional, and international, into operational policies for citizens,[7] that may not fairly be blamed completely on Ghana.

Lessons for Africa from Ghana

These lessons feature as Ghana's contribution to the political economy of healthcare in Africa. The lessons are two-fold and they are illustrative, rather than exhaustive. One, more positive than negative, is about how to build a consensus on healthcare within a political system; the other, more negative than positive, is the need to harmonize production and delivery of healthcare and other social services with the rate of population growth.

How to Build a Consensus on Healthcare Reforms

Africa has made important strides in human rights in the post–Cold War period, monuments of which include the transition of the Organization of African Unity (OAU) into the African Union (AU) in 2000.[8] The Constitutive Act creating the AU stipulates that one of the objectives of the revamped organization shall be to "promote and protect human and peoples' rights in accordance with the African Charter on Human and Peoples Rights and other relevant human rights instruments."[9] Some of the provisions germane to these objectives, enumerated under Article 4 on the "principles" of the new organization, include: "promotion of gender equality; respect for democratic principles, human rights, the rule of law and good governance; and promotion of social justice to ensure balanced economic development."[10]

Going further, the AU created a number of organizations that are critical for safeguarding and promoting human rights, including the African Court of Justice.[11] Still the constraints against realization of these rights remain "daunt[ing]."[12] Part of the reason is probably because, as Chidi Odinkalu said, Africans tend not to use the language of human rights in social struggles.[13] In his observation, "[w]hile Africa's human rights problems are immense [...], most of [its] people do not describe these problems in human rights terms."[14]

Despite the limitations of the NHIS this book recounts, under the Fourth Republic, Ghana presents itself as a textbook case anywhere on how to build a creative consensus on healthcare, a social service embedded in the human right to life. With their supporters, Ghanaian politicians demonstrated that healthcare can form a viable issue for successful political campaigns and for maintaining political office. Years later, Barack Obama did the same in the US, learning from the prior experience of his fellow Democrat Bill Clinton who experimented with healthcare *after* his election into office as president. However, "embracing the politics of Universal Health Coverage"[15] is an orientation many of Ghana's neighbors in West Africa, such as Nigeria, still fight shy of.[16] Notice that even in Ghana, the fire of healthcare as gristmill in the gladiation of partisan politics took some time to ignite, rather than coincide with the beginning of the Fourth Republic, during which period Jerry Rawlings and his NDC held power.

If Ghana handles its healthcare reform initiatives well, it could translate its fledgling comparative advantage in the healthcare field into the status of a medical tourist mecca for Africa in the mold of India in South Asia or Cuba and Costa Rica in the Caribbean.[17] Such an achievement would be consistent with an anticipated transformation of the healthcare sector in Africa in the next 50 years into a "job-creating sector," specifically "a labor-intensive" machine that can create millions of skilled jobs for Africa's youthful population.[18] It is a direction some Ghanaian leaders, such as Nana Akuffo-Addo, appear to have their sights on.[19]

Need to Harmonize Production and Delivery of Healthcare and Other Social Services with the Rate of Population Growth

Some lessons in the political economy of healthcare in Ghana are more negative than positive. One such lesson discussed here is the imbalance between production and delivery of healthcare and the rate of population growth. Unlike the consensus on healthcare in the country discussed above, it is one issue where African countries do not have to emulate Ghana.

To be sure, only humans develop an economy. Arguably, a healthy population is the greatest resource Ghana has. But too much of a good thing can sometimes be a problem. As one Nigerian demographer warned, in a statement we adapt here to Ghana, "[p]opulation is key[,]" and there is little the country "can do to have economic development," if it does not bring population under control.[20] "If [it does not] take care of population, schools can't cope, hospitals can't cope, there's not enough housing."[21] In the space of 60 years from independence in 1957 to 2017, Ghana's population jumped nearly six-fold from about 6 million to over 29 million people.[22] Without dabbling into Malthusian controversy, it is like saying that, over the period of two generations while its landmass remains the same, Ghana's population grew astronomically while the capacity of its governments to produce and delivery health services grew only arithmetically. This is mostly because, as we indicated in Chapter 6 on health as human right, Ghanaian leaders do not take family planning seriously.[23] The moral of the story is that other African countries can emulate the good in the Ghana healthcare reform package, such as the consensus on healthcare reform while jettisoning the bad, such as striving for universal healthcare coverage without reining in on rapid population growth.

Prospects for the Future

For both Ghana and other African countries, the prospects for the future are good—with provisos. With healthcare now part of the policy agenda in Ghana, the next challenge is to maintain and improve it until it becomes a human right. This occurrence brings to mind the memorable story from American national government and politics about how, upon exiting the Constitutional Convention in 1787, Benjamin Franklin was approached by a group of citizens who earnestly quizzed him regarding the sort of government the delegates had created. He responded: "A republic, if you can keep it." The same wisdom applies here. The outbreak of COVID-19 has uncovered many healthcare disparities in Ghana,[24] thereby reinforcing the necessity for a human-rights-oriented healthcare system. Ghana will increase its capacity to maintain affordable healthcare for the masses, if its decision makers, as representatives of the people, fund healthcare adequately, thereby increasing the movement of the country toward health as human right.

For other African countries, despite the known and unknown constraints on realizing human rights, national discourses on healthcare should continue to stress the link between health and human rights.[25] In doing so, these countries should be mindful of the emerging "global movement for health and human rights," including the intricacies of "health as an issue of fundamental human rights and social justice."[26] Though unfinished, the healthcare story from Ghana can lend some measure of encouragement to those discourses on healthcare.

Notes

1 *Achieving a Shared Goal: Free Universal Health Care in Ghana* (Oxford, UK: Oxfam International, March 2011), 10, 34, www.oxfam.org/sites/www.oxfam.org/files/rr-achieving-shared-goal-healthcare-ghana-09033-en.pdf.
2 Our proposition brings to mind the words of St. Paul in the Acts of the Apostles. […] "Men of Athens, I perceive that in every way you are very religious. For as I passed along and observed the objects of your worship, I found also an altar with this inscription: 'To the unknown god.' What therefore you worship as unknown, this I proclaim to you." *The Holy Bible, English Standard Version* (Wheaton, IL: Crossway, 2016), Acts 17:22–23.
3 See Chapter 3, notes 1–33, and accompanying texts ("Healthcare reforms in Ghana before the NHIS").
4 Chapter 2, notes 120–122, and accompanying texts.
5 Chapter 2, note 121, and accompanying text.
6 See generally Samantha Power and Graham Allison, eds., *Realizing Human Rights: Moving from Inspiration to Impact* (New York: St. Martin's Press, 2000).
7 Chapter 1, note 58, and accompanying text.
8 Organization of African Unity (OAU), Constitutive Act of the African Union (July 1, 2000), http://www.refworld.org/docid/4937e0142.html.

108 *Conclusion and Prospects for the Future*

9. Ibid., art. 3(h).
10. Ibid., art. 4
11. See ibid., art. 5 (spelling out the organs of the AU) and art. 18 (establishing the Court of Justice).
12. P.T. Zeleza, "The Struggle for Human Rights in Africa," Keynote Address to the Annual Meeting of the Association of African Studies, University of Toronto (May 17, 2007), 1, 5, http://www.zeleza.com/node/162/print. Reprinted in *Canadian Journal of African Studies*, 41(3) (2007), 474–506.
13. Chidi A. Odinkalu, "Why More Africans Don't Use Human Rights Language," Carnegie Council for Ethics in Int'l Affairs (December 5, 1999), http://www.carnegiecouncil.org/publications/archive/dialogue/2_01/articles/602.html.
14. Ibid.
15. David Heymann and Robert Yates, "Embracing the Politic of Universal Health Coverage," Chatham House: The Royal Institute of International Affairs (June 25, 2014), https://www.chathamhouse.org/expert/comment/14972.
16. See Philip C. Aka and Joseph A. Balogun, *Healthcare and Economic Restructuring: Nigeria in Comparative Perspective* (Palgrave Macmillan, forthcoming 2022).
17. See, for example, Philip C. Aka, *Bosnia as Civic State: Alternative Futures Outside the EU* (Lanham, MD: Rowman & Littlefield, 2021), Chapter 10 (commenting on the statuses of Costa Rica and Cuba as global Good Samaritans); and Philip C. Aka, "Fidel Castro and Socioeconomic Human Rights in Africa: A Multi-Level Analysis," *Fordham International Law Journal*, 43(1) (2019), 41–78 (focusing on Cuba).
18. Mthuli Ncube et al., "Health in Africa over the Next 50 Years," African Development Bank, Economic Brief (March 2013), 20, www.afdb.org/fileadmin/uploads/afdb/Documents/Publications/Economic_Brief_-_Health_in_Africa_Over_the_Next_50_Years.pdf.
19. See Bob Koigi, "Ghana's Eco Medical Village Set to Revolutionize Africa's Medicare and Health Tourism," *Fair Planet* (July 2, 2020), www.fairplanet.org/story/ghana%E2%80%99s-eco-medical-village-set-to-revolutionize-africa%E2%80%99s-medicare-and-health-tourism/.
20. Quoted in Elisabeth Rosenthal, "Nigeria Tested by Rapid Rise in Population," *New York Times* (April 14, 2012), www.nytimes.com/2012/04/15/world/africa/in-nigeria-a-preview-of-an-overcrowded-planet.html?pagewanted=all&_r=0.
21. Ibid.
22. "Ghana Population (Live)," *Worldometer*, www.worldometers.info/world-population/ghana-population/ ("Population of Ghana (2020 and historical)").
23. Chapter 6, note 188, and accompanying text.
24. See "'Agenda 111' to Optimally Advance Ghana's Healthcare Delivery—President," *Ghana Web* (August 18, 2021), www.ghanaweb.com/GhanaHomePage/NewsArchive/Agenda-111-to-optimally-advance-Ghana-s-healthcare-delivery-President-1335367.
25. See Isidore Bonabom, *Health and Human Rights in Ghana: The Political and Economic Aspects of Health* (Champaign, IL: Common Ground Publishing, 2014), *passim* (suggesting that national discourses sometimes overlook that inevitable link).
26. About HHR, www.hhrjournal.org/about-hhr/ (mission statement of the *Health and Human Rights Journal*).

References

Abdullahi, Ali Arazeem. 2011. Trends and Challenges of Traditional Medicine in Africa. *African Journal of Traditional, Complementary, and Alternative Medicine*, 8(115), 123. www.ncbi.nlm.nih.gov/pmc/articles/PMC3252714/.
About HHR. www.hhrjournal.org/about-hhr/.
About Us. 2017. *Official Website of the NHIS*. www.nhis.gov.gh/about.aspx.
Accountability and Transparency: Essential Principles. *Democracy Web: Comparative Studies in Freedom*. http://democracyweb.org/node/42.
Achampong, Emmanuel Kusi. 2012. The State of Information and Communication Technology and Health Information in Ghana. *Online Journal of Public Health Informatics*, 4(2), 4191. doi:10.5210/ojphi.v4i2.4191.
Adlakha, Arjun. 1996. *Population Trends: Ghana*. US Bureau of the Census, International Brief No. 96–1. July. www.census.gov/population/international/files/ib96_01.pdf.
Adler, Jonathan E., and Catherine Z. Elgin (eds.). 2007. *Philosophical Inquiry: Classic and Contemporary Readings*. Indianapolis, IN: Hackett Publishing Co., Inc.
Adu-Gyamfi, Samuel. 2019. What We Can Learn from the Ghanaian Experience of National Health Insurance. *City Press*. September 4. www.news24.com/citypress/voices/what-we-can-learn-from-the-ghanaian-experience-of-national-health-insurance-20190904.
AETNA. *Expat Guide to Health Care in Ghana*. www.aetnainternational.com/en/individuals/destination-guides/expat-guide-to-health-care-in-ghana.html.
Afarikumah, Ebenezer. 2014. Electronic Health in Ghana: Current Status and Future Prospects. *Online Journal of Public Health Informatics*, 5(3), 230. doi:10.5210/ojphi.v5i3.4943.
Africa: The Struggle for Development. 1999. In *Global Studies: Africa*, 8th ed., R. C. Grote, E. L. Harvey, Jeffress H. Ramsay, F. Jeffress Ramsay, E. Jeffress Ramsay, and Wayne Edge (eds.), pp. 1–10. New York: McGraw-Hill.
African (Banjul) Charter on Human and Peoples' Rights. 1982. *OAU Doc*. CAB/LEG/67/3 rev. 5. 21 I.L.M. 58. Adopted June 27, 1981. Entered into force October 21, 1986.
The African Center for Strategic Progress. 2021. *Subregions*. Washington, DC: The African Center for Strategic Progress. https://acstrap.org/subregions/.
African Charter on the Rights and Welfare of the Child. 1990. *OAU Doc*. CAB/LEG/24.9/49 Entered into force November 29, 1999.
African Commission on Human and Peoples' Rights. Ratification Table: African Charter on Human and Peoples' Rights. www.achpr.org/instruments/achpr/ratification/.

References

African Commission on Human and Peoples' Rights. Ratification Table: African Charter on the Rights and Welfare of the Child. www.achpr.org/instruments/child/ratification/.

African Union. *About the African Union*. https://au.int/en/overview.

African Union. 2016. African Union Welcomes Commitments to Achieve Universal Health Coverage by 2030. Press Release. September 1. www.au.int/en/pressreleases/31328/african-union-welcomes-commitments-achieve-universal-health-coverage-2030.

Afrobarometer. 2005. *Parliament of the Fourth Republic of Ghana—Views from the Grassroots*. CDD-Ghana. November. www.afrobarometer.org/files/documents/briefing_papers/AfrobriefNo20.pdf.

Agenda 111: Impeach President Akufo-Addo for Dishonesty—NDC's Brogya Genfi. 2021. *MyNewsGH*. August 18. www.mynewsgh.com/agenda-111-impeach-president-akufo-addo-for-dishonesty-ndcs-brogya-genfi.

Agenda 111 is Ghana's Biggest Ever Investment in Healthcare—Akufo-Addo. 2021. *Modern Ghana*. August 17. www.modernghana.com/news/1098624/agenda-111-is-ghanas-biggest-ever-investment-in.html.

"Agenda 111" to Optimally Advance Ghana's Healthcare Delivery—President. 2021. *Ghana Web*. August 18. www.ghanaweb.com/GhanaHomePage/NewsArchive/Agenda-111-to-optimally-advance-Ghana-s-healthcare-delivery-President-1335367.

Aikins, Moses, Philip Teg-Nefaah Tabong, Paola Salari, Fabrizio Tediosi, Francis M. Asenso-Boadi, and Patricia Akweongo. 2021. Positioning the National Health Insurance for Financial Sustainability and Universal Health Coverage in Ghana: A Qualitative Study among Key Stakeholders. *PLoS One*. June 15. https://doi.org/10.1371/journal.pone.0253109.

Aka, Philip C. 2021. *Bosnia as Civic State and Global Citizen: Alternative Futures Outside the EU*. Lanham, MD: Rowman & Littlefield.

Aka, Philip C. 2020. *Genetic Counseling and Preventive Medicine in Post-War Bosnia*. Gateway East, Singapore: Palgrave Macmillan.

Aka, Philip C. 2019. Fidel Castro and Socioeconomic Human Rights in Africa: A Multi-Level Analysis. *Fordham International Law Journal*, 43(1), 41–78.

Aka, Philip C. 2016. Bridging the Gap Between Theory and Practice in Humanitarian Action: Eight Steps to Humanitarian Wellness in Nigeria. *Willamette Journal of International Law & Dispute Resolution*, 24(1) 1–51.

Aka, Philip C. 2006. Analyzing U.S. Commitment to Socioeconomic Human Rights. *Akron Law Review*, 39(2), 417–463.

Aka, Philip C., and Joseph A. Balogun. Forthcoming 2022. *Healthcare and Economic Restructuring: Nigeria in Comparative Perspective*. Gateway East, Singapore: Palgrave Macmillan.

Aka, Philip C., Ibrahim J. Gassama, A.B. Assensoh, and Hassan Wahab. 2017. Ghana's National Health Insurance Scheme (NHIS) and the Evolution of a Human Right to Healthcare in Africa. *Chicago-Kent Journal of International & Comparative Law*, 17(2), 1–65.

Akufo-Addo Has Packaged NDC's Idea and Named it Agenda 111—Segbefia. 2021. *Ghana Web*. August 19. www.ghanaweb.com/GhanaHomePage/NewsArchive/Akufo-Addo-has-packaged-NDC-s-idea-and-named-it-Agenda-111-Segbefia-1336129.

Akufo-Addo Should Be Removed from Office; Agenda 111 Is a 419 Project—Brogya Genfi. 2021. *PeaceFMOnline*. August 18. www.peacefmonline.com/pages/politics/politics/202108/450318.php.

Anaman, Pauline, and John Darko. 2018. Is Ghana's Petroleum Revenue Management Act (PRMA), 2011 (Act 815) an Effective Public Financial Tool for Public

Investment and Consumption Smoothing?www.bsg.ox.ac.uk/sites/default/files/2018-12/Anaman_Petroleum%20Revenue%20Management.pdf.

Anna, Cara. 2020. As US Struggles, Africa's COVID-19 Response is Praised. 2020. *AP*. September 22. https://apnews.com/article/virus-outbreak-ghana-africa-pandemics-donald-trump-0a31db50d816a463a6a29bf86463aaa9?campaign_id=9&emc=edit_nn_20210307&instance_id=27836&nl=the-morning&regi_id=124708682&segment_id=52986&te=1&user_id=3018d6faed4962db07930c7110d6aad4.

Anyinam, Charles A. 1989. The Social Costs of the International Monetary Fund's Adjustment Programs for Poverty: The Case of Health Care Development in Ghana. *International Journal of Health Services*, 19(3), 531–547.

Asenso-Okyere, W.K. 1995. Financial Health Care in Ghana. *World Health Forum*, 16 (1), 86–91. https://pubmed.ncbi.nlm.nih.gov/7873037.

Asenso-Okyere, W.K., Adote Anum, Isaac Osei-Akoto, and Augustine Adukonu. 1998. Cost Recovery in Ghana: Are There Any Changes in Health Care Seeking Behavior? *Health & Planning*, 13(2), 181–188. doi:10.1093/heapol/13.2.181.

Ashiagbora, George, R. Ofori-Asenso, E.K. Forkuo, and S. Agyei-Frimpong. 2020. Measures of Geographic Accessibility to Health Care in the Ashanti Region of Ghana. *Scientific African*, 9 [e00453]. September. https://doi.org/10.1016/j.sciaf.2020.e00453.

Assensoh, A.B., and Hassan Wahab. 2008. A Historical-Cum-Political Overview of Ghana's National Health Insurance Law. *Journal of African and Asian Studies*, 7, 289–306.

Baidoo, Rhodaline. 2009. *Toward a Comprehensive Healthcare System in Ghana*. MA Thesis. Center for International Studies, Ohio University. March. https://etd.ohiolink.edu/rws_etd/document/get/ohioou1237304137/inline.

Baker, Edward L., Anne J.Menkens, and Janet E.Porter. 2010. *Managing the Public Health Enterprise*. Burlington, MA: Jones Barlett Learning.

Barimah, K.B. 2013. Traditional Healers as Service Providers in Ghana's National Health Insurance Scheme: The Way Forward. *Global Public Health*, 8, 202–208.

Berman, Larry, and Bruce Allen Murphy. 2013. *Approaching Democracy*, 8th ed. Upper Saddle River, NJ: Pearson Education, Inc.

Blanchet, Nathan J., G. Fink, and I. Osei-Akoto. 2012. The Effect of Ghana's National Health Insurance Scheme on Health Care Utilization. *Ghana Medical Journal*, 46, 76–84.

Bonabom, Isidore. 2014. *Health and Human Rights in Ghana: The Political and Economic Aspects of Health*. Champaign, IL: Common Ground Publishing.

Bourret, F.M. 1960. *Ghana: The Road to Independence, 1919–1957*. Redwood City, CA: Stanford University Press.

Brill, Steven. 2015. *America's Bitter Pill: Money, Politics, Backroom Deals, and the Fight to Fix Our Broken Healthcare System*. New York: Random House.

Brookings Institution. 2020. *Telehealth Before and After COVID-19*. Webinar. May 7. www.youtube.com/watch?v=_T-fUjYDfqc.

Brown, Ola. 2018. *Fixing Healthcare in Nigeria: A Guide to Some of the Key Policy Decisions That Will Provide Better Healthcare to All Nigerians*. Self-published. www.dropbox.com/s/g8a2m2n49wlavui/Fixing%20Nigeria%20(2).pdf?dl=0.

Callahan, Michael D. 1999. *Mandates and Empire: The League of Nations and Africa, 1914–1931*. Brighton: Sussex Academic Press.

Carrin, Guy. 2003. *Community-Based Health Insurance Schemes in Developing Countries: Facts, Problems, and Perspectives*. Discussion Paper No. 1. Geneva, Switzerland: World Health Service.

Cennimo, David J. 2021. What is COVID-19? *Medscape*. Updated January 4. www.medscape.com/answers/2500114-197401/what-is-covid-19.

Centers for Disease Control and Prevention. 2019. COVID-19: Frequently Asked Questions: Basics. Atlanta, GA: Centers for Disease Control and Prevention. www.cdc.gov/coronavirus/2019-ncov/faq.html.

Central Intelligence Agency. 2014. *Ghana: CIA Factbook—2014.* www.cia.gov/the-world-factbook/countries/ghana/.

Chappelow, Jim. 2019. Pareto Efficiency. *Investopedia.* Updated September 25. www.investopedia.com/terms/p/pareto.efficiency.asp.

Chan, Margaret. 2010. Message from the Director-General. In *The World Health Report: Health System Financing: The Path to Universal Coverage*, pp. vi–vii. Geneva, Switzerland: World Health Organization.

Christopher, Andrea S. 2016. Single Payer Healthcare: Pluses, Minuses, and What It Means for You. *Harvard Health Blog.* June 27. www.health.harvard.edu/blog/single-payer-healthcare-pluses-minuses-means-201606279835.

Claiming Human Rights. *Claiming Human Rights—in Ghana.* www.claiminghumanrights.org/ghana.html.

Clausen, Lily B. 2015. Taking on the Challenges of Health Care in Africa. *Insights by Stanford Business.* June 16. www.gsb.stanford.edu/insights/taking-challenges-health-care-africa.

Coggi, Paola Testori. 2013. Foreword from the European Commission. In *Health System Performance Comparison: An Agenda for Policy Information and Research*, Irene Papanicolas and Peter C. Smith (eds.), p. xi. Maidenhead: Open University Press.

Colbert, Victoria. 2020. Telemedicine Plays a Bigger Role in Healthcare in Ghana. *Borgen Project* (Blog). July 29. https://borgenproject.org/telemedicine-plays-a-big-role-in-ghana/.

Constitute Project. 2016. Ghana's Constitution of 1992 with Amendments through 1996. April 18. www.constituteproject.org/constitution/Ghana_1996.pdf?lang=en.

Constitute Project. 2021. Ghana's Constitution of 1992 with Amendments through 1996. August 26. www.constituteproject.org/constitution/Ghana_1996.pdf.

Constitution of the World Health Organization. 1948. www.who.int/governance/eb/who_constitution_en.pdf.

Corruption Rank | Africa. *Trading Economics.* https://tradingeconomics.com/country-list/corruption-rank?continent=africa.

Corwin, Samuel Edward, and Jack W. Peltason. 1976. *Corwin and Peltason's Understanding the Constitution*, 7th ed. Oak Brook, IL: Dryden Press.

Cotlear, Daniel. 2013. The World Bank's Universal Health Coverage Studies Series (UNICO). In *The Health Extension Program in Ethiopia.* UNICO Studies Series No. 10, Netsanet W. Workie and Gandham N.V. Ramana (eds.). Washington, DC: World Bank. http://documents.worldbank.org/curated/en/356621468032070256/pdf/749630NWP0ETHI00Box374316B00PUBLIC0.pdf.

Crude Oil Production | Africa. *Trading Economics.* https://tradingeconomics.com/country-list/crude-oil-production?continent=Africa.

Danziger, James N. 2013. *Understanding the Political World: A Comparative Introduction to Political Science*, 11th ed. New York: Pearson.

Darfour, Ernest. 2016. *The Parliament of Ghana: A Countervailing Force in the Governance Process?* London: Political Studies Association. https://psa.ac.uk/sites/default/files/Ghana%20-%20Overview_EDarfour.pdf.

Darkwa, Osei. 2000. An Exploratory Survey of the Applications of Telemedicine in Ghana. *Journal of Telemedicine and Telecare*, 6(3), 177–183. https://doi.org/10.1258/1357633001935185.

Deaton, Angus S., and Robert Tortora. 2015. People in Sub-Saharan Africa Rate Their Health and Healthcare Among the Lowest in the World. *Health Affairs*, 34(3), 3519–3527.

Declaration of Alma-Ata. 1978. International Conference on Primary Health Care, Alma-Atta, USSR. September 6–12. www.euro.who.int/_data/assets/pdf_file/0009/113877/E93944.pdf.

Dickovick, J. Tyler, and Jonathan Eastwood. 2013. *Comparative Politics: Integrating Theories, Methods, and Cases*. New York: Oxford University Press.

Donnelly, Jack. 2013. *International Human Rights*, 4th ed. Boulder, CO: Westview Press.

Donnelly, Jack. 2000. An Overview. In *Human Rights and Comparative Foreign Policy*, David P. Forsythe (ed.), pp. 310–334. Tokyo: United Nations University Press.

Dovi, Efam. 2013. Ghana's "New Path" for Handling Oil Revenue. *Africa Renewal*. January. www.un.org/africarenewal/magazine/january-2013/ghana%E2%80%99s-%E2%80%98new-path%E2%80%99-handling-oil-revenue#:~:text=Petroleum%20revenue%20contributed%204%20per,most%20notably%20for%20fertilizer%20subsidies.

Dubroff, M. Dee. What is the Difference Between a Parliamentary and Presidential System of Government? *InfoBloom*. www.infobloom.com/what-is-the-difference-between-a-parliamentary-and-presidential-system-of-government.htm.

Efficiency. *Merriam-Webster Dictionary*. www.merriam-webster.com/dictionary/efficiency.

Emiljanowicz, Paul. 2021. How Jerry Rawlings Used Democratic Structures to Legitimize Military Rule. *Conversation*. May 23. https://theconversation.com/how-jerry-rawlings-used-democratic-structures-to-legitimise-military-rule-160714.

Eramo, Lisa. 2021. What Is a Medicare Diagnosis Related Group (DRG), and Why Does It Matter for Beneficiaries? *Medicare Advantage*. April 27. www.medicareadvantage.com/coverage/diagnosis-related-group.

Evans, Karen. 1999. *Comparative Successes or Failures? Some Methodological Issues in Conducting International Comparative Research Inpost—Secondary Education*. Education-Line. Paper presented at the British Educational Research Association Annual Conference, University of Sussex at Brighton. September 2–5. www.leeds.ac.uk/educol/documents/00001309.htm.

Fahy, Nick. 2013. Commentary on International Health System Performance Information. In *Health System Performance Comparison: An Agenda for Policy, Information and Research*, Irene Papanicolas and Peter C. Smith (eds.), pp. 313–334. Maidenhead: Open University Press.

Fee-for-Service. *Health Insurance*. www.healthinsurance.org/glossary/fee-for-service/.

Felter, Claire. 2021. How Dangerous Are New COVID-19 Strains? *Council on Foreign Relations*. January 7. www.cfr.org/in-brief/how-dangerous-are-new-covid-19-strains?gclid=Cj0KCQiA1KiBBhCcARIsAPWqoSqLuooY_obXNC_aRxXuELh5kVnMYG8xr-NpA1rHgIvtD8sP0qVZHqwaAnzjEALw_wcB.

Floyd, Colleen M. and Aegal Gross (eds.). 2014. *The Right to Health at the Public/Private Divide: A Global Comparative Study*. New York: Cambridge University Press.

419 Fraud Explained by a Criminal Defense Lawyer in NY. *NYCriminal Defense, Bukh Law Firm*. https://nyccriminallawyer.com/fraud-charge/cross-border-fraud/419-fraud/.

Franck, Thomas M. 1992. The Emerging Right to Democratic Governance. 1992. *American Journal of International Law*, 86(1), 46–91.

Franco, Lynne Miller, François Pathé Diop, Clara R. Burgert, Allison Gamble Kelley, Marty Makinen, and Cheick Hamed Tidiane Simparae. 2008. Effects of Mutual Health Organizations on Use of Priority Health-Care Services in Urban and Rural Mali: A Case-Control Study. *Bulletin of the World Health Organization*, 86(11), 830–838. doi:10.2471/BLT.08.051045.

Frempong, Alexander K.D. 2007. *Constitution-Making and Constitutional Rule in Ghana*. Paper presented at a Colloquium by the Department of Political Science, University of Ghana, March 1–2.

Fuller, Edmund. Oliver Wendell Holmes, Jr.—The Common Law. *Encyclopedia Britannica*. www.britannica.com/biography/Oliver-Wendell-Holmes-Jr/The-Common-Law.

The Future of Healthcare in Africa. 2014. *Economist Intelligence Unit (London)*. www.economistinsights.com/sites/default/files/downloads/EIU-Janssen_HealthcareAfrica_Report_Web.pdf.

Gathara, Patrick. 2021. Charity Alone Will Not End the Calamity of COVID-19 in Africa. *Al Jazeera*. July 31. www.aljazeera.com/opinions/2021/7/31/accountability-is-africas-best-route-out-of-the-pandemic.

General Comments No. 14 on the Right to the Highest Attainable Standard of Health. 2000. Committee on Economic, Social, and Cultural Rights. E/C.12/2000/4. August 11.

George, Alexander L., and Andrew Bennett. 2005. *Case Studies and Theory Development in the Social Sciences*. Cambridge, MA: MIT Press.

Ghana. *Infoplease*. www.infoplease.com/country/ghana.html.

Ghana. *Nations Online*. www.nationsonline.org/oneworld/ghana.htm.

Ghana. 2007. *Worldmark Encyclopedia of Nations*. www.encyclopedia.com/topic/Ghana.aspx.

Ghana: Constitution and Politics. *The Commonwealth*. http://thecommonwealth.org/our-member-countries/ghana/constitution-politics.

Ghana Demographics Profile. 2020. *Index Mundi*. Last updated November 27. www.indexmundi.com/ghana/demographics_profile.html.

Ghana: The Fourth Republic. *Photius*. www.photius.com/countries/ghana/government/ghana_government_the_fourth_republic.html.

Ghana GDP Growth Rate 2006–2016. *Trading Economics*. www.tradingeconomics.com/ghana/gdp-growth.

Ghana Health Service. COVID-19 Ghana's Outbreak Response Management Updates. www.ghanahealthservice.org/covid19/.

Ghana Independence Act 1957. 1957 CH. 6. February 7. www.legislation.gov.uk/ukpga/Eliz2/5-6/6/enacted?view=plain.

Ghana Integrity Initiative (GII). 2018. *Cost and Impact of Corruption on Education and Health Sectors in Ghana*. Accra, Ghana: Ghana Integrity Initiative (GII) Consortium.

Ghana: Location and Size. *Photius*. https://photius.com/countries/ghana/geography/ghana_geography_location_and_size.html.

Ghana Population (Live). *Worldometer*. www.worldometers.info/world-population/ghana-population/.

Ghana: Republic of Ghana. *Nations Encyclopedia*. www.nationsencyclopedia.com/economies/Africa/Ghana.html.

Ghana: Seven-Year Development Plan 1963/64–1969/70. 1964. Accra, Ghana: Office of Planning Commission. https://s3-us-west-2.amazonaws.com/new-ndpc-static1/CACHES/PUBLICATIONS/2017/11/03/SevenYearDevtPlan.pdf.

Ghana [Seven]-Year Development Plan Presentation. 1964. *GhanaHero*. March 11. www.ghanahero.com/Visions/Nkrumah_Legacy_Project/documents/deve_plans/7_Year_Dev_Plan-Ghana-v3_marked.pdf.

Ghana Statistical Service. 2012. *2010 Population and Housing Census: Summary Report of Final Results*. Accra, Ghana: Sakoa Press Ltd. www.statsghana.gov.gh/docfiles/2010phc/Census2010_Summary_report_of_final_results.pdf.

Ghana Swears in Mahama as New President. 2012. *Al Jazeera*. July 25. www.aljazeera.com/news/africa/2012/07/20127259518486684.html.

Ghana's NHIS Wins Major World Award. 2011. *Modern Ghana*. March 22. www.modernghana.com/news/321345/ghanas-nhis-wins-major-world-award.html.

Global Health and Foreign Policy. 2012. *UN Gen. Assembly*. A/67/L.36. December 6. https://ncdalliance.org/sites/default/files/resource_files/Global%20Health%20and%20Foreign%20Policy%20resolution%202012_67th%20GA.pdf.

Global Health Program and Rabin Martin. 2014. *Universal Health Coverage: An Annotated Bibliography*. Geneva, Switzerland: Graduate Institute. http://graduateinstitute.ch/files/live/sites/iheid/files/sites/globalhealth/ghp-new/publications/UHC_Bibliography_v9_web.pdf.

Gobah, Freeman F.K., and Zhang Liang. 2011. The National Health Insurance Scheme in Ghana: Prospects and Challenges: A Cross-Sectional Evidence. *Global Journal of Health Science*, 3, 90. October.

Hannum, Hurst. 1996. The Status of the Universal Declaration of Human Rights in National and International Law. *Georgia Journal of International & Comp. Law*, 25(1), 287–397.

Hassim, Adila, Mark Heywood, and Jonathan Berger. 2007. A Background to Health Law and Human Rights in South Africa. 2007. *Health and Democracy*. June 1. www.section27.org.za/wp-content/uploads/2010/04/Chapter1.pdf.

Health and Welfare. 1994. In *Ghana: A Country Study*, ed. La Verle Berry. Washington, DC: GPO for the Library of Congress.

Health Insurance in Ghana. *GhanaWeb*. www.ghanaweb.com/GhanaHomePage/health/national_health_insurance_scheme.php.

Henkin, Louis. 2000. Human Rights: Ideology and Aspiration, Reality and Prospect. In *Realizing Human Rights: Moving from Inspiration to Impact*, Samantha Power and Graham Allison (eds.), pp. 3–38. New York: St. Martin's Press.

Herbst, Jeffrey. 1993. *The Politics of Reform: Ghana, 1982–1991*. Berkeley, CA: University of California Press.

Heymann, David, and Robert Yates. 2014. *Embracing the Politic of Universal Health Coverage*. London: Chatham House, The Royal Institute of International Affairs. June 25. www.chathamhouse.org/expert/comment/14972.

HHS. *What is the Difference between Medicare and Medicaid?* https://www.hhs.gov/answers/medicare-and-medicaid/what-is-the-difference-between-medicare-medicaid/index.html.

History of Ghana. *HistoryWorld.Net*. www.historyworld.net/wrldhis/PlainTextHistories.asp?historyid=ad43.

HIV/AIDS: The Basics. 2020. *National Institutes of Health*. https://hivinfo.nih.gov/understanding-hiv/fact-sheets/hivaids-basics#:~:text=HIV%20stands%20for%20human%20immunodeficiency,stands%20for%20acquired%20immunodeficiency%20syndrome.

The Holy Bible: English Standard Version. 2016. Wheaton, IL: Crossway.

Huber, B. Rose. 2015. *Sub-Saharan Africans Rate Their Health and Health Care Among the Lowest in the World*. Woodrow Wilson School of Public & International Affairs, Princeton University. February 25.

Human Rights Watch. 2012. *Ghana: People with Mental Disabilities Face Serious Abuse*. October 2. www.hrw.org/news/2012/10/02/ghana-people-mental-disabilities-face-serious-abuse.

Hunt, Paul. 2014. Foreword. In *The Right to Health: A Multi-Country Study of Law, Policy and Practice*, Brigit Toebes, Rhonda Ferguson, Milan M. Markovic, and Obiajulu Nnamuchi (eds.), pp. v–vi. Berlin: Springer.

Hunt, Paul, Alicia Ely Yamin, and Flavia Bustreo. 2015. Editorial: Making the Case: What Is the Evidence of Impact of Applying Human Rights-Based Approaches to Health? *Health & Human Rights Journal*, 17(2). November 2. www.hhrjournal.org/2015/11/editorial-making-the-case-what-is-the-evidence-of-impact-of-applying-human-rights-based-approaches-to-health/.

Independence, Coups, and the Republic, 1957–Present. 2016. In *The Ghana Reader: History, Culture, Politics*, Kwasi Konadu and Clifford C. Campbell (eds.). Durham, NC: Duke University Press.

Information Communication Technology in Healthcare. 2016. *Front Enders* (Blog). November 6. www.frontenders.in/blog/information-communication-technology-healthcare.html.

International Covenant on Economic, Social and Cultural Rights. 1966. G. A. Res. 2200A (XXI). Opened for signature December 9. 993 U.N.T.S. 3. Entered into force January 3, 1976.

International Covenant on Civil and Political Rights. 1966. G.A. Res. 2200A (XXI), U.N. GAOR, Supp. No. 16, U.N. Doc. A/6316, 999 U.N.T.S. 171. 6 I.L.M. 368 (1967).

Ismi, Asad. 2004. *Impoverishing a Continent: The World Bank and the IMF in Africa*. Ottawa: Canadian Center for Policy Alternatives.

Is There a Role for Trado-Medicine in the Nigerian Health Sector?2018. *Nigeria Health Watch*. October 4. https://nigeriahealthwatch.medium.com/is-there-a-role-for-trado-medicine-in-the-nigerian-health-sector-d824d13a47e8.

Janda, Kenneth, Jeffrey M. Berry, and Jerry Goldman. 1999. *The Challenge of Democracy: Government in America*, 6th ed. Boston, MA: Houghton Mifflin.

Jerry J. Rawlings, Head of State, Ghana. 2021. *Encyclopedia Britannica*. Last updated June 18. www.britannica.com/biography/Jerry-J-Rawlings.

Jerry Rawlings: Why He Divided Opinion in Ghana. 2020. *BBC News*. November 12. www.bbc.com/news/world-africa-27193658.

Kagan, Julia, and Thomas J. Catalano. 2021. Capitation Payments. *Investopedia*. July 6. www.investopedia.com/terms/c/capitation-payments.asp.

Kaiser, Frederick M. 2001. Congressional Oversight. *CRS Report for Congress*. 97–936 GOV. Updated January 2. http://156.33.195.33/artandhistory/history/resources/pdf/CRS.Oversight.pdf.

Kangoye, Thierry. 2013. Does Aid Unpredictability Weaken Governance? Evidence from Developing Countries. *Developing Economies*, 51(2), 121–144.

Kenton Will, and Michael J. Boyle. 2021. Political Economy. *Investopedia*. Updated February 25. www.investopedia.com/terms/p/political-economy.asp.

Kesse-Tachi, Agyenna, Alexander Ekow Asmah, and Ebenezer Agbozo. 2019. Factors Influencing Adoption of eHealth Technologies in Ghana. *Digital Health*, 5:2055207619871425. September 5.

Kim, Jim Yong. 2014. *Speech at Conference on Universal Health Coverage in Emerging Economies*. Washington, DC: Center for Strategic and International Studies. January 14.

Kim, Jim Yong. 2013. *Poverty, Health and the Human Future*. Speech at the World Health Assembly. May 21. www.worldbank.org/en/news/speech/2013/05/21/world-bank-group-president-jim-yong-kim-speech-at-wirkd-health-assembly.

Kingdom of Ghana. *USHistory.org*. www.ushistory.org/civ/7a.asp.

Kipling, Rudyard. 1891. The English Flag. *Bartleby*. bartleby.com/364/122.html.

Kipo-Sunyehzi, Daniel Dramani, Martin Amogre Ayanore, Daniel Kweku Dzidzonu, and Yakubu Ayalsuma Yakubu. 2019. Ghana's Journey toward Universal Health Coverage:

The Role of the National Health Insurance Scheme. *European Journal of Investigation in Health, Psychology, and Education*, 10, 94–109. doi:10.3390/ejihpe10010009.

Kirchner, Sarah. 2021. Facts about Healthcare. *The Borgen Project*. February 25. https://borgenproject.org/facts-about-healthcare-in-ghana/.

Koigi, Bob. 2020. Ghana's Eco Medical Village Set to Revolutionize Africa's Medicare and Health Tourism. *Fair Planet*. July 2. www.fairplanet.org/story/ghana%E2%80%99s-eco-medical-village-set-to-revolutionize-africa%E2%80%99s-medicare-and-health-tourism/.

Kokutse, Francis. 2007. Ghana Leader: Oil Reserves at 3b Barrels. *Associated Press* (Internet Archives). December 22. http://web.archive.org/web/20071226200944/http://news.yahoo.com/s/ap/20071222/ap_on_re_af/ghana_oil_discovery_3

Konadu-Agyemang, Kwadwo. 2010. The Best of Times and the Worst of Times: Structural Adjustment Programs and Uneven Development in Africa: The Case of Ghana. *Professional Geographer*, 52, 469–483.

Kruk, Margaret E., Michael Myers, S. Tornorlah Varpilah, and Bernice T. Dahn. 2015. What is a Resilient Health System? Lessons from Ebola. *Lancet*, 385(9980), 1910–1912. doi:10.1016/S0140-6736(15)60755-3.

Kwame Nkrumah, President of Ghana. *Encyclopedia Britannica*. www.britannica.com/biography/Kwame-Nkrumah.

Lassey, Marie L., William R. Lassey, and Martin J. Jinks. 1996. *Health Care Systems Around the World: Characteristics, Issues, Reforms*. New York: Pearson.

Lasswell, Harold D. 1990. *Politics: Who Gets What, When, and How?* Gloucester, MA: Peter Smith Pub. Inc.

Lauren, Paul Gordon. 2011. *The Evolution of International Human Rights: Visions Seen*. Philadelphia, PA: University of Pennsylvania Press.

Legal Information Institute. *Customary International Law*. Cornell Law School. www.law.cornell.edu/wex/customary_international_law.

Legislature. *Encyclopedia Britannica*. www.britannica.com/topic/legislature.

Lensink, Robert. 1996. *Structural Adjustment in Sub-Saharan Africa*. New York: Longman.

Lessons from COVID-19: Building a Stronger Global Health System. 2020. *Foreign Policy*. May 26. https://foreignpolicy.com/events/fp-virtual-dialogue-lessons-from-covid-19/.

London, Leslie. 2008. What is a Human-Rights Based Approach to Health and Does it Matter? *Health & Human Rights Journal*, 10(1), 65–80. www.hhrjournal.org/2013/09/what-is-a-human-rights-based-approach-to-health-and-does-it-matter/.

MacNaughton, Gillian, Fiona Haigh, Mariah McGill, Konstantinos Koutsioumpas, and Courtenay Sprague. 2015. The Impact of Human Rights on Universalizing Health Care in Vermont, USA. *Health & Human Rights Journal*, 17(2), 83–95. www.hhrjournal.org/2015/12/the-impact-of-human-rights-on-universalizing-health-care-in-vermont-usa/.

Mahomoodally, M. Fawzi. 2013. Traditional Medicines in Africa: An Appraisal of Ten Potent African Medicinal Plants. *Evidence-Based Complementary and Alternative Medicine*. Article ID 617459. https://doi.org/10.1155/2013/617459.

Maps of Ghana. *World Atlas*. www.worldatlas.com/maps/ghana.

Martić, Marko, and Ognjen Dukić. 2017. Friedrick Ebert Stiftung Sarajevo. *Health Care System in BiH: Financing Challenges and Reform Options?* October 20. Bonn: Friedrich Ebert Foundation.

Maxfield, Michael G., and Earl R. Babbie. 2015. *Research Methods for Criminal Justice and Criminology*, 7th ed. Stamford, CT: Cengage Learning.

McLure, Jason. 2010. Ghana Oil Reserves to be 5 Billion Barrels in 5 Years. *Bloomberg.* December 1. www.bloomberg.com/news/articles/2010-12-01/ghana-oil-reserves-to-be-5-billion-barrels-in-5-years-as-fields-develop

McNeill, William H. 1976. *Plagues and Peoples.* Garden City, NY: Anchor Press/Doubleday.

Méndez, Juan E. 2014. *Report of the Special Rapporteur on Torture and Other Cruel, Inhuman or Degrading Treatment or Punishment. Human Rights Council Twenty-Fifth Session. Agenda item 3.* A/HRC/25/60/Add.1. March 5.

Mensah, Kent. 2014. Ghana's Successful but Unpopular Healthcare. *Al Jazeera.* August 6. www.aljazeera.com/news/africa/2014/07/ghana-successful-but-unpopular-healthcare-2014722101651828127.html.

Mental Health Act. Act 846. 2012. https://ijmhs.biomedcentral.com/articles/10.1186/1752-4458-8-16.

Ministry of Health. Republic of Ghana. 2021. Government Secures US$100 Million Start-up Fund for 'Agenda 111' Hospital Project. August 17. www.moh.gov.gh/agenda-111-construction-of-largest-number-of-hospital-projects.

Ministry of Health. Republic of Ghana. COVID-19: Government to Begin Construction of 88 District Hospitals This Year–Nana Addo. www.moh.gov.gh/covid-19-government-to-begin-construction-of-88-district-hospitals-this-year-nana-addo/.

Mobarak, Ahmed Mushfiq, and Rifaiyat Mahbub. 2020. What the US Can Learn from How African Countries Handled COVID. *CNN.* November 3. www.cnn.com/2020/11/03/africa/africa-coronavirus-lessons-opinion-intl/index.html.

Mohammed, Abdul-Rahim. 2012. *"Cash and Carry" or Health Insurance in Ghana?* Sunnyvale, CA: Lambert Academic Publishing.

Morrison, Minion K.C. 2004. Political Parties in Ghana through Four Republics: A Path to Democratic Consolidation. *Comparative Politics*, 36(4), 421–442. July.

Muller, Elena. COVID-19 Ushering in the Age of Telehealth. *Health Recovery Solution.* www.healthrecoverysolutions.com/blog/covid-19-ushering-in-the-age-of-telehealth.

Musgrove, Philip. 2010. The Five Cs of Universal Health Care: Canada, Chile, Colombia, Costa Rica, and Cuba Take Different Paths to the Same Goal. *Americas Quarterly.* July 21. www.americasquarterly.org/node/1691.

National Development Planning Commission. 2009. *2008 Citizens' Assessment of the National Health Insurance Scheme: Toward a Sustainable Health Care Financing Arrangement that Protects the Poor.* Accra, Ghana: National Development Planning Commission.

National Health Insurance Act. Act 650. 2003. August. http://d1020125.u42.pws-servers.com/UploadFiles/Publications/National%20Health%20Insurance%20Act090407134319.pdf.

National Health Insurance Authority. 2018. *Guidelines for Private Health Insurance Schemes in Ghana.* Accra, Ghana: National Health Insurance Authority. July. nhis.gov.gh/files/PHISGUIDELINES.pdf.

The National Health Insurance Scheme Functions. *EHealth Insurance.* www.ehealthinsurance.com.ng/the-national-health-insurance-scheme-functions.

Nazzah, Noble Kofi. 2020. Jerry Rawlings Is Dead, but He Still Looms Large in Ghanaian Politics. *Foreign Policy.* December 30. https://foreignpolicy.com/2020/12/03/jerry-rawlings-is-dead-but-he-still-looms-large-in-ghana-politics/.

Ncube, Mthuli, Aly Abou-Sabaa, Charles L. Lufumpa, and Agnes Soucat. 2013. *Health in Africa over the Next 50 Years.* African Development Bank. Economic Brief. March. www.afdb.org/fileadmin/uploads/afdb/Documents/Publications/Economic_Brief_-_Health_in_Africa_Over_the_Next_50_Years.pdf.

Neubauer, Chuck. 2010. Ghana Discovery Sparks Fight Over Oil. *Washington Times.* March 26. www.washingtontimes.com/news/2010/mar/26/ghana-discovery-sparks-fight-over-oil/?page=all.

A New Nation: Gold Coast Becomes Ghana in Ceremony. 1957/03/07. 2006. July 3. https://archive.org/details/1957-03-07_A_New_Nation.

New Patriotic Party. 2005. The Manifesto: Development in Freedom, Agenda for Change. *Ghana Web.* September 20. www.ghanaweb.com/GhanaHomePage/election2004/npp_manifesto.pdf.

New Patriotic Party. *Who We Are.* www.newpatrioticparty.org/index.php/the-party/who-we-are/who-we-are.

Ngwena, Charles. 2000. The Recognition of Access to Health Care as a Human Right in South Africa: Is it Enough? *Health & Human Rights,* 5(1), 22–44.

NHIS Active Membership Soars. 2020. *NHIS: National Health Insurance Scheme.* July 2. www.nhis.gov.gh/News/nhis-active-membership-soars-5282.

Nossiter, Adam. 2020. Jerry Rawlings, From Coup-Plotter to Ghanaian Stateman, Dies at 73. *New York Times.* November 12. www.nytimes.com/2020/11/12/world/africa/jerry-rawlings-dead-version.html.

Novartis Foundation. *Ghana Telemedicine.* www.novartisfoundation.org/past-programs/digital-health/ghana-telemedicine.

NS Energy Staff Writer. 2020. Top Five Gold Mining Countries of Africa from Ghana to Burkina Faso. *NS Energy.* August 28. www.nsenergybusiness.com/news/top-gold-mining-countries-africa/.

Ntiamoa, Ken. 2005. Ghana Needs a Population Control Policy. *Modern Ghana.* January 18. www.modernghana.com/news/116094/1/ghana-needs-a-population-control-policy.html.

Nwachukwu, Emmanuel. 2021. Health Sector Decay: Nigerians Dying Needlessly. *New Watcher.* September 13. https://thenewwatcher.com/health-sector-decay-nigerians-dying-needlessly-10119.html.

Nyonator, Frank, and Joseph Kutzin. 1999. Health for Some? The Effects of User Fees in the Volta Region of Ghana. *Health Policy & Planning,* 14(4), 329–341. December. doi:10.1093/heapol/14.4.329.

Odinga, Oginga. 1968. *Not Yet Uhuru: The Autobiography of Oginda Odinga.* New York: Heinemann.

Odinkalu, Chidi A. 1999. Why More Africans Don't Use Human Rights Language. Carnegie Council for Ethics in International Affairs. December 5. www.carnegiecouncil.org/publications/archive/dialogue/2_01/articles/602.html.

OECD. *Official Development Assistance (ODA).* Paris: OECD. www.oecd.org/dac/financing-sustainable-development/development-finance-standards/official-development-assistance.htm.

Office of the UN High Commissioner for Human Rights. 1990. *CESCR General Comment No. 3: The Nature of States Parties' Obligations. Doc. E/1991/23.* December 14. www.refworld.org/pdfid/4538838e10.pdf.

Ogbuoji, Osondi, Ipchita Bharali, Natalie Emery, and Kaci Kennedy McDade. 2019. Closing Africa's Health Financing Gap. *Brookings Institution.* March 1. www.brookings.edu/blog/future-development/2019/03/01/closing-africas-health-financing-gap/.

Ohene, Elizabeth. 2015. Letters from Africa: What Can Ghana Learn from Norway? *BBC News.* December 22. www.bbc.com/news/world-africa-34710175.

Ohnesorge, John. 2010. Administrative Law in East Asia: A Comparative-Historical Analysis. In *Comparative Administrative Law*, Susan Rose-Ackerman and Peter L. Lindseth (eds.), pp. 78–91. Northampton, MA: Edward Elgar.

Oksman, Olga. 2016. We Need Fundamental Changes: U.S. Doctors Call for Universal Healthcare. *Guardian*. May 5. www.theguardian.com/us-news/2016/may/05/us-doctors-calling-universal-healthcare-system-affordable-care-act.

Onwujekwe, Obinna. 2013. *Moving Nigeria from Low Coverage to Universal Health Coverage: Health System Challenges, Equity and the Evidence-Base*. 74th Inaugural Lecture. University of Nigeria, Enugu Campus. April. www.researchgate.net/publication/317267470_Moving_Nigeria_from_low_coverage_to_universal_health_coverage_national_health_system_challenges_equity_and_the_evidence-base.

O'Regan, Kate, and Nick Friedman. 2011. Equality. In *Comparative Constitutional Law*, Tom Ginsburg and Rosalind Dixon (eds.), pp. 473–503. Northampton, MA: Edward Elgar Publishing.

Organization of African Unity (OAU). 2000. *Constitutive Act of the African Union*. July 1. www.refworld.org/docid/4937e0142.html.

Osei-Boateng, Clara, and Edward Ampratwun. 2011. The Informal Sector in Ghana. *Friedrick Ebert Stiftung*. Bonn: Friedrich Ebert Foundation. http://library.fes.de/pdf-files/bueros/ghana/10496.pdf.

Our Creed. *Official website of the New Patriotic Party*. www.newpatrioticparty.org/index.php/who-we-are/what-we-stand-for/our-creed.

Oxfam. 2021. *History of Oxfam International*. Oxford: Oxfam International. www.oxfam.org/en/countries/history-oxfam-international.

Oxfam International. 2013. *Universal Health Coverage: Why Health Insurance Schemes are Leaving the Poor Behind*. October 9. Oxford: Oxfam International.

Oxfam International. 2011. *Achieving a Shared Goal: Free Universal Health Care in Ghana*. March. Oxford: Oxfam International. www.oxfam.org/sites/www.oxfam.org/files/rr-achieving-shared-goal-healthcare-ghana-09033-en.pdf.

Oxfam International. 2021. *Our Commitment to Human Rights*. Oxford: Oxfam International. www.oxfam.org/en/our-commitment-human-rights.

Oxfam International. *Who We Are*. https://www.oxfam.org/en/about.

Owusu-Ansah, David. 2014. *Historical Dictionary of Ghana*, pp. 92–93. Lanham, MD: Rowman & Littlefield.

Owusu-Dapaah, Ernest. 2015. Empowering Patients in Ghana: Is There a Case for a Human Rights-Based Health Care Law? *Lancaster University Ghana Law Journal*, 1, 91. www.lancaster.edu.gh/uploads/law/Advisory%20and%20Editorial%20Board.pdf.

Papanicolas, Irene, Liana R. Woskie, and Ashish K. Jha. 2018. Health Care Spending in the United States and Other High-Income Countries. *Journal of the American Medical Association*, 319(10), 1024–1039. doi:10.1001/jama.2018.1150.

Parliament of Ghana. *Parliament of Ghana*. www.parliament.gh/mps.

Patient-Centered Outcomes Research Institute (PCORI). 2020. *Confronting COVID-19: The Changing Role of Telehealth*. Webinar. May 5. www.pcori.org/events/2020/part-6-changing-role-telehealth.

The Permanent Mission of Ghana to the United Nations. *Map and Regions of Ghana*. www.ghanamissionun.org/map-regions-in-ghana/.

Petchenkine, Youry. 1993. *Ghana: In Search of Stability, 1957–1992*. Santa Barbara, CA: ABC-CLIO.

Petroleum Revenue Management (Amendment) Act. Act 893. 2015. www.mofep.gov.gh/sites/default/files/reports/petroleum/PRMA-Amendment-2015.pdf.

Pipes, Sally C. 2014. The Many Failures of Single Payer. *National Review.* December 1. www.nationalreview.com/article/393679/many-failures-single-payer-sally-c-pipes.

Poen, Monte M. 1996. *Harry S. Truman Versus the Medical Lobby: The Genesis of Medicare.* Columbia, MO: University of Missouri Press.

Population Growth: Friend or Foe? *Econedlink.* www.econedlink.org/lessons/projector.php?lid=32&type=educator.

Powell, Anita. South Africa Debates Bill for National Health Care. *Learning English.* https://learningenglish.voanews.com/a/south-africa-debates-bill-for-national-heath-care/5127964.html.

Power, Samantha, and Graham Allison (eds.). 2000. *Realizing Human Rights: Moving from Inspiration to Impact.* New York: St. Martin's Press.

Protocol to the African Charter on Human and Peoples' Rights on the Establishment of an African Court on Human and Peoples' Rights. 1998. *OAU Doc.* OAU/LEG/EXP/AFCHPR/PROT (III). June 9. Entered into force January 25, 2004.

Quadagno, Jill. 2006. *One Nation, Uninsured: Why the U.S. Has no National Health Insurance.* New York: Oxford University Press.

The Rectification of Names. *Cultural China.* www.cultural-china.com/chinaWH/History/en/165History878.html.

Regions of Ghana. *Statoids.* www.statoids.com/ugh.html.

Republic of Ghana. 2012. National Health Insurance Act, 2012. Act 852. October. https://s3.amazonaws.com/ndpc-static/CACHES/NEWS/2015/07/22//NHIS+Act+2012+Act+852.pdf.

Roberson, Mary-Russell. 2020. *Ghana: Healthcare for a Country in Transition.* Duke Global Health Institute. March 15. https://globalhealth.duke.edu/news/ghana-healthcare-country-transition.

Roberts, Marc J., William Hsiao, Peter Berman, and Michael R. Reich. 2008. *Getting Health Reform Right: A Guide to Improving Performance and Equity.* New York: Oxford University Press.

Roberts, Mark, Caroline Mogan, and Joseph B.Asare. 2014. An Overview of Ghana's Mental System: Results from an Assessment Using the World Health Organization's Assessment Instrument for Mental Health Systems (WHO-AIMS). *International Journal of Mental Health Systems*, 8(16), May 4. doi:10.1186/1752-4458-8-16.

Rosen, Ruth. 2003. Time for Single Payer? *San Francisco Chronicle.* December 29. www.sfgate.com/opinion/article/Time-for-single-payer-2544505.php.

Rosenthal, Elisabeth. 2012. Nigeria Tested by Rapid Rise in Population. *New York Times.* April 14. www.nytimes.com/2012/04/15/world/africa/in-nigeria-a-preview-of-an-overcrowded-planet.html?pagewanted=all&_r=0.

Roth, Kenneth. 2000. Human Rights Organizations: A New Force for Social Change. In *Realizing Human Rights: Moving from Inspiration to Impact,* Samantha Power and Graham Allison, (eds.), pp. 225–248. New York: St. Martin's Press.

Rudiger, Anja. 2016. Human Rights and the Political Economy of Universal Health Care: Designing Equitable Financing. *Health & Human Rights Journal,* 18(2). December 5. www.hhrjournal.org/2016/12/human-rights-and-the-political-economy-of-universal-health-care-designing-equitable-financing/.

Sadik, Nafis. Population Growth and the Food Crisis. FAO Corporate Doc. Repository. www.fao.org/docrep/U3550t/u3550t02.htm.

Saksena, Priyanka, Adélio Fernandes Antunes, Ke Xu, Laurent Musango, and Guy Carrin. 2010. Impact of Mutual Health Insurance on Access to Health Care and Financial

Risk Protection in Rwanda. World Health Report. Background Paper No 6. www.who.int/healthsystems/topics/financing/healthreport/6whr-bp.pdf.

Sasu, Doris Dokua. 2021. Share of Population with National Health Insurance Scheme (NHIS) Membership in Ghana from 2014 to 2017. *Statista*. February 9. www.statista.com/statistics/1172722/share-of-people-with-active-national-health-insurance-membership-in-ghana/.

Savedoff, William. 2004. *Tax-Based Financing for Health Systems: Options and Experiences*. Geneva, Switzerland: World Health Organization.

Schudel, Matt. 2020. Jerry Rawlings, Coup Leader Who Ruled Ghana for 20 Years, Dies at 73. *Washington Post*. November 12. www.washingtonpost.com/local/obituaries/jerry-rawlings-coup-leader-who-ruled-ghana-for-20-years-dies-at-73/2020/11/12/d8453a32-2504-11eb-a688-5298ad5d580a_story.html.

Schwelb, Egon. 1960. The Republican Constitution of Ghana. *American Journal of Comparative Law*. Vol. 9.

Sen, Amartya. 2015. Universal Healthcare: The Affordable Dream. *Vanguard*. January 6. www.theguardian.com/society/2015/jan/06/-sp-universal-healthcare-the-affordable-dream-amartya-sen.

Sharman, Alice. 2016. Oxfam International to Move Headquarters to Nairobi. *Civil Society News*. July 26. www.civilsociety.co.uk/news/oxfam-international-to-move-headquarters-to-nairobi.html.

Singleton, Jennifer L. 2006. *Negotiating Change: An Analysis of the Origins of Ghana's National Health Insurance Act*, Honors Project, Paper 4. Macalester College. May 1. http://digitalcommons.macalester.edu/soci_honors/4.

The Six Regions of the African Union. *West Africa Brief*. www.west-africa-brief.org/content/en/six-regions-african-union.

Smith II, George P. 1983. Acid Rain: A Transnational Perspective. *New York Law School Journal of International & Comparative Law*, 4, 459–502.

Social Health Insurance Report of a Regional Expert Group Meeting New Delhi, India, 13–15 March 2003. 2003. World Health Organization Regional Office for South-East Asia New Delhi. June 2003.

Sodaro, Michael J. 2008. *Comparative Politics: A Global Introduction*, 3rd ed. New York: McGraw-Hill.

Sodzi-Tettey, Sodzi, M. Aikins, J.K. Awoonor-Williams, and I.A. Agyepong. 2012. Challenges in Provider Payment under the Ghana National Health Insurance Scheme: A Case Study of Claims Management in Two Districts. *Ghana Medical Journal*, 46(4), 189–199.

The State of Healthcare in Africa: Full Sector Report. 2012. Nairobi, Kenya: KPMG Africa Ltd. www.kpmg.com/Africa/en/IssuesAndInsights/Articles-Publications/Documents/The-State-of-Healthcare-in-Africa.pdf.

Stoecker, Helmut (ed.). 1987. *German Imperialism in Africa: From the Beginning Until the Second World War*. Translated by Bernd Zöllner. Atlantic Highlands, NJ: Humanities Press International.

Stuart Mill, John. 2002. *The Basic Writings of John Stuart Mill: On Liberty, the Subjection of Women and Unilateralism*. New York: Modern Library.

Sulzbach, Sara, Bertha Garshong, and Gertrude Owusu-Banahene. 2005. *Evaluating the Effects of the National Health Insurance Act in Ghana: Baseline Report*. Bethesda, MD: The Partners for Health Reformplus Project, Abt Associates Inc. December. www.abtassociates.com/files/Insights/reports/2005/national_health_insurance_ghana_1205.pdf.

Sustainable Development Goals Fund. 2021. *From MDGs to SDGs*. New York: Sustainable Development Goals Fund. www.sdgfund.org/mdgs-sdgs.

Suuk, Maxwell. 2020. Ghanaians Question President's Promise of New Hospitals. *Deutsche Welle*. April 29. www.dw.com/en/ghanaians-question-presidents-promise-of-new-hospitals/a-53282310.

There Ain't No Such Thing as a Free Lunch—TANSTAAFL. *Investopedia*. www.investopedia.com/terms/t/tanstaafl.asp.

Togo. *Infoplease*. www.infoplease.com/country/togo.html.

The Top Cocoa-Producing Countries. *World Atlas*. www.worldatlas.com/articles/top-10-cocoa-producing-countries.html.

Torres, Fernando Montenegro. 2013. *UNICO Studies Series 14: Costa Rica Case Study: Primary Health Care Achievements and Challenges Within the Framework of the Social Health Insurance*. Washington, DC: World Bank. January. www.tpg-iha.com/wp-content/uploads/2016/02/TPG-IHA-Costa-Rica-Briefing-Materials.pdf.

Transparency International. *What Is Corruption?* www.transparency.org/en/what-is-corruption.

Travel Documents System. *Ghana*. www.traveldocs.com/world-atlas/Ghana-atlas84.

Umozurike, U. Oji. 1997. *The African Charter on Human and Peoples' Rights*. Leiden, Netherlands, and Boston, MA: Brill.

UN General Assembly. 2012. *Resolution on Foreign Policy Resolution*, 67th Session, 53rd Plenary Meeting. Agenda Item 123. U.N. Doc. No. A/RES/67/81. December 12. www.un.org/en/ga/search/view_doc.asp?symbol=A/RES/67/81.

UN General Assembly. 2000. *United Nations Millennium Declaration*. Doc. A/RES/55/2. September 18. www.un.org/en/development/desa/population/migration/generalassembly/docs/globalcompact/A_RES_55_2.pdf.

United Nations. 2021. *Human Rights Day*, 10 December. New York: United Nations. www.un.org/en/observances/human-rights-day#:~:text=2020%20Theme%3A%20Recover%20Better%20%2D%20Stand,are%20central%20to%20recovery%20efforts.

United Nations Economic Commission for Africa. 2020. *Policy Brief: Impact of COVID-19 in Africa*. May 28. www.uneca.org/sites/default/files/PublicationFiles/sg_policy_brief_on_covid-19_impact_on_africa_may_2020.pdf.

United Nations Economic Commission for Africa. 2019. *The Great Debate Focuses on How to Fix Africa's Healthcare*. February 12, 2019. https://uneca.org/stories/great-debate-focuses-how-fix-africa%E2%80%99s-healthcare.

United Nations Human Rights Treaty Bodies. *UN Treaty Body Database. Ratification Status for Ghana*. https://tbinternet.ohchr.org/_layouts/15/TreatyBodyExternal/Treaty.aspx?CountryID=67&Lang=EN.

US Census Bureau. Oregon. *QuickFacts*. http://quickfacts.census.gov/qfd/states/41000.html.

Universal Declaration of Human Rights. 1948. G.A. Res. 217 A (III). U.N. GAOR, 3d Sess. U.N. Doc. A/810.

Universal Health Coverage Coalition. http://universalhealthcoverageday.org/welcome/.

Value-Added Tax—VAT. *Investopedia*. www.investopedia.com/terms/v/valueaddedtax.asp.

Victora, Cesar G., J.P. Vaughan, F.C. Barros, A.C. Silva, and E. Tomasi. 2000. Explaining Trends in Inequities: Evidence from Brazilian Child Health Studies. *Lancet*, 356(9235), 1093–1098. September 23. doi:10.1016/S0140-6736(00)02741-0.

Vincent, R.J. 1986. *Human Rights and International Relations*. New York: Cambridge University Press.

Waddington, C.J., and K.A. Enyimayew. 1990. A Price to Pay, Part 2: The Impact of User Charges in the Volta Region of Ghana. *International Journal of Health Planning & Management*, 5(4), 287–312. https://doi.org/10.1002/hpm.4740050405.

Wahab, Hassan. 2019. Are Members of Parliament in Ghana Responsive to their Constituents? Evidence from Parliamentary Debates on Health Care. In *Ghanaian Politics and Political Communication*, Samuel Gyasi Obeng and Emmanuel Debrah (eds.), pp. 99–114. London: Roman & Littlefield.

Wahab, Hassan. 2019. The Politics of State Welfare Expansion in Africa: Emergence of National Health Insurance in Ghana, 1993–2004. *Africa Today*, 65(3), 91–112.

Wahab, Hassan. 2015. *The Politics of State Welfare in Africa: Ghana's National Health Insurance Scheme in Comparative Perspective*. PhD Dissertation, Indiana University Bloomington. September.

Wahab, Hassan. 2014. Universal Healthcare Coverage: Assessing the Implementation of Ghana's NHIS Law. In *Intellectual Agent, Mediator and Interlocutor: A. B. Assensoh and African Politics in Transition*, Toyin Falola and Emmanuel M. Mbah (eds.), pp. 188–199. Newcastle: Cambridge Scholars Publishing.

Wahab, Hassan. 2008. *Assessing the Implementation of Ghana's NHIS Law*. Paper prepared for Workshop in Political Theory and Policy Analysis Mini-Conference. Spring. http://ostromworkshop.indiana.edu/seminars/papers/wahab_mcpaper08.pdf.

Wahab, Hassan, and Philip C. Aka. 2021. The Politics of Healthcare Reforms in Ghana under the Fourth Republic since 1993: A Critical Analysis. *Canadian Journal of African Studies*, 55(1), 203–221. https://doi.org/10.1080/00083968.2020.1801476.

Waiswa, Peter. 2012. *The Impact of User fees on Access to Health Services in Low- and Middle-Income Countries*. RHL: The WHO Reproductive Health Library. May 1. http://apps.who.int/rhl/effective_practice_and_organizing_care/cd009094_waiswaw_com/en/.

Wallis, William. 2020. Jerry Rawlings, a Showman President of Varied Ideologies. *Financial Times*. November 20. www.ft.com/content/c23175d4-a39e-4550-bcfd-bc66a2b2a8cf.

Wang, Huihui, Nathaniel Otoo, and Lydia Dsane-Selby. 2017. *Ghana National Health Insurance Scheme: Improving Financial Sustainability Based on Expenditure Review*. Washington, DC: World Bank. https://openknowledge.worldbank.org/bitstream/handle/10986/27658/9781464811173.pdf.

Wendimagegn, Netsanet Fetene, and Marthie C. Bezuidenhout. 2019. Integrating Promotive, Preventive, and Curative Health Care Services at Hospitals and Health Centers in Addis Ababa, Ethiopia. *Journal of Multidisciplinary Healthcare*, 12, 243–255. April 5. doi:10.2147/JMDH.S193370.

Wilson, Frank L. 1996. *Concepts and Issues in Comparative Politics: An Introduction to Comparative Analysis*. Upper Saddle River, NJ: Prentice Hall.

Wilson, Mary E. 1995. Travel and the Emergence of Infectious Diseases. *Emerging Infectious Diseases*. 1(2), 39–46. doi:10.3201/eid0102.950201.

Witter, Sophie, and Bertha Garshong. 2009. Something Old or Something New? Social Health Insurance in Ghana. *BMC International Health & Hum. Rights*. 9, 20. August 28. https://doi.org/10.1186/1472-698X-9-20.

World Health Assembly. 2005. *Sustainable Health Financing*, Universal Coverage, and Social Health Insurance. Doc. A58/20. WHA58.33. 58th World Health Assembly. May 25. https://cdn.who.int/media/docs/default-source/health-financing/sustainable-health-financing-universal-coverage-and-social-health-insurance.pdf?sfvrsn=f8358323_3.

World Health Organization. 2021. *What is Universal Coverage?* Geneva, Switzerland: World Health Organization. www.who.int/health_financing/universal_coverage_definition/en/.

World Health Organization. 2016. *Act with Ambition: Universal Health Coverage (UHC) Day 2016.* Event Notice. December 7. www.who.int/health_financing/events/uhc-day-2016/en/.

World Health Organization. 2016. *Public Financing for Health in Africa: From Abuja to the SDGs.* Geneva, Switzerland: World Health Organization.

World Health Organization. 2014. *Health in All Policies: Helsinki Statement Framework for Country Action.* Geneva, Switzerland: World Health Organization.

World Health Organization. 2013. *Global Action Plan for the Prevention and Control of Noncommunicable Diseases 2013–2020.* Geneva, Switzerland: World Health Organization.

World Health Organization. 2011. *The Abuja Declaration: Ten Years On.* www.who.int/healthsystems/publications/abuja_declaration/en/.

World Health Organization. 2010. Executive Summary: Why Universal Coverage? In *The World Health Report: Health Systems Financing: The Path to Universal Coverage*, pp. ix–xxii. Geneva, Switzerland: World Health Organization.

World Health Organization. 2010. *The World Health Report: Health Systems Financing: The Path to Universal Coverage.* Geneva, Switzerland: World Health Organization.

World Health Organization. 2005. *Social Health Insurance.* 58th World Health Assembly. Provisional Agenda Item 13.16.

World Health Organization. 2000. *World Health Report 2000: Health Systems: Improving Performance.* Geneva, Switzerland: World Health Organization.

World Health Organization. 1995. *World Health Report 1995: Bridging the Gap.* Geneva, Switzerland: World Health Organization.

World Health Organization. 1978. *Declaration of Alma-Ata.* International Conference on Primary Health Care, Alma-Ata, USSR. September 6–12. www.who.int/publications/almaata_declaration_en.pdf.

World Health Organization. *Countries.* www.who.int/countries/en/.

World Health Organization. *Employment: Who We Are.* www.who.int/employment/about_who/en/.

World Health Organization. *Employment: Who We Need.* www.who.int/employment/who_we_need/en/.

World Health Organization. *Our Contributors.* www.who.int/about/funding/contributors.

World Health Organization. Executive Board. 2004. *Social Health Insurance: Report by the Secretariat.* 15th Session. Provisional Agenda, Item 4.5. EB115/8. December.

World Health Organization. Media Center. *World Health Assembly.* www.who.int/mediacentre/events/governance/wha/en/.

World Health Organization. Regional Office for the Eastern Mediterranean. 2006. *The Role of Government in Health Development.* July. http://applications.emro.who.int/docs/em_rc53_tech.disc.1_en.pdf.

World Health Organization and the World Bank. 2017. *Healthy Systems for Universal Health Coverage: A Joint Vision for Healthy Lives.* Geneva, Switzerland: World Health Organization, and Washington, DC: World Bank.

The World Health Organizations Ranking of the World's Health Systems, by Rank. *Countries of the World.* photius.com/rankings/healthranks.html.

Wright, Quincy. 1968. *Mandates Under the League of Nations.* Westport, CT: Greenwood Press.

Yergin, Daniel, and Joseph Stanislaw. 1998. *Commanding Heights: The Battle Between Government and the Marketplace that is Remaking the Modern World*. New York: Simon & Schuster.

Zakariah, Afisah, Daniel Degbotse, Dan Osei, Anthony Ofosu, Nicholas Nyagblornu, and Andreas Bjerrum. 2014. *Holistic Assessment of the Health Sector Program of Work 2013*. Accra, Ghana: Ministry of Health.

Zeleza, P.T. 2007. *The Struggle for Human Rights in Africa. Keynote Address to the Annual Meeting of the Association of African Studies. University of Toronto. May 17*. http://www.zeleza.com/node/162/print. (Reprinted in *Canadian Journal of African Studies*. 41(3) (2007), 474–506).

Zimmerman, Mary Ko. 2020. Comparative Health-Care Systems. *Encyclopedia of Sociology*. Updated February 10. www.encyclopedia.com/social-sciences/encyclopedias-almanacs-transcripts-and-maps/comparative-health-care-systems.

Zuniga, José M., Stephen P. Marks, and Lawrence O. Gostin (eds.). 2013. *Advancing the Human Right to Health*. New York: Oxford University Press.

Index

Notes: Page numbers in *italics* indicate tables and page numbers followed by 'n' refer to notes.

Abuja Declaration 49, 68, 69, 73, 73n4
[US] Affordable Care Act (2010) 47, 92
African Charter on the Rights and Welfare of the Child (ACRWC) 80, 81, 95n30, 96n46, 96n48
African Charter on Human and Peoples' Rights (ACHPR) 42, 54n83, 80, 95n29, 96n45
African Union (AU) 11n47, 18, 31n52, 31n53, 105, 107n,
Akufo-Addo, Nana, President 6, 41, 61, 86
Agenda 111 13n72, 13n73, 62, 66n22, 66n26, 66n28, 66n29, 66n32, 66n35, 66n36, 66n37, 66n38, 86, 98n99, 108n24
Aka, Philip C. 29n4, 29n23, 52n36, 53n47, 65n2, 65n4, 67n42, 74n10, 74n12, 75n42, 94n7, 99n105, 108n16, 108n17,

Bourne, Sir Frederick (Bourne Commission) 2

capitation fees 43
"cash and carry" xii, 4, 37, 38, 59, 82, 83, 99n124, 104
community health insurance (CHI) 44
comparative analysis xii, 7, 15, 20, 21–23, 33n90, 104
comparative method xii, 21, 22, 34n111
"complexity" of ranking healthcare systems 20, 28
Confucius 15
consensus on healthcare reforms xiii, 105
Constitution of the Republic of Ghana (1992) xi

Corwin, Samuel Edward 33n84
COVID-19 pandemic 6, 7, 12n64, 12n65, 12n67, 12n68, 13n69, 13n70, 61, 62, 66n34, 88, 100n135, 107
curative over preventive medicine 17, 83, 84, 91, 92

Declaration of Alma-Ata (1978) 17, 30n31, 70, 73, 74n21
Diagnosis-related Grouping (DRG) 43
Disability-Adjusted Life Expectancy (DALE) 25, 35n132
Dickovick. J. Tyler 22, 34n111
District Mutual Insurance (DMI) 40, 41
Donnelly, Jack 33n83, 94n3

Eastwood, Jonathan 22, 34n111
Economic Commission for Africa (UNECA) 6

fee-for-service (FFS) 43
First Republic (1960–1966) 3
Fourth Republic (1993–) 2–4, 7, 15, 23, 36, 41, 50, 58–61, 63–65, 68, 70, 77, 104–106
four hallmarks as guidepost for healthcare assessment. *See* Guide to healthcare reforms in Ghana, four hallmarks as 15, 23, 24, 28, 50, 58, 77, 104
Franklin, Benjamin 101n180, 17

General Comment No. 3 to the ICESCR 67n44
Ghana (formerly Gold Coast) 1, 2, 8n9, 8n14, 9n20, 37
Ghana, regional and regional capitals, *3*

128 *Index*

Ghana Health Service (GHS) 6
Ghana Independence Act (1957) 8n18
Ghana Investment Infrastructure Fund (GIIF) 62
Ghana Ministry of Health 41
Ghana Revenue Authority (GRA) 41
Ghana under the NHIS, recap of health as human right 77, 82, *84*
Ghana's 1992 Constitution 39, 53n46
Ghana's Fourth Republic, leaders since 1993 *41*, 64
Ghana's performance, recap on the four hallmarks, *26*

good laws 6, 23, 24, *26*, 27, 58, 59, 64, 65, 104
good funding 24, *26*, 73, 104
good politics 23, 24, *26*, 27, 28, 58, 59, 61, 63, 64, 65, 104
guide to healthcare reforms in Ghana, four hallmarks 7, 15, 23, 24, *26*, 28, 50, 58, 77, 104; good laws 6, 23, 24, *26*, 27, 58, 59, 64, 65, 104; good funding 24, *26*, 73, 104; good politics 23, 24, *26*, 27, 28, 58, 59, 61, 63, 64, 65, 104; health as human right 77, 104

healthcare debate in Africa 1, 6
health as human right xii, 1, 4, 7, *26*, 41, 42, 50, 58, 60, 65, 68, 69, 70, 71, 77, 82, 83, *84*, 87, 88, 94, 104, 106, 107
"healthcare for all" 17, 20, 40, 45, 47, 79, 83
healthcare as social struggle xii, 77–79, 103n208
healthcare system 6, 7, 15–17, 21, 23, 24, 25, *26*, 27, 28, 38, 47–49, 59, 60, 62, 73, 77, 85, 87–90, 92, 107
health system statuses and performances of WHO members in 2000, juxtaposition of Ghana with 13 neighboring and non-neighboring countries, *25*
Henkin, Louis 33n84, 33n85
Heymann, David 35n139
Holmes, Oliver Wendel 35n124
human rights 4–7, 15, 20, 21, 24, 27, 40, 64, 69, 77–80, 86, 89, 93, 94, 105, 107
Hunt, Paul 5, 12n59, 94n5,
hybrid model 46

Information and Communication Technology (ICT) 88
inefficient 83, *84*, 87, 90
inequitable 45, 83, *84*, 90

insufficiently accountable *84*, 88, 90
International Covenant on Economic, Social, and Cultural Rights (ICESCR) 24, 33n85, 42, 64, 67n44, 69, 80, 95n28,
International Covenant on Civil and Political Rights (ICCPR) 33n85, 96n35
International Conference on Primary Health Care 17, 74n21
International Monetary Fund (IMF) 19, 37

Kim, Jim Yong 19, 22
Kipling, Rudyard 21
Kufuor, John A. 38–40, *41*, 50, 60

League of Nations 1–2
legislative oversight 65
less than comprehensive 83
less than free 83

Magnetic Resonance Imaging (MRI) 7
Mahama, John D. *41*, 60
"Medicare for all," single-payer as 47
Mental Health Act 86
Mill, John Stuart 33n88
Mills, John A. 41, 44
most-different-systems design (MDSD) 22
most-similar-systems design (MSSD) 22
mutual health organization (MHO) 44

National Democratic Congress (NDC) 3, 39
National Health Insurance Act (NHIA) 39, 86
National Health Insurance Act, Act 650 *26*, 40, 53n54, 59–61
National Health Insurance Act, Act 852 *26*, 40, 53n58, 59–61, 90
National Health Insurance Fund (NHIF) 39, 89
National Health Insurance Scheme (NHIS) 3, 11n48, 36, 38
New Patriotic Party (NPP) 3, 38, 52n33, 53n55
Nigeria 419 scam 63
Nkrumah, Kwame 2, 9n21, 9n22, 37, 104
non-governmental organizations (NGOs) 5, 18, 93

Odinkalu, Chidi 78, 94n6, 105
Official/Overseas Development Assistance (ODA) 75n41
oil discovery in Ghana 3, 76n50

Index

Organization of African Unity (OAU) 11n47, 18, 105, 107n8
Organization for Economic Cooperation and Development (OECD) 75n41
Oxford Committee for Famine Relief 5
Oxfam International 4, 5, 45, 47–49, 79, 82, 85, 87, 89–93, 97n73, 99n111, 99n124, 101n152, 104

Peltason, Jack W. 33n84
Petroleum Revenue Management Act (PRMA), Act 815 72
Power, Samantha, et al. 5
principle of exemptions 39, 44, 48, 87, 91
Private Commercial Health Insurance (PCHI) 39, 41
Private Mutual Insurance (PMI) 41
Public Interest and Accountability Committee (PIAC) 73

Rawlings, Jerry J. 3, 37, 40, *41*, 50, 106
rapid population growth inconsonant with supply of healthcare services 92
Resolution 58.33 17
Roberts, Marc J., et al. 24, 35n127
Roth, Kenneth 33n87

Second Republic (1969–1972) 3
Sen, Amartya K. 5, 17–20
single-payer, tax-funded system 36, 39, 42, 47–49, 91
Sisyphus 105
social determinants of health 18, 81, *84*, 92
social health insurance (SHI) 18, 22, 45–48, 83
Social Security and National Insurance Trust (SSNIT) 44, 55n105
Stage 2½ 104, 105
Structural Adjustment Program (SAP) 37, 38

(UN) Sustainable Development Goals (SDGs) 62, 74n15,

tax-funded healthcare financing 45, 46, 49
Third Republic (1979–1981) 3

uhuru (freedom in Swahili) 83
United Nations Organization (UNO or UN) 2
universal healthcare 4, 15, 17–20, 22, 27, 31n48, 40, 47, 49, 59, 61, 71, 82, 107
universal health coverage (UHC) 29n7, 49
"Universal Health Coverage (UHC) Day" 18
UN Special Rapporteur on the Right to Health 5
UN Millennium Development Goals (MDGs) 69, 83
Universal Declaration of Human Rights (UDHR) 32n60, 33n85, 69, 80
The United Kingdom of Great Britain and Northern Ireland (UK) *25*
The United States of America (USA) *25*

value-added tax (VAT) 41, 42, 54n64, 90

Wahab, Hassan 11n48, 52n21, 52n36, 52n41, 65n12
World Bank 19, 22, *26*, 37, 52n29, 68, 90, 96n41
World Health Assembly 17, 22, 30n33, 32n63
World Health Organization (WHO) 12n64, 17, 28n3, 69
WHO Constitution (1948) 17, 28n3
WHO Report (2000) *25*, 29n21
within-case comparison (WCC) 22, 104

Yates, Robert 35n139

Zimmerman, Mary Ko 34n93

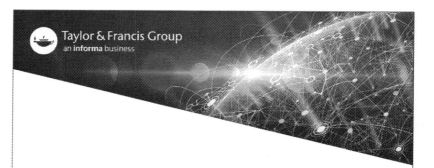